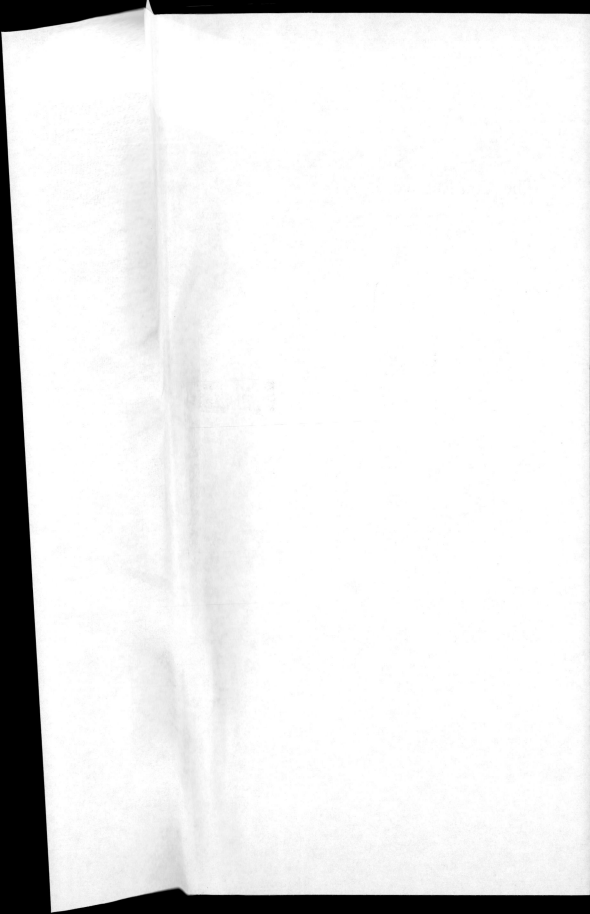

The Asia Recovery

To Souraya, Danielle and Cybele

The Asia Recovery

Issues and Aspects of Development, Growth, Trade and Investment

Edited by

Tran Van Hoa

Associate Professor of Economics, University of Wollongong, Australia

Edward Elgar
Cheltenham, UK • Northampton, MA, USA

Published by
Edward Elgar Publishing Limited
Glensanda House
Montpellier Parade
Cheltenham
Glos GL50 1UA
UK

Edward Elgar Publishing, Inc.
136 West Street
Suite 202
Northampton
Massachusetts 01060
USA

A catalogue record for this book
is available from the British Library

Library of Congress Cataloguing in Publication Data

The Asia recovery: issues and aspects of development, growth, trade and investment/
edited by Tran Van Hoa.
     p. cm.
   Includes index.
   1. Asia—Economic conditions—1945– 2. Investments—Asia. I. Tran,
   Van Hoa.
HC412.A724153 2001

330.95′043—dc21   2001023013

ISBN 1 84064 475 3

Printed and bound in Great Britain by MPG Books Ltd, Bodmin, Cornwall

Contents

Tables

Figures

Editor's biographical notes

Professor Tran Van Hoa, a graduate from the University of Western Australia, holds higher degrees from Monash University, Victoria, Australia. He has taught widely at universities in Australia, Asia and the USA, and visited major international research institutes and universities, including Cambridge University (UK), the London School of Economics (UK), CORE at the Université Catholique de Louvain (Belgium), Stanford University (USA), the University of Southern California (USA), the University of California in San Diego (USA), University of Florida (USA), INSEE (France), CEPII (Prime Minister's Office, France), Chulalongkorn and Thammasat Universities (Thailand), the People's University of China (Beijing) and the National Economics University (Vietnam). Dr Tran Van Hoa has published 18 books and over 100 refereed articles in the major applied and theoretical areas of economics, business, finance, energy and econometrics in Australian and international professional journals, and numerous commissioned reports. He is listed in *Who's Who in the World, Who's Who in Asia and the Pacific Nations, Who's Who in Science and Engineering, 2000 Outstanding People of the 20th Century* and in the *Dictionary of International Biography*. He also is a director of T&M Enterprises P/L (Australia) which provides education and consulting services, and in the past few years he has been a consultant to a number of organizations and authorities in Australia and China and various ministries in Thailand and Vietnam.

Acknowledgements

The book is the fourth in a series of books on the Asia crisis that started in July 1997 in Thailand and has spread, with damaging impact, economic, financial, political and social, to other countries in the neighbouring region and, to some significant extent, Russia, Latin America, the USA, and the European Union. This volume complements the three previous books (*Causes and Impact of the Asian Financial Crisis, The Asia Crisis: The Remedies, their Effectiveness and the Prospects After,* and *The Social Impact of the Asia Crisis*) by looking at the situation of major Asian crisis countries in the first half of 2000 where major economic and financial benchmarks, provided by national and international organizations (such as the national statistical offices, the Asian Development Bank, the International Monetary Fund and the World Bank), indicated almost uniformly that an economic recovery was on the way.

The book contains a collection of important studies on major problems associated with this emerging Asia recovery and provides a comprehensive survey and critical analysis of issues and aspects not only of development and growth but also of trade, investment and business of the crisis countries. Of particular importance are the derived pertinent policy implications useful for international economic relations, corporate and government management and governance, and international business strategic planning. In this respect, the book's coverage is of interest not only to national and international economic policy makers, academics, researchers and consultants, and students of economics and commerce, but also to corporate planners and business analysts.

The editor wishes to thank Edward Elgar for his strong and prompt support for the book concept which arose from the former's sabbatical study visit to the Department of Economics at the University of California in San Diego late in 1999. Discussions with UCSD colleagues on the interest and aspects of the Asia crisis were most useful in developing the idea of a new book on the subject. The editor also wishes to thank his contributing authors for their great efforts to meet the strict deadline for the book typescripts.

The support and sacrifice of my family during the preparation of this book are deeply appreciated.

Tran Van Hoa
Melbourne, July 2000

Notes on the contributors

Charles Harvie is Associate Professor, Department of Economics, and Deputy Director, International Business Research Institute, University of Wollongong.

Hyun-Hoon Lee is Associate Professor, Division of Economics and International Trade, Kangwon National University, Korea, and managing director of the *Journal of the Korean Economy*.

Jong Won Lee is Professor of Economics, Department of Economics, Sungkyunkwan University, Korea.

Jingping Li is Assistant Professor, Department of Statistics and Economics, the Renmin University of China, Beijing.

The Dzung Nguyen is National Projects Officer, United Nations Development Program (UNDP) in Hanoi, Vietnam, and a doctoral candidate in Economics at the University of Wollongong.

Tran Van Hoa is Associate Professor of Economics, and Director, Vietnam Research Program, University of Wollongong.

Ma. Rebecca Valenzuela PhD, is Lecturer in Economics, Faculty of Business and Economics, Monash University.

Mei Wen PhD, is Senior Research Fellow, the Australian National University.

Doo Yong Yang is an Economist at the Korea Institute for International Economic Policy, Seoul, Korea.

Xiaokai Yang is Professor of Economics, Faculty of Business and Economics, Monash University, and Fellow, Harvard Institute for Economic Development, USA.

Yanyun Zhao is Professor of Economics and Chairman of the Department of Statistics and Economics, the Renmin University of China, Beijing, and an adviser to the central government, China.

1. The Asia recovery

Tran Van Hoa

The Asia crisis, also known as the economic and financial turmoil or melt-down in Asia, that started in July 1997 in Thailand had brought untold damage to a large number of countries worldwide and intolerable hardships and poverty to millions of people in Asia and, to a lesser extent, in Russia, Latin and North America and the European Union. After nearly three years of wide-spread economic and financial turmoil and social unrest, there were signs in mid-2000 that a slow but promising economic recovery in the crisis countries in Asia was on the way. Since the recovery was only emerging it would be reasonable to assume that there may be numerous problems in reading the signs accurately and, more importantly, in extracting, analysing and summa-rizing the right information contained in them for scholarly studies, govern-ment and corporate policy analysis, or practical applications in business planning.

While a number of studies and reports have occasionally been brought out by national and international organizations and agencies (such as the International Monetary Fund, the World Bank, the Asian Development Bank and several non-government organizations) with ample research funding and policy interest in the Asia crisis, there has been no significant and systematic work on the Asia recovery *per se*, and most of these studies and reports leave much to be desired. This observation can be amplified as follows.

First, the studies and reports principally provide casual and descriptive analysis of a short-term nature that is based essentially on recent trends (of a few years' duration) in economic and financial aggregates and, importantly, also strong *a priori* assumptions on the direction and causality of the relevant cause-and-effect variables on the subject matter in the crisis countries. It is well known in economic and business literature that output growth for a country, for example, can be equally attributed to a number of contributing factors in an interdependent, complex and continually dynamic way (for example through that country's accumulated knowledge, temporally changed perspective and motivation, capital formation and built up infrastructure in key industries over the years). In this context, a casual, descriptive and short-term analysis, however carefully done it may be, may be regarded as

'rushed'; lacking a deep or thorough and rigorous investigation of the underlying multidirectional causes and effects of national and international
economic activities. In the environment of countries with fast changing information technology-based industries (such as Malalysia) and a complex global
economy, a long-term analysis taking into account a long process of development and growth would be more appropriate to understand the important
aspects necessary to restart the economy's growth and to sustain the recovery.

Second, the studies and reports often lack an on-site perspective of local or
national experts who have had to live through the crisis and witness its development and who may in all probability understand and report better the issues,
problems and the underlying thinking of policy makers in the countries in
trouble.

This book is an attempt to provide a significant complement to studies and
reports of a casual, descriptive and short-term kind in the sense that it is
focused essentially on the long-term analysis of the Asia recovery, tracing, for
the selected countries under study, a long process of development and its over-
riding and lasting features, using, in some cases, historical data going back to
the countries' initial Schumpeterian-type take-off stage up to more than three
decades ago. The book is also a collection of soundly researched and analysed
and concisely articulated studies by respected national and international
experts in the crisis economies in the areas covered to explore in depth the
major issues and important aspects of the Asia economic and financial recovery and their potential impact on growth, development, trade and investment,
for use by government, academics, business, non-government organizations
and all interested in this significant current event. It will also map out the
global directions in international economic and financial relations, corporate
and public governance, and the challenges we have to face and manage in the
21st century.

OVERVIEW

In Chapter 2, Tran Van Hoa gives an overview of the Asia recovery as
observed and reported by economic and financial analysts in mid-2000, and
briefly discusses pertinent issues and important aspects of the recovery so far
as they are related, in the medium and long term, to output growth, economic
development, international trade and investment in the crisis economies in
Asia, and with implications for their trading partners. The problems of or
obstacles to the recovery process in the major crisis countries are then briefly
analysed country by country, and recommendations are suggested for adoption
by government or policy makers.

KOREA

Chapter 3, written by Jong Won Lee, Hyun-Hoon Lee and Doo Yong Yang, aims to evaluate the post-crisis performance of the Korean economy. The emphasis is on the Korean government's structural reform efforts under the International Monetary Fund rescue programme and current development progress in a number of major economic sectors. The chapter also identifies potential dangers and challenges lying ahead, and further discusses the problems and prospects of a full recovery and sustainable growth of the Korean economy for 2000 and thereafter.

INDONESIA

In Chapter 4, Charles Harvie first discusses the pre-crisis macroeconomic outcomes and factors behind the collapse of the Indonesian economy, and then focuses upon the initial policy responses to the crisis. Highlights of the current key issues and policies for sustained economic recovery are further evaluated, and the new democratically elected government's medium-term economic strategy is discussed. Finally, the chapter identifies the government of Indonesia's medium-term macroeconomic policy framework and presents a summary of the major issues identified in the analysis.

MALAYSIA

Chapter 5, written by Tran Van Hoa, provides first a brief survey of Malaysia's fundamentals in its development and growth over the last 30 years, and discusses the pertinent trends, significant patterns and plausible prospects of the major tradable commodities in its international trade in the medium term. Special focus is on the 'new' economy, its past development, its role and treatment in the Asia crisis, and its current bottlenecks. Problems and issues of the economic recovery in Malaysia are then analysed in detail and recommendations suggested for adoption and implementation in a number of important areas. These include economic management, international trade policy, development and growth aspects, skilled labour and human resource development, and trade competitiveness.

THE PHILIPPINES

Ma. Rebecca Valenzuela reports on the issues and aspects of the recovery in the Philippines in Chapter 6, touching on the question why the country has seemingly escaped the impact or contagion of the Asia turmoil starting in 1997 without much damaging effect. The main factor is probably the economic reforms initiated by the government many years before the emergence of the Asia crisis. However, she continues to argue that the social impact of the Asia crisis on the Philippines is still lingering and it is foolish to rely on the good fortune to date for recovery; much work needs to be done to ensure that the recovery efforts are made to rest on firm ground and to adopt sensible growth strategies that will enable the economy to pursue sustainable long-term growth amid expanding globalization, increased competition and the political reality in the Philippines' long-term recovery.

The four subsequent chapters deal exclusively with two major transition economies in Asia, namely, Vietnam and China, and discuss issues and aspects of their development, growth, trade, investment and social policy in the context of the Asia recovery. Emphasis is also placed on the interaction between these economies and the regional economic development environment.

VIETNAM

Chapter 7, prepared by The Dzung Nguyen, argues that the underlying driving force of the development and economic recovery in Vietnam was and remains the process of economic reform called 'Doi Moi', starting in 1987. The chapter first provides an overview of Vietnam's recent economic performance and analyses major factors influencing its recovery. It then reviews the country's major deep-rooted social issues, existing problems, the impact of the slowdown and recovery, and discusses potential solutions. The information used in the chapter is based on government statistics and official data collected by international agencies operating in Vietnam, particularly the World Bank and the United Nations Development Programme.

CHINA

Three perspectives on issues and aspects of China's development, growth, trade and investment during the Asia recovery are given in Chapters 8–10. In Chapter 8, Zhao Yanyun and Li Jingping focus especially on China's merchandise trade and foreign direct investment as these two categories form the majority of its trade and investment. The chapter first describes the general medium-term situation of exports and foreign direct investment (FDI) in China. It then analyses issues and aspects of China's exports and FDI after the Southeast Asian financial crisis. As a novel approach to studying development, growth, trade and investment, the authors provide a quantitative long-term analysis with a simple model of China's trade and investment and their impact on development and growth. This analysis makes use of the modern techniques of Engel–Granger cointegration or long-term causality and Granger error-correction modelling to provide empirical answers to the important question with far-reaching policy implications: what is the role of exports and FDI in China's development and growth in the long term?

Chapter 9, written by Mei Wen, deals in great detail with key issues and important aspects of China's fast growth in the past two decades and its sustainability via continuing economic reforms. These include state-owned enterprises reform, financial system reform and land management reform. The chapter also discusses China's long-term economic growth and development plan in the context of both transition and development and attempts to present a picture of China's growth and development perspective during the Asia recovery.

In Chapter 10, Xiaokai Yang provides another perspective on China's economic development process and deep-rooted crisis issues, using principally a theoretical framework. He first surveys the approaches to understanding transition economies and especially China's success in its development and growth in the past two decades. He then discusses how this kind of long-term understanding can be used to study and manage economic crises of the 1997 Asia turmoil type and the recovery from them. In the author's view, the Asia crisis can be regarded as a crisis of success, and the present diagnosis of a moral hazard problem (for example, state monopoly or cronyism) or the lack of an IMF-inspired financial insurance scheme as the possible causes of the crisis is inappropriate. Using several general equilibrium models with endogenous network size of labour division to formalize economic crises, the author finds that each of the two sides of the policy debate on the Asian financial crisis should be complemented by its opponent. Other issues on incentive provision and sensitive feedback and its stability in understanding economic crises are also discussed.

2. The Asia recovery and sustainable development and growth: an overview

Tran Van Hoa

1 INTRODUCTION

After the emergence of the economic and financial crisis in Thailand in early July 1997, a number of major 'economic miracle' countries or 'economic tigers' in Asia had seen their hard-won development and high growth achieved over the previous 30 years or so suddenly stalled or drastically reduced. The damage of this regional turmoil had spread beyond the spheres of economics and finance and affected, politically and socially, millions of people in the five major crisis economies (Indonesia, Korea, Malaysia, the Philippines and Thailand) and also in other countries or regions (for example, China, Russia and Latin America – including Brazil in 1998 and Argentina in 1999). Late in 1999 and, especially, early in 2000, however, there were significant signs that the worst effects of the Asia crisis were truly over and that the five crisis countries in Asia, at least, had started posting long-awaited results of positive development and growth. The recovery, if confirmed, would have a widespread economic, political and social impact on the crisis countries and beyond.

2 SIGNS OF RECOVERY

Within the crisis countries in Asia, statistics collected by international organizations such as the Asian Development Bank (ADB) and the International Monetary Fund (IMF) revealed in mid-2000 some telling signs of an economic recovery. These included a moderate-to-strong upswing replacing negative growth in several of these countries, a decrease in the IMF-inspired high interest rates and the stabilization of exchange rates. Domestic demand and, especially, export growth also improved. Other signs that seemed to show some degree of confidence in the region's economic and trade potential and prospects included strengthened foreign capital inflows, increased vitality of equity markets and revived consumer confidence.

Many countries in the region and beyond were affected by the Asia turmoil but to varying degrees. As a result, the recovery processes of these countries were different. China and South Asia, for example, were to some extent insulated from the economic crisis and their recovery therefore fared better than that in the crisis economies. As an example, in 1999, growth in China slowed down slightly but that in South Asia accelerated by the same margin. On the other hand, the five Asian countries that were most seriously affected by the crisis and experienced negative growth in 1998 were able to post positive growth in 1999. The interdependence of the regional economies can also be seen in the correlation of their growth rates and economic activities of their trading partners or neighbours. For example, growth in Central Asia showed a strong increase as the perceived effect of the Russian crisis dissipated. Finally, the performance of the Pacific countries in 1999 improved, as compared to 1998 (Chino, 2000).

3 POLICIES TO RESTORE AND SUSTAIN DEVELOPMENT AND GROWTH IN ASIA

To sustain and further promote the growth process in Asia, the developing economies in Asia will, as recommended by international organizations such as the ADB and the IMF, have to continue with their plans for nationally or internationally inspired reforms and institutional innovation in areas that are considered weak and vulnerable. The areas of weakness as revealed by the Asia crisis include the banking system, capital markets and corporate sectors of the crisis economies. While admitting that the scope and complexities of the reforms were enormous, the ADB, for example, has proposed a list of restructuring plans and actions that it considered urgently relevant to sustain an economic recovery.

These plans include collaboration with other international donors in providing emergency financial assistance to stabilize the affected economies and to support urgent structural reforms. For its part, the ADB also focused on a structural agenda that involved restructuring insolvent financial institutions, improved corporate governance, and deregulated and opened domestic markets. Among the ADB's actions were loans to assist Indonesia, Korea and Thailand in implementing financial sector reforms. In June 2000, the ADB reported that the crisis countries in Asia had made significant progress in bank and corporate sector restructuring and had created new organizational and administrative entities to deal with these issues, but while much progress has been made, much remained to be done by the governments concerned (Chino, 2000).

4   ISSUES AND ASPECTS OF THE RECOVERY

The road back to fast and sustainable development, growth and continuing prosperity for the Asian crisis economies seemed to be in view, but, in our assessment, it was a slow and hard road with many problems and obstacles along the way. Some of these problems and obstacles have also been acknowledged by national and international economic experts.

The May update of the Asian Recovery Report 2000 (Asian Development Bank, 2000c) for example lists recent developments and problems in four key areas of Asia's recovery: (a) asset markets and the real sector; (b) bank and corporate restructuring; (c) social recovery, governance and competitiveness; and (d) prospects and risks. It also briefly reviews economic performance, medium-term prospects and policy issues of the Asian economies that have not been much affected by the crisis, namely, the People's Republic of China, Singapore and Vietnam. Additional indicators have been collated to capture important structural and social dimensions of Asia's recovery and to develop and implement appropriate policies.

A brief survey of issues, aspects and prospects for development, growth, trade and investment of each of the countries in our present study is given below, country by country. The summary has been collated from various national and international statistics and reports available as at July 2000.

Korea

In sharp contrast to a GDP growth rate of –6·7 per cent in 1998, Korea posted a remarkable growth rate of 10·7 per cent in 1999. This significant reversal of output was due to the country's adoption of a rescue package, led and recommended by the IMF, in 1997/98, continuing financial and corporate sector restructuring, and a favourable export environment.

One could argue that the recovery in GDP growth could also have been spurred to some significant extent by the Korean government's expansionary macroeconomic policy, adopted in mid-1998. This policy involved allocation of funds for financial restructuring and recapitalization, strengthened social safety nets and boosted the economy. This interventionist policy had resulted in a budget deficit, a rather extraordinary situation, as the government had long maintained a balanced budget tradition. With the public debt burden increasing explosively in 1998, the government announced in January 1999 a medium-term fiscal plan for a balanced budget. According to this plan, the consolidated budget balance is expected to be attained in 2004. However, there may be numerous obstacles to this fiscal consolidation. These obstacles include the government's huge interest payments (W8–10 trillion in 2001–2), sharp increases and depleted funds in the social welfare budget, and laxity in fiscal discipline in which both the public and policy makers may take a budget deficit for granted or as something they can comfortably live with.

Other obstacles or challenges to Korea's economic recovery include increases in structural unemployment, the slowing down of comprehensive deregulation efforts, and an overhaul of the social welfare system to provide an effective safety net for workers and, at the same time, strengthening work incentives.

Indonesia

After two years of economic and financial turmoil, Indonesia recorded a 0·2 per cent growth rate in GDP in 1999, as compared to a –13·2 per cent rate in 1998. The crisis-induced level of poverty appeared to have peaked in early 1999. The economic rebound was due to growth in agriculture in the first half of 1999, but gradually spread to other sectors of the economy. Growth in agriculture, however, slowed down to 0·7 per cent in the third quarter of 1999.

With projected increases in investment and exports in the non-primary sectors and agricultural production, Indonesia should expect a growth rate of 4 per cent in 2000 and 5 per cent in 2001. These rates can be achieved mainly with the following necessary conditions: continuing but declining budget deficits (5 per cent of GDP in 2000 and 3·1 per cent in 2001), greater macroeconomic stability and adequate reserve cover, reducing domestic and external debt-service expenditures (currently at 41 per cent of total expenditures and 61 per cent of total tax revenues), resource mobilization through revenue-raising measures such as asset sales through privatization, and strong financial and corporate restructuring. Other conditions the government has to fulfil include addressing the negative perception about governance in judicial processes, combating corruption, new regulations to reform public procurement and project implementation practices, and combating poverty through decentralization and anti-corruption measures.

Other obstacles to Indonesia's recovery have been the uncertainties of the newly elected democratic government, ethnic and religious unrest, pro-independence movements in some regions of the country and the problems associated with East and West Timor.

Malaysia

Malaysia has made remarkable progress from its economic recession in 1998. In the first three months of 2000, industrial production increased by 17·9 per cent on a year-on-year basis, and the trade balance stood at RM16·2 billion. Annual manufacturing sales value grew by 38·7 per cent in February 2000, while the annual inflation rate reached only 1·5 per cent in March 2000. The country's current account surplus was RM13·7 billion in the third quarter of 1999.

The much-maligned policy of capital controls has enabled the authorities to carry out, as in other Asian crisis countries, an expansionary fiscal and monetary policy, but without capital flight. In spite of the relative success of capital controls, a market orientation policy has been deemed more appropriate to support and sustain the country's recovery in the long term. Another pressing problem for Malaysia is its current shortage of skilled labour, due to income reduction of households during the crisis and severe budget cuts in education expenditure as remedial government policy. Until the problem is resolved, Malaysia will face a serious disadvantage in economic competitiveness and in long-term development programmes.

The Philippines

In 1998, the Philippines posted a growth rate of –0·5 per cent, as compared to 5·2 per cent in 1997. However, in 1999, the economy achieved a rate of 3·2 per cent. This positive but relatively slow growth was due to the modest performance of the industry sector, which grew by only 0·5 per cent. Agriculture recorded a strong recovery from the El Niño drought of 1998, and reached 6·6 per cent of growth. Services which had remained stagnant during the Asia crisis grew by 3·9 per cent in 1999, and this was due mainly to growth in retail trade. In 2000, GDP growth may reach 3·8 per cent as the economy continues its moderate recovery.

Problems were evident, however, in the Philippine economy even with these signs of a slow recovery. First, the level of non-performing loans (NPLs), at 15 per cent of total loans, has acted as a brake on the financial system and restrained credit growth. Second, investor confidence has apparently sagged during the crisis, and its restoration requires of necessity the government's commitment to reform as well as social consensus in favour of its policies and programmes. At the beginning of 1999, changes in a number of important departments in the government were announced, and the Economic Coordination Council was established to start the implementation of stalled reforms. The business community and the public welcomed these as significant efforts by the government to speed up reforms. Third, the huge budget deficits, used by the government to stimulate the economy, are likely to generate inflation pressure and interest rate hikes. This would call for better fiscal management of government resources to fund priority investments without resorting to high budget deficits, and a revamping of tax administration to improve revenue collection.

Other important issues that may hinder the country's faster economic recovery and growth include the need for poverty reduction, proper environmental management and adequate infrastructure.

Vietnam

While Vietnam has not been severely affected by the Asia crisis, its economy slowed down significantly during 1997–9 owing to the contagion of this economic and financial turmoil. Vietnam posted a growth rate of 8·2 per cent in 1997, 4·4 per cent in 1998 and 4·4 per cent also in 1999. It is remarkable that Vietnam was one of the very few countries in Asia that still recorded a positive growth rate in 1998.

However, foreign direct investment into the country fell for the second year in a row. Before the crisis, two-thirds of FDI inflows came from Asia and, as a result, were vulnerable to weaker regional GDP growth. The decline in FDI continued in 2000 as investor sentiment remained lukewarm because of uncertainties about the direction and pace of reform. A problem with this slowdown and the loss of reform momentum is that poverty reduction programmes of the country, one of the poorest in the world, are at stake.

In addition, government revenue as a percentage of GDP has been declining since 1997 in terms of both non-tax and, especially, tax (corporate income tax and international trade tax). This downward trend in revenue is a crucial concern as it affects government expenditure on education and social programmes. An important issue for Vietnam therefore is revenue target realignment without macroeconomic stability being jeopardized.

Rapid economic growth from the early 1990s until the arrival of the Asia crisis had a significant impact on poverty reduction in Vietnam. It also increased inequality and especially urban/rural income gaps, even though foreign welfare experts working in Vietnam have asserted that the country is still a relatively egalitarian society. Slow growth will have the disastrous impact of increases in poverty incidence in Vietnam. Other challenges include poverty among the ethnic minorities and the population of the highland regions of Vietnam. The issue has been recognized as a high priority and requires urgent attention and appropriate policies from both the government and the international donor and development communities.

China

Like Vietnam, China is another major transition economy in Asia that has not been severely affected by the Asian economic and financial crisis. While the country began to decelerate in the fourth quarter of 1998 and continued the same trend up to the second quarter of 1999, its prudent macroeconomic policy seemed to have assisted it in adjusting reasonably well to the impact of the crisis.

For example, the government introduced a fiscal stimulus (giving rise to a Y346 billion budget deficit in 1999, as compared to Y260 billion in 1998) and a tax package to boost growth, to discourage households from saving with banks, and to encourage private consumption. Also in response to the economic slowdown, the government reduced, in 1999, the benchmark one-year lending rate from 6·39 per cent to 5·85 per cent, and the benchmark one-year deposit rate from 3·78 per cent to 2·25 per cent. However, fixed investment grew by only 5·2 per cent in 1999, down from 14 per cent in 1998. Private investment, which made up about 25 per cent of total investment in the economy, has been slowing since 1996. While FDI reached a peak level during 1995–8, it fell in 1999 for the first time since 1990.

The pressing issues of China's economic recovery seem to be to counteract deflationary trends, to maintain robust economic growth, to stabilize the yuan–US dollar exchange rate at around Y8·3 per dollar, to strengthen an unemployment insurance scheme and to establish a sound legal framework. Unemployment is high especially owing to the reform of state-owned-enterprises (SOEs) that have been playing a key role in growth and employment generation. The Asia crisis has also exposed weaknesses in the financial and enterprise sectors, both of which need urgent attention and appropriate policies from the government. Many of the problems in the financial sector were related to ailing SOEs that accounted for a large portion of Chinese banks' NPLs.

BIBLIOGRAPHY

Asian Development Bank (2000a), *Asian Recovery Review 2000*, Internet, May 2000.
Asian Development Bank (2000b), *Asian Development Outlook 2000*, Internet, June 2000.
Asian Development Bank (2000c), *Asian Recovery Report 2000: May Update*, Internet, July 2000.
Chino, Tadao (2000), 'Foreword', *Asian Development Outlook 2000*, Internet, June 2000.
Dunning, J.H. (ed.) (1999), *Globalization, Trade and Foreign Direct Investment*, Amsterdam: Elsevier Science.
International Monetary Fund, *2000 World Economic Outlook*, Internet, July 2000.

PART I

Major ASEAN and East Asian Economies

3. Structural reform in Korea: its process and consequences

Jong Won Lee, Hyun-Hoon Lee and Doo Yong Yang

1 INTRODUCTION

On 21 November 1997, Korea turned to the International Monetary Fund (IMF), as the rollover ratio of short-term external borrowings by domestic financial institutions kept decreasing and the country's usable foreign exchange reserves plummeted to US$7·3 billion, from US$22·3 billion only a month earlier. On 3 December 1997, Korea and the IMF signed an agreement on a financial aid package totalling US$58·3 billion. The IMF Stand-by Arrangement was subject to a broad range of conditions, including macroeconomic stabilisation and structural reform.

As emergency measures, the Korean government was required to implement a tight monetary policy, fiscal austerity and the immediate closure of insolvent financial institutions. In the longer term, the Korean government was required to pursue economic reform programmes in the financial sector, the corporate sector and the labour market. Because the Korean crisis had its roots in the weakened fundamentals of the Korean economy, attempting to stabilize only the financial market without an emphasis on structural reforms is like treating symptoms without addressing the cause.[1] Thus, since the onset of the financial crisis in 1997, the Korean government has pursued structural reforms in the areas that the IMF required. In addition, the Korean government has pursued public sector reform to achieve the efficiency necessary to keep up with other sectors' reforms.

This chapter aims to evaluate the post-crisis performance of the Korean economy with special emphasis on the Korean government's structural reform efforts under the IMF programme. Having done this, the chapter identifies potential dangers and challenges lying ahead, and further discusses the prospects of a recovery of the Korean economy. The remainder of the chapter is as follows. Section 2 presents the structural reform programmes of the financial sector, the corporate sector, the labour market and the public sector. In Section 3, economic developments after the crisis are presented. Section 4 discusses the problems associated with the structural reforms and the challenges that the Korean economy has to overcome so as to attain full recovery from the crisis and a sustainable growth. Section 5 concludes.

2   STRUCTURAL REFORM

Financial Sector Restructuring

Before the financial crisis, the Korean government was actively involved in the market. This government-led economic policy was once considered to have led the nation to its remarkable economic successes in the 1960s–1980s. However, after the crisis, the IMF, and others, criticized the government-led economic policies as they had resulted not only in corruption but also in moral hazard among enterprises and banks. They also criticized the Korean government's imprudent liberalization of the financial market during the early 1990s; appropriate supervision and prudential regulation had not accompanied the rapid liberalization of the financial market.

Most Korean financial institutions borrowed short-run foreign capital at low rates, denominated in the US dollar, and made long-term loans at higher rates. These financial institutions believed that the government would not allow them to fail. This led to a serious mismatch in maturities between borrowing and lending. On the eve of the financial crisis, short-term loans accounted for 63 per cent of the total foreign debts of Korea. This fragile debt structure played a crucial role in triggering the financial crisis. Soon after, the financial crisis exposed the many weaknesses of the financial sector, such as its unsound lending practices, unhedged foreign borrowing, weak liquidity positions and its ineffective supervisory system.

Thus the financial sector was the area most urgently in need of reform. Financial sector restructuring was to stabilize the financial system in the short run, and enhance the soundness and efficiency of financial institutions in the long run. In order to facilitate the financial sector reform, several financial supervisory authorities were created or modified in early 1998. The Financial Supervisory Commission (FSC) was created and the Korea Asset Management Corporation (KAMCO) and the Korea Deposit Insurance Corporation (KDIC) were modified.

In the wake of the financial crisis, authorities closed or suspended the operations of a number of non-viable financial institutions. Nine insolvent merchant banks, which had been suspended on 2 December 1997, were required to submit a rehabilitation plan within 30 days. If their plans did not meet approval, the institution's licence would be revoked. The remaining merchant banks were each required to submit a recapitalization programme by

31 December 1997. They were required to at least meet the 4 per cent capital adequacy ratio of the Bank for International Settlements (BIS) by 31 March 1998.

Commercial banks were also each required to prepare a plan to meet the BIS 8 per cent minimum requirement. Of the 25 commercial banks, 12 'unsound' banks, which did not satisfy the BIS ratio requirement of 8 per cent by the end of 1997, were classified into two categories. Five banks were 'disapproved' and seven banks were 'conditionally approved'. The five 'disapproved' non-viable banks were liquidated through purchases and acquisitions in July 1998. The seven 'conditionally approved' banks took corrective actions imposed by the FSC to further improve their soundness. By 31 December 1998, 86 financial institutions (five commercial banks and 81 non-bank financial institutions) had either been closed or had their operations suspended.

The disposal of non-performing loans (NPLs) and recapitalization were also important parts of the financial sector restructuring. By the end of 1998, KAMCO and the KDIC together financed a total of W40·9 trillion to settle NPLs and to recapitalize certain financial institutions. Meanwhile, the number of people employed by the financial sector had been cut by a third.

Capital market liberalization and the promotion of foreign direct investment (FDI) were also important aspects of the restructuring. Various measures were taken by the Korean government to liberalize the capital market and to promote FDI. The ceiling on foreign investment in Korean equities was raised from 26 per cent to 55 per cent in December 1997, and was completely abolished in May 1998. Thus foreign financial institutions have been allowed to establish subsidiary banks and security companies, and to set up joint-venture banks. Virtually all restrictions on foreign investors' access to the bond markets had been lifted by 1 January 1998.

The restructuring of financial institutions continued through 1999, when an additional W23·1 trillion in public funds were provided for the financial sector restructuring. Thus, by the end of 1999, a total of W64 trillion in public funds had been injected since the outbreak of the financial crisis in 1997. Thanks to the injection of public funds and the massive rights offerings, the BIS ratios of domestic banks continued to rise. As of the end of 1999, the average BIS ratio of the 17 commercial banks was 10·8 per cent, which was well above the BIS recommended level of 8 per cent. At the same time, the total amount of the domestic financial institutions' NPLs had rapidly decreased. As of December 1999, they amounted to W51·3 trillion, which was only 9 per cent of the total credit in Korea.

Thus far, the restructuring of the financial sector has focused on the clearance of depressed assets under government supervision. However, the increasing presence of foreign financial companies in Korea is likely to further drive market-oriented reforms. With new players in the market, competition among financial companies will become stiffer. Moreover, as major international banks become larger and more diversified, strategic alliances and mergers and acquisitions (M&As) among financial companies in Korea will increase. Financial holding companies will be established in an effort to nurture larger financial institutions. Therefore a universal banking system with financial holding companies will emerge.

Up to the end of 1999, the financial sector restructuring had primarily focused on the commercial and merchant banks. However, the restructuring of non-bank financial institutions has only just started. In fact, many of the investment trust companies (ITCs), which had expanded their exposure to the corporate sector in 1998 and 1999, are undercapitalized and hence vulnerable to the corporate sector's turmoil. However, the restructuring of ITCs has been postponed several times. The government had already declared Korea Investment Trust and Daehan Investment Trust to be insolvent financial institutions, and had agreed to inject W8 trillion into the two largest investment-trust firms, yet only W3 trillion in public funds were injected in early 2000. Confidence in the trust companies has ebbed quickly, their investors withdrawing, and this has put the squeeze on the huge family-controlled conglomerates, or *chaebols*, the trust companies' biggest borrowers. The Korean government has decided to provide an additional W4·9 trillion in public funds for the two troubled investment trust companies, but many suspect that the public funds will not cover the total amount of the two investment companies' liabilities.

Corporate Sector Reform

The very high leverage of Korean firms played another crucial role in causing the financial crisis. In particular, the *chaebols* in Korea tended to borrow excessively through cross-payment guarantees among interlinked subsidiaries.[2] By the end of 1997, the top 30 *chaebols* had debt–equity ratios of 519 per cent, in sharp contrast to the 154 per cent in the United States and 193 per cent in Japan. Poor corporate practices and governance also contributed to the 1997 crisis in the form of inaccurate company financial information, no credible exit threat, insufficient financial institution monitoring, and few legal rights and forms of protection for minority shareholders (Joh, 1999). Hence the priority in corporate sector reform has been to focus on achieving a major reduction in corporate indebtedness and bringing corporate practices into line with international standards.

In January 1998, the then president-elect, Kim Dae-jung, and the leaders of the five largest *chaebols* made an agreement on five principles of corporate sector reform: (a) heightening of the transparency of corporate management, (b) prohibition of cross-guarantees between affiliates, (c) improvement of the corporate financial structure, (d) business concentration on core competence, and (e) responsibility reinforcement of governing shareholders and management. Under these five principles, the top five *chaebols* and their creditors reached an agreement on debt reduction and other restructuring measures in early 1998, and verbalized the agenda for *chaebol* reform as follows:

- adoption of consolidated financial statements from fiscal year 1999;
- compliance with international standards of accounting;
- strengthening of voting rights of minority shareholders;
- compulsory appointment of at least one outsider director from 1998;
- establishment of an external auditors committee;
- prohibition of cross-subsidiary debt guarantees from April 1998;
- resolution of all existing cross-debt guarantees by March 2000.

The Korean government led the way in corporate sector restructuring through the revision of related legislation and the periodic checking of the progress in those agreed measures. Ten laws related to corporate sector restructuring, such as the Commercial Law and the Securities Exchange Law, were revised in February 1998. Legal proceedings for corporate rehabilitation and bankruptcy filing were simplified to facilitate market exit for non-viable firms, and ensure better representation of creditor banks in the resolution process. At least 50 per cent of the board members should be outside directors. The rights of minority shareholders were strengthened by lowering the minimum shareholding requirements for many shareholder rights. For example, any shareholder with 0·01 per cent of firm ownership can file a mismanagement derivative suit.

The top five *chaebols* were to follow a programme of business swaps named the 'Big Deal.' The 'Big Deal' was pursued to streamline overinvestment and enhance efficiency in such key industries as semiconductors, petrochemicals, aerospace, railway vehicles, oil refining, power plant facilities and vessel engines. The plan involved 17 subsidiaries of the five *chaebols*. In December 1998, the *chaebols* reached agreement on many of the deals. Tax incentives were provided for those companies. The agreement involved 19 companies. (There were three non top-five *chaebol* companies.) The Big Deal, for the semiconductors, oil refining, aerospace and railway vehicles industries, was completed. However, the Big Deal for the other industries eventually failed or were delayed.

In addition, the top five *chaebols* were required to reduce their debt–equity ratios to 200 per cent by the end of 1999 and improve their financial structure by asset sales, recapitalization and foreign capital inducement. Excluding the dismantled Daewoo Group, the average debt–equity ratio of the top four *chaebols* fell to below 200 per cent by the end of 1999, down from 352 per cent in 1998. The number of affiliates of the top five *chaebols* had decreased from 262 in April 1997 to 177 by December 1999. (The number of affiliates of the top 30 *chaebols* decreased from 819 to 589 during the same period.)

For the sixth to 64th largest *chaebols*, restructuring was to be carried out through workout programmes. Financial institutions signed the Corporate Restructuring Agreement, which provided informal debt workouts as an alternative to the formal procedures of the insolvency law regime. These programmes involved term extensions, deferred payments and/or the reduction of principal and interest. As of February 2000, 77 corporations of the sixth to 64th *chaebols* were under workout programmes.

Under the current workout programmes, creditor banks are required to oversee the management of workout firms as well as the rescheduling of their debts. The creditor banks, however, lack management expertise and their role is limited to external supervision, leaving management responsibilities in the hands of company officials. To promote more efficient management of insolvent firms under workout programmes, the Korean government is currently considering the establishment of Corporate Restructuring Vehicles (CRVs). A CRV is an independent agency specializing in corporate restructuring. In place of creditor banks, it will assume the authority to manage workout firms.

Despite the corporate reform efforts, however, there has been little evidence of success. For example, the *chaebols* are actually strengthening their grip on the economy. According to the Fair Trade Commission, the total amount of the top five *chaebols'* assets increased by 13·8 per cent in 1998. Furthermore, the total debts of the top five *chaebols* increased to W234 trillion in 1998, up from W221 trillion in 1997. Nonetheless, the debt–equity ratios of the top five *chaebols* decreased as a consequence of the fact that their mode of financing has changed drastically in favour of direct financing through the stock market. Some *chaebols* attracted liquidity through trusts and mutual funds.

The effectiveness of the Big Deal remains unclear. The new firms made by the Big Deal remain in financial distress because of unimproved finances as there has been no debt reduction or injection of new capital. Without lay-offs and plant closures, excess capacity problems also remain and reducing the number of firms is likely to reduce competition and facilitate collusive behaviour. As for the workout programmes, some critics argue that preferential financial treatment for the indebted firms might unnecessarily prolong the lives of failing firms, eat away at banks' assets and exacerbate the credit problems of other firms.

The Korean government has repeatedly announced that the structural reforms have been and will be driven by market forces. However, it is fair to say that the structural reform efforts have been driven by government initiatives. The government intervened widely in the pace and methods of the restructuring process. For example, it supported the Big Deal for the *chaebol* subsidiaries, informally selected the bankrupt firms for workout programmes, set a uniform reduction of the debt–equity ratio regardless of the characteristics of the business, and implicitly placed a limit on *chaebols*' entry into new business (Samsung Economic Research Institute, 2000).

Thus the Korean government needs to reduce its level of corporate intervention and institutionalize a basic corporate governance system; the direction of corporate sector reforms should be more concentrated on profit maximization, or cost minimization, rather than just fitting the standard required by the government itself.

Labour Market Reform

The rigidity of the labour market was also pointed out as a key factor that had contributed to the weakening of the international competitiveness of Korean firms and thereby helped cause the financial crisis. According to Fitch ICBA (1999), with the advent of democratization in 1987 and the subsequent liberalization of trade unions, nominal wages increased by 15 per cent per annum up to 1996, exceeding productivity, which rose by 11 per cent. However, tight labour market conditions and strong trade union power ensured that labour market reform went untouched. The labour market was plagued by rigidity. An excessive degree of job protection prevented lay-offs and encouraged overmanning, inflexible working hours and few limits on strike action. Therefore a major goal of the reform was to ensure flexibility in the labour market.

The Tripartite Commission, composed of representatives from labour, management and government, was established in January 1998, and the Tripartite Social Accord was signed in February 1998. The Accord covers not only labour-related matters, but also a wide range of socioeconomic matters. It includes issues such as the promotion of freedom of association, management transparency, business restructuring, labour market policy, reform of the social security system, wage stabilization, the improvement of labour–management cooperation and the enhancement of labour market flexibility.

In February 1998, greater labour market flexibility was instituted with the revision of the Labour Standard Act (LSA), which legalized lay-offs for 'managerial reasons'. Specifically, lay-offs became possible if four preconditions could be met. First, there must be an urgent managerial need; second, all efforts to avoid lay-offs should have been exhausted; third, workers to be laid off should be selected by a reasonable and fair standard; and fourth, agreement should be reached with labour union representatives. In spite of its very demanding preconditions, the new LSA facilitated necessary lay-offs in the process of financial and corporate sector reform. In addition to the new LSA, legislation allowing the establishment of manpower dispatching businesses took effect in July 1998. Manpower dispatching businesses provide employment outsourcing services for 26 work types and 118 job classifications, including computer professionals, interpreters, secretaries and tour guides. This measure is also expected to further enhance labour market flexibility.

On the other hand, the basic rights of workers have been strengthened. Teachers have been allowed to organize labour unions. The coverage of both unemployment insurance and industrial accident compensation insurance has been widened. Indeed, many policies and programmes were designed to assist the unemployed, although they have been able to provide support for only a fraction of those who have lost their jobs because of the financial crisis (Lee and Lee, 2000).

Public Sector Reform

Poor productivity and rampant inefficiency in the public sector have been notorious. In the wake of the financial crisis, the Korean government declared it would launch its own reforms aimed at remodelling the government's role, and improving the efficiency and transparency of public administration.

The 'downsizing' of the government has been an important feature of the public sector reform. The Korean government has pursued streamlining of its organizational structure. In February 1998, the first reshuffling of the central government structure was implemented, and 11 chambers, 42 bureaux and 53 departments were scrapped. As a result, the number of government employees is to be reduced by 11 per cent by the end of the year 2000. In addition, another downsizing plan has been set up to reduce as many as 16 per cent of total employees by the year 2001. Local governments have also streamlined their organizations; by October 1998, 12 per cent of total jobs had been eliminated. Additionally, the quasi-government sector, including public institutions and various associations, has been streamlined.

State-owned enterprises (SOEs) have also been subject to drastic overhaul by means of privatization or management reform. In August 1998, a plan of SOE privatization was announced. Among the 108 SOEs, 38 would be immediately privatized, 34 gradually privatized, 9 would be merged into others or liquidated, and 21 would go through restructuring. Six SOEs remained untouched. Twenty of the 108 SOEs were privatized in 1998. The 89 subsidiaries of the 30 parent SOEs are also subject to privatization or management reform. Out of 24 non-financial SOEs (parent companies), 5 are to be privatized by 1999, 6 will be gradually privatized by 2002, while the remaining SOEs are earmarked for managerial reform and consolidation.

Elimination of excessive regulation has been another important task in the public sector reform. The Regulation Reform Committee (RRC) announced that in 1998 it abolished approximately 49 per cent of the total 11 125 government regulations pertaining to the private sector.

If is fair to say, however, that many of the public sector reform tasks, and their actual implementation, have been hardly satisfactory. Many critics argue that the government, in particular, which has led the structural reform in other sectors, has not followed through with its own public sector restructuring.

3 ECONOMIC PERFORMANCE

Evolution of the Crisis in 1998[3]

As briefly mentioned in the Introduction, the immediate IMF programme required that the Korean government implement tight monetary and fiscal policies, as an emergency stabilization measure. In particular, the Korean government was asked to raise interest rates sharply. This measure was expected to stem the outflow of foreign funds and the rapid depreciation of the exchange rate. The call rate was raised from 12·3 per cent on 1 December 1997 to 20·7 per cent on 3 December, and further to 30·1 per cent on 23 December. As a consequence, yields on three-year corporate bonds soared from around 14 per cent, before the crisis, to more than 20 per cent, and yields on 91-day commercial paper rose sharply from 13–14 per cent to a peak of 40·8 per cent on 31 December. (See Figure 3.1.) Broad money growth (M3) was reduced to

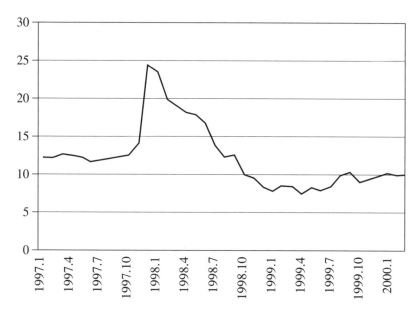

Source: The Bank of Korea, 2000.

Figure 3.1   Yields on three-year corporate bonds (per cent)

13·9 per cent by the end of December 1997, from 16·3 per cent at the end of
November 1997. The IMF also asked Korea to address its fiscal surplus of 0·2
per cent of GDP in 1998 by making contractionary adjustments.

As discussed regarding financial sector reform, many troubled financial
institutions were suspended or closed and commercial banks were required to
meet the BIS 8 per cent minimum requirement by September 1998. However,
the rollover ratio of short-term debt declined sharply and usable official
reserves were almost depleted in mid-December. For example, the rollover
ratio of the seven largest commercial banks fell to 32·2 per cent in December,
from 58·8 per cent in November and 86·5 per cent in October. After a brief
increase to 435 on 6 December, from 379 on 3 December, the Korea Stock
Price Index (KOSPI) kept sliding to reach 351 on 24 December. (See Figure
3.2.) As the speed of depreciation accelerated, the exchange rate rose from
about 1150 W/US$ at the beginning of the month to over 1600 W/US$ at the
end of the year.[4] (See Figure 3.3.) All of these figures were in fact much worse
than the IMF had predicted.

When Korea faced imminent default by 24 December, the IMF decided to
press the foreign commercial banks to roll over their short-term credits on an
enforced basis. The IMF insisted on the comprehensive debt rollover as a

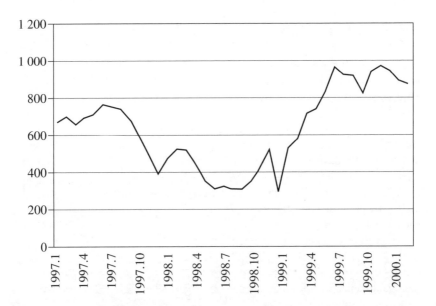

Source: The Bank of Korea, 2000.

Figure 3.2   Korea Stock Price Index (1980 = 100)

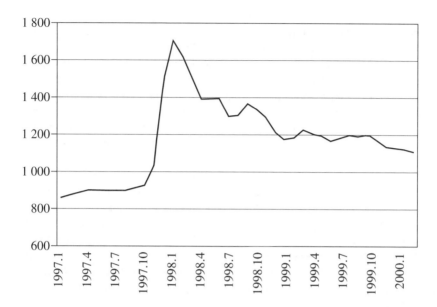

Source: The Bank of Korea, 2000.

Figure 3.3 Exchange rate (W/US$)

condition for further disbursements of the IMF lending package. Initially, the banks and the Korean government announced a freeze on debt servicing. On 16 January the Korean government and the banks formally agreed to a complete rollover of all short-term debts falling due in the first quarter of 1998. On 28 January an agreement was reached to convert US$24 billion in short-term debt into claims of maturities between one and three years (Radelet and Sachs, 1998, p.30). The new arrangements put a brake on the fall of the won and on the decline in Korea's stock market.

As the market interest rates soared to the 30 to 40 per cent level, the financial difficulties of corporations deepened. As the IMF programme required financial institutions to meet the BIS capital adequacy ratios, they became reluctant to provide corporations with funds for fear of incurring new NPLs. Even strong banks came under intense pressure as foreign creditors refused to roll over loans and domestic depositors fled to foreign-owned banks. The merchant banks, in particular, which used to provide corporations with short-term funds, virtually suspended new lending to corporations and tended to refuse rolling over loans falling due.

This, in turn, made the situation even worse for the debt-ridden corporations, resulting in a boost in the number of insolvencies to three times the pre-crisis level. Bankruptcies in Korea hit 3197 in December 1997, rising to 3323 in January 1998, before falling back to 2749 in March 1998. The ratio of dishonoured bills rose drastically to 2·1 per cent in December 1997, from 0·5 per cent in November 1997. As a consequence, the external liquidity crisis became a full-fledged economic crisis as the full extent of the collateral damage to the real sector became apparent. During the first quarter of 1998, real gross domestic product (GDP) recorded a negative growth rate of –4·6 per cent on a year-on-year basis, for the first time in 18 years, followed by –8·0 per cent, –8·1 per cent and –5·9 per cent in the second, third and fourth quarters. In 1998, real GDP dropped by 6·7 per cent. The unemployment rate increased sharply to 6·8 per cent in 1998, in sharp contrast to the 2·6 per cent of 1997. (See Figure 3.4.) Per capita gross national product (GNP) is estimated to have remained at about US$6300 in 1998, down sharply from US$9511 in 1997 and US$10 542 in 1996, and fell short of the US$6745 recorded in 1991.[5]

Meanwhile the current account, which recorded a deficit every month until October 1997, has recorded surpluses since November 1997. In 1998, the current account recorded a surplus of US$40 billion, which was the largest in history. (See Figure 3·5.) However, this was brought about mainly by a decline

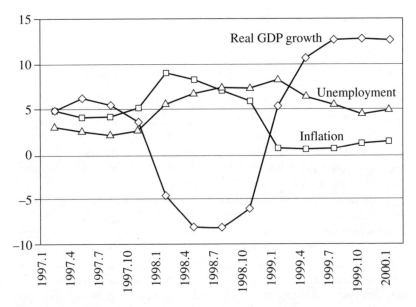

Source: The Bank of Korea, 2000; Ministry of Finance and Economy, 1999b.

Figure 3.4   Real GDP growth rate, inflation rate and unemployment rate (per cent)

in imports rather than an increase in exports. Despite the potential for increased profitability from the exchange rate depreciation, exporters were also badly affected because those with confirmed orders were unable to obtain trade credits and export demand for Korean products shrunk as the Asian crisis spread. In 1998, Korean exports declined by 2·8 per cent on a year-on-year basis to US$132·3 billion, while imports plunged 35·5 per cent to US$93·3 billion.

Signs of Recovery in 1999

Signs of recovery started to appear in early 1999. In the first and second quarters of 1999, real GDP rose by 5·4 per cent and 10·8 per cent, respectively, on a year-on-year basis. Overall, real GDP rose 10·7 per cent in 1999. After peaking at a 17-year high of 8·6 per cent in February 1999, the unemployment rate declined steadily. The annual average jobless rate in 1999 was 6·3 per cent. The current account balance reached US$25 billion in 1999. Thanks to large current account surpluses, Korea's usable foreign exchange reserves grew continuously, reaching US$74·1 billion in December 1999, in sharp contrast with the US$8·8 billion at the end of 1997. The total external liabilities of

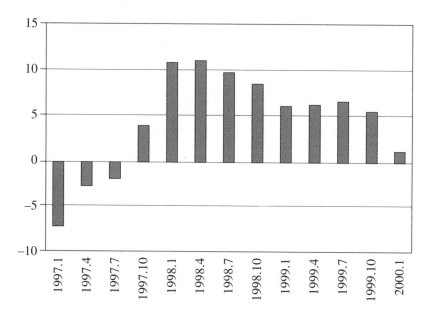

Source: The Bank of Korea, 2000.

Figure 3.5   Current account balances (US$ billions)

Table 3.1   Korea: external liabilities and credit (US$ billions)

	End 1997	End 1998	End 1999	End April 2000
Total external liabilities	159·2	148·7	136·4	140·4
Long-term liabilities	95·7	118·0	98·3	94·2
Short-term liabilities	63·6	30·7	38·1	46·2
Short-term debt/total debt (%)	39·9	20·6	27·9	32·9
Total external credit	105·2	128·5	145·7	156·0
Net external liabilities	−54·1	−20·2	93·0	15·6
Foreign exchange reserves	8·8	48·5	74·1	84·6
Short-term debt/FX reserves (%)	722·7	63·3	51·5	54·6

Source: Ministry of Finance and Economy; Bank of Korea.

Korea were US$136·4 billion at the end of December 1999, which is US$22·8 billion smaller than that at the end of 1997. (See Table 3.1.) Reflecting the economic recovery, foreign capital inflows have rapidly increased. Korea attracted about US$15·5 billion of FDI in 1999, nearly twice the US$8·9 billion achieved in 1998. Not surprisingly, the role of FDI in the Korean economy has increased; it accounted for approximately 8 per cent of GDP in 1999, in contrast to less than 3 per cent in 1996. The W/US$ exchange rate has appreciated to below 1200 and remains stable, mainly owing to the current account surplus and inflows of foreign investment. (See Figure 3.3.) In February 1999, Standard & Poor, an international credit rating agency, raised Korea's sovereign credit rating to BBB−, almost the same level as before the outbreak of the crisis.

Higher than expected economic growth resulted from the rebound of the world economy as well as the restoration of financial confidence in Korea, reflected in lower interest rates, the stock market boom and increasing industrial production. Low interest rates since mid-1998 have produced favourable economic conditions for financial market and corporate restructuring in Korea. In 1999, the domestic interest rates remained stable at a lower level of between 7 to 8 per cent. (See Figure 3.1.) As a result of the lower interest rates, the investors turned to the stock market. In 1999, the benchmark Korea Stock Price Index (KOSPI) recorded a 75 per cent rise from 588 points at the beginning of the year to close to 1000 points by year-end. (See Figure 3.2.) Due to the booming stock market, listed companies raised more than W46 trillion on the Korea Stock Exchange (KSE) and W3·5 trillion on the Korea Securities Dealers Automated Quotation (KOSDAQ) market.

Even though the general economic conditions of Korea have improved, some adverse consequences have emerged during the process of crisis resolution. Specifically, the government and public debt have grown as a consequence of the expenditures on financial restructuring and expanded social programmes. The ratio of national debt to GDP increased from 11·7 per cent in 1997 to almost 20 per cent in 1999.

4   CHALLENGES TO THE ECONOMIC RECOVERY AHEAD

In April 2000, Korea's usable foreign exchange reserves reached US$84·6 billion (see Table 3.1). The Korean economy also showed a high growth rate of 12·8 per cent (see Figure 3.4) and the unemployment rate decreased steadily, reaching 5·1 per cent in the first quarter of 2000. The exchange rate has strengthened and interest rates have remained at levels below where they stood before the crisis erupted. (See Figure 3.3.) It now seems that the Korean economy has overcome the worst of the crisis and the possibility of a repetition of 1997's external liquidity crisis has been significantly reduced. However, unstable elements and conditions are increasingly appearing both inside and outside the nation. Among the destabilizing factors inside Korea are the ailing investment trust companies and the reduction of the current account surpluses. Globally, the slowdown of the US economy, high oil prices and the financial instability in Southeast Asia are casting a shadow over the Korean economy.

Internal Challenges

On the surface, the financial market and corporate sector reforms have been successful. For instance, the banks and the *chaebols* have more than met the government's conditions, imposed following the financial crisis. At the end of 1999, the average BIS ratio of the 17 domestic commercial banks was well above the BIS recommended level of 8 per cent, and the *chaebols* had lowered their borrowing to below 200 per cent of their equity.

However, in June 2000, Korea's financial market was once again severely rattled and, as *The Economist* (3 June 2000) puts it, the country seemed to be back on the brink of a financial crisis. Specifically, on 26 May 2000, lenders to the two subsidiaries of the largest *chaebol*, Hyundai, refused to renew short-term loans. As a consequence, the stock market plunged. Hyundai's troubles began with fears over the health of the group's investment trust company, Hyundai Investment Trust & Securities, which was thought to have a W1·2 trillion hole in its finances and had debts of approximately W3 trillion that will fall due by the end of 2000. Hyundai Investment Trust is 51 per cent owned by two other Hyundai companies, which are also owned by other Hyundai companies, and so forth. This cross-ownership means that the collapse of Hyundai Investment Trust can put the entire group at risk. Therefore creditors lost faith in the Hyundai group's resolve to cut its debts, and finally refused to renew short-term loans falling due. At the urging of the government, Hyundai announced a hasty restructuring plan, which includes the retirement of Hyundai's founding family members. This restored some calm to the markets.

However, Korea's financial distress does not seem to be over yet, because Hyundai Investment Trust is not alone. Korea Investment and Daehan Investment are also in danger. All this renewed financial distress proves that the financial and corporate reforms have been superficial, and the financial markets are still very fragile. The capital adequacy ratio of the commercial banks was significantly improved by the injection of public funds and the infusion of subordinated debt. However, the bad loans still remain high and may increase with potential further distress of the corporate sector. The recent Daewoo and Hyundai cases showed the possibility of such distress. Investment trust companies were at the root of the recent damage to Korea's financial stability. However, banks seem to be running into some trouble as well, as they are also large shareholders in the trust companies. In fact, most domestic banks in Korea are still classified as non-investment grade by major international credit rating agencies.

Thanks to large current account surpluses in 1998 and 1999, the banks and the *chaebols* have repaid or refinanced some of their short-term foreign debts, and the government has amassed huge foreign exchange reserves. As imports grow more rapidly than exports, however, the current account surpluses are shrinking rapidly. (See Figure 3.5.) Korea may soon experience a current account deficit and become a net importer of capital again. In fact, Korea's external liabilities were US$140·4 billion in April 2000, up from US$136·4 billion in December 1999. The nation's short-term external liabilities also rose, from US$38·1 billion in December 1999 to US$46·2 billion in April 2000, recording a weight of 32·9 per cent of the nation's total foreign debt and 54·6 per cent of its official foreign exchange reserves, which reached US$84·6 billion in April. (See Table 3.1.) This suggests that the financial and corporate sector reforms should be pursued in a timely manner.

The social consequences of the financial crisis and subsequent structural reforms also warrant a close look. There have been tumultuous and painful side-effects for most Koreans in all segments of Korean society. In particular, the crisis and Korea's structural reform process have had significant and adverse effects on equitable growth in Korea. Specifically, low-income households and marginal workers, such as women, young workers, the less educated, wage earners and first-time jobseekers, were the hardest hit and the existing social protection systems have been unable to cope adequately with the social consequences of the crisis and, as a consequence, income distribution in Korea has deteriorated (Lee and Lee, 2000). Therefore, special efforts to strengthen social protection systems are sorely needed.

External Challenges

First of all, there is a risk that the US stock market may collapse if the foreign capital inflow slows down as a result of the vast current account deficit and external liabilities of the United States. As the *Los Angeles Times* reports, 'a sharp U.S. slowdown could spread pain at home and damaging fallout in a closely connected world economy' (12 June 2000). Even though this scenario is a remote possibility, the US economy will slow down because of its successive interest rate hikes. Korea's exports to the United States will then see a downturn as US private expenditure declines.

The European Union (EU) has also raised its interest rates in an effort to prevent the devaluation of the Euro. This worldwide trend of high interest rates can become a serious threat to Korea and to other East Asian countries whose financial markets are still fragile. This is because, unless the East Asian countries also increase their interest rates, foreign capital may pull out of these countries. And if they increase interest rates to avoid such a situation, the interest burden of firms will increase and extra financial stress will follow.

On the other hand, the Southeast Asian financial markets have become increasingly unstable since the end of 1999. This is due to the uncertainties of the world economy and the diminished confidence of foreign investors in these markets in the face of the political unrest and delays in their restructuring processes. If the Southeast Asian countries face a threat similar to the 1997 financial crisis and competitive currency devaluation, there can be no doubt that Korea will again be adversely affected.

The current upward trend of international oil prices is also worrisome. The price of West Texas Intermediate oil, for example, surpassed US$30 on 18 May 2000, the highest level in the past nine years. As a result, Korea's energy imports during the first quarter of 2000 surged by 120 per cent on a year-on-year basis to a total of US$9·1 billion. If the oil prices remain high, this will put intense pressure on the Korean economy by pushing domestic prices up while simultaneously pulling current account surpluses down.

5 CONCLUDING REMARKS

On the basis of post-crisis economic developments in Korea, it is fair to say that the likelihood of a repetition of the turmoil in the Korean economy has declined considerably. However, there remain many internal and external obstacles to the full recovery of the Korean economy. If any of the obstacles are not adequately confronted, the crisis could turn out to be an even more enduring pain for the Korean people. On the other hand, if positive preconditions are met and the structural reforms are accomplished smoothly, the crisis could turn out to be a blessing in disguise that will pave the way for another economic miracle and sustainable growth for Korea in the 21st century (Lee, 1999).

There is therefore a strong need for continued efforts to safeguard macro-economic stability, implement structural reforms and attain sustained growth through increases in efficiency and productivity. In line with this, Korea has to establish a true market economy – an economy led by the private sector and the basic principles of transparency, accountability and fair competition, but guided by prudential supervision.

NOTES

1. Drawing upon the analogy between a financial crisis and a human stroke, Lee (1999) shows how numerous factors, such as fundamental weaknesses, unfriendly environment, policy mistakes and exogenous shocks, were systematically intertwined in causing the financial crisis. See also Lee (2000).
2. For more discussion of the *chaebols*, see Yoo (1995), and Lee and Lee (1996).
3. This section draws heavily upon Lee (1999).
4. Before the crisis Korea maintained the so-called 'market average foreign exchange rate system which was adopted in 1990. Even though the daily fluctuation band had been widened gradually with the progress of financial liberalization, it remained at only ±2·25 per cent just before the crisis. On the eve of its turning to the IMF, the Korean government widened the daily band for exchange rate fluctuations to ±10 per cent of the market average rate. On 16 December it shifted to a free-floating exchange rate system.
5. The sharp fall in per capita GNP was attributed not only to the economic contraction, but also largely to the Korean won's sharp depreciation.

REFERENCES

The Economist (2000), 'Korea's New Wobbles', 3–9 June, pp.85–6.

Fitch ICBA (1999), *Rating Report: Republic of Korea.*

Joh, Sung Wook (1999), 'The Korean Corporate Sector: Crisis and Reform', KDI Working Paper no. 9912, Korea Development Institute, Seoul.

Los Angeles Times (2000), 'Economic Rebound Abroad a Boon to U.S.', 12 June.

Lee, Hyun-Hoon (1999), 'A "Stroke" Hypothesis of Korea's 1997 Financial Crisis: Causes, Consequences and Prospects', University of Melbourne Research Paper no. 696. (Available at http://www.ecom.unimelb.edu.au/ecowww/research/696.pdf)

Lee, Jong Won (2000), 'Success and Failure of the Korean Economy and its Prospects', mimeo, presented at the International Conference on 'International Economics and Asia', Hong Kong, July.

Lee, Kyu-Uck and Jae-Hyung Lee (1996), 'Business Groups (*Chaebols*) in Korea: Characteristics and Government Policy', occasional paper no. 23, Korea Institute for Industrial Economics and Trade, Seoul.

Lee, Young-Youn and Hyung-Hoon Lee (2000), 'Financial Crisis, Structural Reform and Social Consequences in Korea', in Tran Van Hoa (ed.), The *Social Impact of the Asia Crisis*, London: Macmillan.

Ministry of Finance and Economy (MOFE) (1999a), 'Second Round Reforms in Financial, Corporate, Labor and Public Sectors', *Economic Bulletin*, Korea Development Institute, Seoul, March, pp.24–35.

Ministry of Finance and Economy (MOFE) (1999b), 'The Road to Recovery: Korea's Ongoing Economic Reform', Korea Development Institute, Seoul, May. (Available at http://epic.kdi.re.kr/ecobul/19905/19905-2.htm)

Radelet, Steven and Jeffrey Sachs (1998), 'The East Asian Financial Crisis: Diagnosis, Remedies, Prospects', mimeo. (Available at http://www.stern.nyu.edu/~nroubini/asia/AsiaHomepage.html)

Samsung Economic Research Institute (2000), 'Two Years after the IMF Bailout: A Review of the Korean Economy's Transformation', mimeo, March.

Yoo, Seong Min (1995), '*Chaebol* in Korea: Misconceptions, Realities and Policies', KDI Working Paper no. 9507, Korea Development Institute, Seoul.

4. Indonesia: charting the road to recovery

Charles Harvie

1 INTRODUCTION

The Indonesian economy experienced a dramatic economic collapse in 1998 after the financial convulsions in the second half of 1997 and the early part of 1998, with GDP declining by some 13·7 per cent. The speed and intensity of this economic and social collapse surprised many, particularly given the economy's impressive pre-crisis economic and social outcomes. GDP grew by an average of more than 7 per cent per year between 1990 and 1996, and even during 1997 the overall growth rate was 5 per cent. This 19 per cent turnaround in economic growth in a single year represented one of the most dramatic economic collapses recorded anywhere in the world since the Great Depression. During this period foreign and domestic investors fled the country; hundreds of non-bank corporations became effectively bankrupt; the banking system effectively ground to a halt, with very little new lending taking place and dozens of banks becoming insolvent; imports fell by 34·4 per cent in 1998, reflecting a collapse of domestic demand, and in particular that of investment expenditure; thousands of Indonesians lost their jobs in the formal sector and sought employment in the informal sector; and millions faced a substantial reduction in their standard of living. There is no quick fix to the country's plight,[1] and it will take many years before the country can hope to regain pre-crisis rates of economic growth. However, a glimmer of hope occurred during 1999, when there were signs that the economy was recovering, albeit at a very low level.

The remainder of this chapter proceeds as follows. In Section 2, pre-crisis macroeconomic outcomes and factors behind the collapse of the Indonesian economy are discussed. Section 3 focuses upon the initial policy response to the crisis. Section 4 highlights the key issues and policies for sustained economic recovery. Section 5 outlines the new democratically elected government's medium-term economic strategy. Section 6 identifies the government's medium-term macroeconomic policy framework. Finally, section 7 presents a summary of the major issues identified in this chapter.

2 PRE-CRISIS MACROECONOMIC OUTCOMES AND WEAKNESSES

Between 1970 and 1996, Indonesia achieved one of the fastest growth rates in the world, with GDP growing on average by 7·2 per cent per year and contributing to an annual average increase of 5·1 per cent in per capita income. For the average Indonesian, real annual income was nearly four times higher in 1996 than it was in 1970. In addition, compared to many other developing economies, these gains in income were spread fairly equitably. Between 1976 and 1990, income per person in the poorest quintile of Indonesia's population grew by 5·8 per cent per year, while the average income of the entire population grew by 4·9 per cent per year (Gallup *et al.*, 1998). Poverty reduction in Indonesia during this period was the largest recorded anywhere in the world, with official estimates which indicated that over 60 per cent of Indonesia's population were below the official poverty line in 1970 falling to 11 per cent by 1996. While the precise magnitude of these numbers has been disputed, acceptance of Indonesia's impressive achievement in reducing abject poverty is not. Additional social indicators support this success. For example, life expectancy at birth increased from 49 years to 65 years, adult literacy rates jumped from 57 per cent to 84 per cent, and infant mortality rates fell from 114 per thousand to 49 per thousand (World Bank, 1998). In the context of a relatively poor developing country, such developments are very impressive.

A number of factors have been advanced to explain Indonesia's rapid economic growth during the period under discussion.[2] The first of these is the country's abundant and diverse natural resources, including oil and gas, copper, tin, gold, rubber and palm oil, which played a particularly important role during the high commodity price era of the 1970s. This contributed to a rapid expansion of export revenues, then utilized to pay for improvements in infrastructure, including that of ports, roads, agricultural irrigation and the expansion of primary school provision. Despite the extensive nature of corruption and nepotism that existed in the country, and the resulting waste and abuse of resources, its investment in infrastructure enabled it to perform well in comparison to many resource-abundant developing economies during the 1970s and 1980s.

A second factor is the agricultural sector. Output in this sector grew steadily from the early 1970s, supported by green revolution technologies that rapidly increased rice production on Java and some of the outer islands. Emphasis by the government was placed on offering relatively stable and remunerative prices to rice farmers, with the objective of offering farmers adequate returns rather than providing large subsidies for consumers.[3] As indicated previously, it also supported agriculture by providing substantive investments in irrigation and other agricultural infrastructure, and by connecting villages to larger markets through the construction of new roads.

A third factor, arising from the fall in world oil prices in the mid-1980s, was the active promotion by the government of labour-intensive manufactured exports. In particular, exports increased rapidly in the textiles, clothing, footwear, toys, furniture and other products industries, contributing to a major expansion in manufacturing jobs, a resulting improvement in productivity, and acquisition of new technology. To take advantage of the benefits deriving from foreign direct investment, the government reduced investment barriers during the 1980s and 1990s in many sectors of the economy. However, some sectors still remained off limits to foreign investors. This development exposed domestic producers to increased competition and facilitated their integration with globalized production networks.

A fourth factor was the adoption by the country of prudent macroeconomic policies that kept the fiscal budget basically in balance, inflation low, exports competitive and the current account deficit at reasonable levels. Competent economic management enabled Indonesia to come through well the period of oil prices increases and decreases during the 1970s and 1980s, and this was maintained until the onset of the crisis in mid-1997. The government's strategy of essentially proscribing domestic financing for the budget resulted in both expenditures and monetary growth being kept under reasonable control. Over the period 1992 to 1996, inflation averaged only 8 per cent per year, the budget balance was slightly positive and the current account deficit averaged 2·7 per cent of GDP.

Despite these apparently healthy macroeconomic indicators, weaknesses in the Indonesian economy began to appear during the 1990s. Four developments were of particular concern: an increasing reliance on capital inflows, particularly that on a short-term basis; the development of an overvalued exchange rate which was contributing to a slowdown in export growth; a weak banking system arising from financial reform dating back to the late 1980s; and the rapidly growing business interests of President Suharto and his family and close associates. The latter becoming most prevalent as Suharto's family came of age, and began to have extensive business interests. Each of these developments is now briefly discussed in turn.

In terms of the first development, between 1990 and 1996, Indonesia received capital inflows averaging about 4 per cent of GDP. Foreign creditors were keen to provide financing to Indonesia during this period, and most especially through bank loans. Indonesia's total debt outstanding to foreign commercial banks amounted to US$59 billion by mid-1997. Table 4.1 shows that Indonesian banks owed about US$12 billion of this amount, while Indonesian non-bank corporations owed about US$40 billion.[4] Although much of this financing was used for productive investment projects, an increasing and significant amount was being directed to weaker projects, many of which were controlled by the Suharto family and their associates. Foreign

Table 4.1   *Indonesian debt outstanding to foreign commercial banks (US$ billion)*

	Total	Banks	Public	Non-bank private	Short-term debt	Foreign reserves (excl. gold)
			Debt by Sector			
June 1997	58·7	12·4	6·5	39·7	34·7	20·3
December 1997	58·4	11·7	6·9	39·7	35·4	16·6
June 1998	50·3	7·1	7·6	35·5	27·7	17·9

	Total	Japan	United States	Germany	Other European	All Others
	Banks' Claims on Indonesia by Country of Origin					
June 1997	58·7	23·2	4·6	5·6	16·9	8·4
December 1997	58·1	22·0	4·9	6·2	17·1	7·9
June 1998	48·4	19·0	3·2	5·9	16·1	4·2

Sources: Debt data: Bank for International Settlements; reserves: International Monetary Fund.

lenders believed that these projects carried an implicit guarantee from the government, and consequently financed these projects often without under-taking adequate risk analysis. In addition, most creditors believed that rapid growth would continue, so that even marginal projects would be able to service their loans.

While the quantity of loans was substantial, of more importance, in terms of the economy's vulnerability, was the maturity structure of the foreign borrowing. Of the US$59 billion owed to foreign banks in mid-1997, US$35 billion was short-term debt due within one year. In addition to this amount, Indonesian firms had taken out substantial lines of short-term credit in foreign currencies from Indonesian banks, adding to the short-term foreign currency exposure of Indonesian firms. By comparison, foreign exchange reserves in mid-1997 totalled about US$20 billion, so short-term debts owed to foreign commercial banks were about 1.75 times the size of Indonesia's total foreign exchange reserves (see Radelet and Sachs, 1998).

Short-term foreign currency loans were particularly attractive to Indonesian firms, since they generally carried relatively low interest rates. Firms assumed, in addition, that in a rapidly growing economy they would easily be able to roll over these loans when they were due for repayment, and indeed this was the case until mid-1997. In addition, the exchange rate system adopted by Indonesia further encouraged the accumulation of short-term foreign debt. Indonesia adopted a crawling peg system in the mid-1980s, with the rupiah depreciating by between 3 and 5 per cent per year, primarily against the US dollar, with little variation in the trend. Such exchange rate predictability made short-term dollar loans seem much less risky, and therefore much more attractive, and reduced the incentive for firms to hedge against their exposure to exchange rate movements. Indeed, very few firms covered their exposure. Indonesia's vulnerability was all the greater because its largest creditors were Japanese banks, which supplied about 40 per cent of the total credit from foreign banks. The underlying weakness of Japanese banks made them more likely to try and quickly withdraw their loans once the crisis started. Indeed, this appears to have been precisely what happened.

A second problem development was the contribution of Indonesia's slowly crawling peg to a mostly overvalued exchange rate and slowing export growth. As prices for many non-traded Indonesian goods and services grew in the early 1990s, the rupiah became increasingly overvalued (Radelet, 1996). After the US dollar began to appreciate against the Japanese yen in 1995, this trend accelerated, resulting in the rupiah also appreciating against the yen. Between 1990 and mid-1997, the rupiah appreciated approximately 22 per cent in real terms,[5] and growth in Indonesia's non-oil exports slowed from an annual average of 26 per cent in 1991–2 to 14 per cent between 1993 and 1995, to just 10 per cent in 1996 and 1997. Although smaller than in the other Asian crisis countries, Indonesia's overvalued currency and export slowdown indicated a need for some moderate adjustments to re-establish the international competitiveness of Indonesian firms.

A third area of weakness was the country's financial system, especially its banks. Beginning in the late 1980s, Indonesia began a series of initiatives and reforms aimed at opening and expanding the financial sector. Privately-owned banks were allowed to operate and compete directly with the large state-owned banks that had long controlled financial activities. The government substantially reduced the extent of state-directed lending, giving the banks much more leeway in their lending decisions. Bank capitalization requirements were eased, and the number of banks more than doubled to well over 200 between 1988 and 1993. The government also moved to deregulate equity, bond insurance and other financial activities, although these did not expand as quickly as banking. These changes were encouraged and generally applauded by the international community. Indeed, financial deregulation brought many benefits to the economy by diminishing the role of the state in allocating credit, providing Indonesians with many more options for financial services and reducing the costs of financial intermediation.

However, the government did not develop the supervisory and regulatory capacity needed to keep up with the greatly expanded and more sophisticated financial system. A number of banks, especially state-owned banks, were undercapitalized or allowed to violate other prudential regulations without penalty. Several large business groups opened their own banks, using bank deposits to finance their own activities with little scrutiny. As a result, many banks had substantial exposure to affiliated companies. In addition, the state-owned banks had large exposures to firms controlled by the Suhartos and their friends, and few of these loans were fully serviced.

Such problems in the banking system were relatively well known, and indeed efforts were made between 1993 and 1997 to improve the situation, with some progress being achieved. Many banks, indeed, were much weaker in 1993 and 1994 than they were in 1997, at the onset of the crisis. Non-performing loans rose quickly in the early 1990s, especially following a major monetary contraction in early 1991, but they declined in subsequent years as banks regained profitability and were able to write off some bad loans. The World Bank, in a report on Indonesia issued just before the onset of the crisis, concluded that 'the quality of commercial bank portfolios continued to improve during 1996, albeit slowly' (World Bank, 1997).

Unlike banks in Thailand and Korea, Indonesian banks had accumulated considerably less foreign debt from borrowing offshore by mid-1997. A major factor behind this was that the government introduced limits on offshore borrowing by commercial banks, the government and state-owned enterprises in 1991, as foreign borrowing began to grow. However, the government did not impose limits on foreign borrowing by private companies, arguing instead that private sector borrowing decisions were best left to the market. When the crisis hit, despite this apparently prudent policy, it created more difficulty for the country, in that it had to restructure debts owned by Indonesia's diffuse private sector firms in comparison to the more limited number of debtors, mostly banks, in Korea and Thailand. This goes a long way to explaining the comparatively slow progress the country has made in restructuring its foreign debt.

A final weakness was the business corruption and cronyism that had long been a feature of the Indonesian economy, compounded by the rapid expansion of the business interests of the family and close allies of President Suharto and, especially, his children. From the late 1980s and 1990s, Suharto's children came of age and became involved in a growing range of businesses, including shipping of oil and gas, production of petrochemicals, clove marketing, hotels, toll roads and a plethora of other activities. Suharto's apparent unwillingness to compromise these interests for the benefit of the country provided a major undoing for the country during the early stages of the crisis. At a broader level, Indonesia's rapid economic development was not matched by similar political and institutional development. President Suharto consolidated his power during the 1970s and 1980s, and tolerated no political opposition or discourse.

Although significant, these growing weaknesses, on their own, do not sufficiently explain the magnitude of the economic crisis experienced by Indonesia from late 1997. The following section analyses the Indonesian government and IMF's response to the crisis, to identify other factors resulting in the financial crisis developing into an economic crisis and, later, political crisis.

3   POLICY RESPONSE TO THE CRISIS

During the early stages of the financial crisis, Indonesia was widely praised for having taken swift and appropriate action. In early July 1997, the government widened the trading band on the rupiah and then in August let it float, being unwilling to run down its foreign exchange reserves in a futile and wasteful defence of the currency. Interest rates were increased sharply in August, so that overnight inter-bank rates rose by a factor of six from 15 per cent at the end of June to as high as 98 per cent on 20 August. Inter-bank interest rates remained at around three times their pre-crisis level in the months that followed, far higher than in the other crisis countries. The government postponed several large investment projects, and quickly eased restrictions governing foreign direct investment. It was generally anticipated that Indonesia would be much less affected by the crisis than its neighbours. For example, the IMF described Indonesia's initial response as 'timely and broadly appropriate'.

Ultimately, however, considerable blame for the Indonesian crisis can be directed at mismanagement by both Suharto and the IMF. Suharto's unwillingness to enforce policies that might damage the business interests of his family and close associates, his inconsistency and, ultimately, his confrontational approach undermined confidence and accelerated Indonesia's economic contraction. In conjunction the IMF's lack of familiarity with the Indonesian economy and its key institutions, and its poorly conceived reform programme did the economy more harm than good. Together, they contributed to making the initial financial crisis develop into a full-scale economic and, later, financial crisis of a magnitude far greater than that observed elsewhere in the region.

Indications of a lack of commitment by the Suharto government to reform of the economy, particularly where it conflicted with family and close associates' business interest, came in early September 1997, when the government postponed some 150 investment projects only to announce several days later that 15 of the biggest would be allowed to go forward. All 15 of these projects were controlled by Suharto's close associates. In mid-October, the government called in the IMF, and the two parties reached agreement on Indonesia's first programme on 31 October. The timing of this decision has been questioned by some,[6] since the central bank had not depleted its reserves, Indonesia's early handling of the crisis, other than the reversal of the 15 investment projects, had been widely praised and a relatively strong group of economic managers were in place.[7]

IMF policy response

The IMF programme had three basic components: tighter fiscal and monetary policies, financial reforms based on bank closures, and a range of other structural reforms aimed at specific sectors. We focus upon the first two.

Tighter fiscal and monetary policies

The first priority of the programme was to generate a fiscal surplus of 1 per cent of GDP. The tightening of fiscal policy was not appropriate since excess demand was not the primary cause of Indonesia's problems, and the capital withdrawals already well under way meant that the economy was already contracting significantly. The initial fiscal tightening simply added to the contraction, further undermining investor confidence in the short-term economic outlook and adding to the capital flight that was under way. The IMF later recognized its mistake and eased up on its fiscal targets for Indonesia, but the initial damage had been done. The IMF also aimed to keep monetary policies tight. Overnight inter-bank lending rates, after their initial huge jump in August, fluctuated at around three times their pre-crisis level in September and October 1997, and they remained high after the IMF programme was introduced. The higher interest rates did not produce the desired effect upon the exchange rate; instead they further weakened the financial condition of both corporations and banks.[8]

Financial reforms through bank closures

Indonesia's banking system was weak, poorly supervised and in need of substantial reform. The crisis highlighted in October 1997 the urgent need to restructure the financial system. However, the IMF programme called for a sudden closure of 16 banks in November 1997, in an attempt to send a strong signal to foreign investors that the government was serious about reform. But the closures were very hastily conceived, and were not accompanied by a comprehensive strategy to restructure appropriately the financial system.[9] The IMF's insistence on bank closures ignored the fact that there was no deposit insurance in place and failed to take into consideration how depositors in other banks would react. The bank closures caused a series of bank runs, adding to the withdrawal of bank deposits already under way, that seriously undermined the rest of the banking system, including healthy banks. The closures did not engender confidence but rather exacerbated the current liquidity squeeze in financial markets, making it much more difficult for all banks to continue their normal lending operations. These bank closures were a mistake, and this was recognized later on, even by the IMF itself and the World Bank.

The bank closures débâcle was made even worse by Suharto. One of the closed banks was owned by his son, who publicly threatened legal action to keep his bank open. Within a few weeks he was allowed to open a new bank, using the same buildings and employees. Doubts about the efficacy of the IMF programme, arising from the bank closure policy, certainly added to the government's reluctance to follow the IMF's advice at later critical periods.

The original IMF programme contained an additional flaw, by providing only a very minimal amount of financing to ease Indonesia's enormous liquidity squeeze. The first IMF programme scheduled Indonesia to receive US$3 billion in November 1997 and nothing else for at least five months, with the next disbursement scheduled for March 1998. This was a clearly inadequate amount of financing to engender confidence and stop Indonesia's panic.

Indonesia signed its second agreement with the IMF on 15 January 1998. The new programme eased up slightly on fiscal policy and on the required capital adequacy ratio for banks, but otherwise kept the same basic strategy as the first programme. The markets immediately reacted negatively, with the rupiah falling 11 per cent in two days. One key reason was that there was almost nothing in the new programme about a strategy for dealing with Indonesia's short-term foreign debt, which was at the heart of the market turmoil. Given the success of the IMF and US Treasury-backed rollover of Korea's short-term debt in late 1997 and early 1998, this seemed surprising. Debt restructuring in Indonesia, in fact, was not to become a priority of the IMF until its third programme in April 1998. By this time, however, it appeared to be happening too late. As mentioned previously, debt restructuring in Indonesia was made more difficult because it was mainly corporate rather than commercial bank debt. While this did make the process of debt restructuring more difficult, its delay in implementation simply compounded the country's financial and economic difficulties.

Earlier, in late January 1998, the government had acted on its own by announcing a 'voluntary' suspension of private sector debt repayments. At the same time the government announced that it would guarantee all commercial bank liabilities, including both foreign and domestic creditors and all deposits. The government had little choice given the disintegration of the banking system that was under way. The government also began to renege on several structural reforms in the programme, such as dismantling the clove marketing board, controlled by Suharto's son, removing tax breaks that heavily protected production of a national car, also controlled by his son, and other issues.[10] Of particular concern was Suharto's flirtation with the adoption of a currency board in Indonesia.

Indonesia's contraction was deepened by two additional economic shocks. First, the country was hit by a severe drought in 1997, which seriously undermined agricultural production just as the financial crisis was beginning to evolve. In particular, rice production fell sharply, leading to price increases that added significantly to overall inflationary trends. Weak farm production also meant that there were fewer employment opportunities for urban day workers that were laid off as the financial crisis began. Second, export prices, specifically for commodities, declined sharply in 1997 and continued to be low throughout 1998. Weak oil prices, in particular, hurt both export earnings and budget revenue.

4   KEY ISSUES AND POLICIES FOR ECONOMIC RECOVERY

There are a number of key areas in which policy will need to be focused if a sustained recovery of the economy is to be possible. In particular, these include the attainment of political stability, the need to reform and recapitalize the banking system, the restructuring of corporate sector debt, restarting the growth of exports, and keeping the budget deficit within manageable limits.

The financial and economic crisis was compounded by the political crisis arising from the delay in the departure of President Suharto. The dislike for his regime throughout the country and his protection of family and close allies' interests at the expense of the country's interests contributed to considerable political turmoil and instability. The riots of May 1998 that ultimately brought about his demise simply ushered in another leader, President B.J. Habibe, already tainted by his close relationship with the outgoing leader. A key to restoring investor confidence, and to signal a clear break with the past and to usher in fundamental changes and reform, has occurred with the coming to power of a new leader supported by Indonesia's first democratically elected parliament – President Abdurrahman Wahid. While this has signalled a break with the past, there is still some concern over the fragile leader and his ability to unite the country as well as bring about the necessary changes that will set Indonesia on a path to long-term growth and development. The country desperately requires the establishment of political stability without which economic stability is unlikely. Potential investors are unlikely to make significant commitments until they know the new government's reform credentials.

The Indonesian banking system is essentially moribund, with most banks undercapitalized and illiquid and normal lending operations seriously curtailed. Non-performing loans (NPLs), by some estimates, have reached as high as 60–75 per cent of total loans. Over 60 banks have been closed and dozens of others are under the supervision or management of the Indonesian Bank Restructuring Agency (IBRA), established in early 1998. IBRA initially focused its efforts on recovering at least part of the Rp130 billion in liquidity credits with which Bank Indonesia had provided ailing banks in late 1997 and early 1998. The owners of these banks pledged US$16 billion in assets to the government to cover the loans, and had four years to repay the loans or lose their assets.

In September 1998, the government announced its basic strategy to recapitalize the banking system. Banks were separated into three groups. First, any bank with a capital adequacy ratio (CAR) of less than –25 per cent would be closed. Second, those banks with a CAR greater than 4 per cent would be allowed to operate normally, and would be expected to increase their CAR to 8 per cent by 2001. Third, banks with a CAR between –25 per cent and 4 per cent would be eligible to apply for government recapitalization plans. Owners of banks in that category that meet certain eligibility requirements will be expected to provide immediately 20 per cent of the funds necessary to increase their bank's CAR to 4 per cent. The government would supply the remaining 80 per cent of the recapitalization funds. The owners of the banks would have the option to repurchase the government's shares within three years and would have the right of first refusal to buy the shares over five years. In addition, these banks would be able to remove some of the NPLs from their books by swapping them for government bonds. Any amounts the banks collect on these loans can be used to buy back the government's capital share.

Even with this recapitalization many banks still remain illiquid, and have little incentive to begin lending. Most banks prefer to put the few available funds they have in instruments such as one month Bank Indonesia certificates rather than in new loans. Moreover, the move to recapitalize the banking system effectively represents a temporary nationalization of the banking system. Extricating the state from the banking sector in the coming years represents a major challenge to the authorities.

The short-term foreign debt owed by non-bank corporate firms was at the heart of the crisis in Indonesia. Despite this almost nothing was done, with the exception of voluntary debt suspension, about the issue until June 1998. At the end of June 1998, Indonesian firms owed about US$36 billion to foreign banks, down only slightly from the US$40 billion owned just prior to the crisis. Indonesia's short-term debt fell from US$35 billion to US$27 billion between mid-1997 and mid-1998. Thus, even after a full year, the debt burden remained very high, both because debtors were unable to pay the debts and because creditors were unwilling to reschedule them.

In June 1998, the government reached agreement, the 'Frankfurt Agreement', with a group of private creditors on restructuring Indonesian debt. First, Indonesian commercial banks were expected to repay US$6 billion in trade credit arrears, in return for which foreign banks would try to maintain trade credits at the April 1998 level. All new trade credits would be guaranteed by Bank Indonesia. Second, about US$9 billion in debts owed by Indonesian commercial banks and falling due before March 1999 would be exchanged for new loans of maturity between one and four years. This was also guaranteed by Bank Indonesia. These two facilities have been seen as generally success-ful, albeit at least six months too late. The third portion of the agreement covered corporate debts. Indonesia established the Indonesian Debt Restructuring Agency (INDRA) to facilitate repayment of an estimated US$64 billion in corporate debt. INDRA acts as an intermediary between creditors and debtors and is designed to provide protection against further real depreca-tion of the rupiah, and to provide adequate assurances that adequate foreign exchange will be available to make payments.

The agreement provided little cash relief for debtors, however, and little incentive for creditors to write down their loans. To further encourage restruc-turing, the government announced the 'Jakarta Initiative' in September 1998. The initiative offered guidelines on the formation of creditor committees, standstill arrangements, exchange of information, subordination of old loans to new credits and other related issues. However, it did nothing to address the fundamental problem of burden sharing between debtors and creditors.

A major hurdle for Indonesian debt restructuring has been the reluctance of Japanese banks to offer any substantial relief or write-down on Indonesian debt. Since Japanese banks are by far the biggest of Indonesia's creditors, this problem is of particular importance. Many Japanese banks were fairly weak to begin with before the crisis, and had not made adequate provisioning to write off substantial amounts of Asian debts. Following the onset of the crisis, non-Japanese banks were willing to move forward with substantial debt relief, but no such willingness has been demonstrated by the Japanese banks. They continued to insist that borrowers make interest payments on time, so that the loans remain current in their books. More active participation and assistance by the Japanese government was clearly essential before progress in alleviat-ing Indonesian debt could be made.

One of Indonesia's main hopes for a recovery was through an expansion of exports. The large depreciation of the rupiah substantially increased the inter-national competitiveness of Indonesian firms, and made Indonesia one of the lowest cost producers in the world of many commodities and other products. While export volumes expanded, many foreign buyers became convinced that Indonesian firms could no longer be relied upon for timely delivery of prod-ucts. As a consequence they switched their orders to firms in other countries. Once foreign buyers switch their suppliers it is very hard to convince them to come back, especially given the then uncertainty over the political situation. This will be a major problem that the country will face in the foreseeable future.

Finally, after years of prudent fiscal policy with essentially balanced budgets, Indonesia's budget deficit escalated in 1998/99 to around 4 per cent of GDP, and was expected to reach 6 per cent of GDP in 1999/2000. Domestic tax revenues collapsed with the fall in economic activity. In addition, revenues from exports of oil fell by about one-third in US dollar terms. These forces put tremendous pressure on the budget. The crisis increased the need for critical social welfare programmes, in addition to the cost of recapitalizing the banks. The result is a substantial increase in budget deficits. Receipts from new privatizations are unlikely to be large enough to make much of a difference, and any further depreciation of the exchange rate would only make the deficit larger.

Financing the budget deficit is the most immediate challenge, and will persist for several years into the future. There is not enough liquidity in the economy to float a major domestic bond issue. Monetizing the budget risks sparking inflation, which could jump very quickly. That leaves foreign financing as the only viable option. The government has received significant commitments from donor countries, and will be dependent upon this for several years in the future.

5   THE MEDIUM-TERM ECONOMIC STRATEGY

With the establishment of Indonesia's first democratically elected parliament in October 1999 and the coming to power of a new president, President Wahid, a new economic reform programme was introduced designed to reinvigorate the economic reform agenda and to provide the basis for sustained economic growth based on social justice and good governance. The performance of the programme is to be monitored through quantitative performance criteria and indicative targets in the monetary, fiscal and external sectors.

The completion of Indonesia's political transition, and the election of a government with a wide popular mandate, appeared to place the country in a better position to implement transparent restructuring policies to achieve strong recovery and improve the well-being of the Indonesian people. While progress under the Habibe administration in restoring macroeconomic stability,[11] dealing with the financial crisis, advancing structural reforms and assuring food security was recognized by the incoming government, much still remains to be done to revive the real economy and lay the foundations for a sustained recovery that would increase employment, reduce poverty and assure equality of opportunity. These challenges constitute the principal agenda of the State Policy Guidelines approved by Indonesia's elected parliament. Based on these the government adopted, in January 2000, a comprehensive economic strategy that would accelerate the restructuring of Indonesia's economy and meet these challenges.

The so-called Medium Term Economic Strategy (MTES) contained four main planks: first, to make the macroeconomic policy mix fully supportive of recovery while entrenching basic price stability; second, to reinvigorate bank, corporate and other restructuring policies; third, to rebuild key public institutions with the objective of strengthening Indonesia's capacity to implement economic and social policies with popular support, transparency and good governance; and fourth, to improve natural resource management, arrest the long-term deterioration of the environment, and ensure the sustainable use of natural resources for future generations.

Medium-term Macroeconomic Framework[12]

The MTES envisages restoring a GDP growth rate of 5–6 per cent over the medium term, and Bank Indonesia has adopted a target of keeping inflation below 5 per cent annually. Although the external current account is anticipated to weaken over the next several years, as investment picks up, official financing and improvements in private capital flows, including the return of capital flight, are anticipated to offset the decline in the current account surplus. The import coverage of liquid reserves would be maintained at about six months. The government debt to GDP ratio is anticipated to decline from its recent peak of about 100 per cent to about 65 per cent by 2004, helped by falling interest rates and IBRA's asset recovery. Key to attaining this will be a range of fiscal reforms, affecting both revenues and expenditures. These reforms will be introduced concurrently with the implementation of fiscal decentralization by June 2001, consistent with the Regional Governance and Fiscal Balance Laws, and without increasing the general government deficit.

Restructuring policies

To ensure that the economic recovery is sustainable and that the benefits are widely shared amongst the Indonesian people, the strategy includes a wide range of structural measures. The most important are in the following areas.

Banking sector   Financial and corporate reforms lie at the heart of the strategy, and the government is resolved to carry these forward in an integrated and coherent way. Reflecting this a Financial Sector Policy Committee (FSPC), which reports directly to the president, has been established to give clear political leadership and direction in the areas of banking and corporate restructuring. The strategic objectives of the government's bank restructuring programme in particular are fourfold: (a) to recapitalize all banks to at least an 8 per cent CAR by the end of 2001, as a precondition to the eventual replacement of the comprehensive guarantee on deposits by 2004 with a limited deposit insurance fund financed by the banking system. Linked to this is the need to sustain banking system profitability; (b) to ensure that the banking system is restructured at minimum public cost; (c) to enhance supervision and instill much improved governance in the banking sector; and (d) to deepen bond and equity markets, allowing dependence on bank finance to be reduced.

Table 4.2   Indonesia: medium-term macroeconomic framework, 1998/99–2002[a]

	Actual 1998/99	Estimate 1999/2000	Projections 2000	2001	2002
			(percentage change)		
Output and prices					
Real GDP	−14.2	1.8	3 to 4	4 to 5	5 to 6
CPI inflation (average)	64.7	8.5	3 to 4	4 to 5	4 to 5
CPI inflation (end-of-period)	45.4	0.0	5 to 6	4 to 5	4 to 5
			(percentage of GDP)		
Savings and investment					
Gross domestic investment	12.1	13.4	16.3	18.1	19.2
Gross national savings	16.6	16.6	18.1	18.7	19.1
Central government operations					
Revenue and grants	15.3	14.5	15.1	15.5	16.0
Expenditure and net lending, of which:	17.4	18.3	20.1	19.2	18.6
interest payments on bank restructuring bonds	0.6	2.2	4.7	4.1	3.6
Overall balance	−2.2	−3.8	−5.0	−3.7	−2.6
Overall balance including arrears	−2.2	−5.0	−5.0	−3.7	−2.6
Domestic financing, of which:	−2.3	3.5	2.4	2.6	2.6
Privatization receipts	0.2	0.8	0.7	0.7	0.8
Recovery of bank assets (cash basis)	0.0	1.5	1.8	1.8	1.7
Foreign financing[b]	4.5	1.5	2.5	1.2	0.1
			(end-of-period, in annual percentage change)		
Money and credit					
Credit to the private sector[c]	−2.6	1.9	10.4	n.a.	n.a.
Broad money	33.8	16.0	11.8	n.a.	n.a.
Base money	27.4	9.5	8.3	n.a.	n.a.
			(billions of US dollars)		
Balance of payments					
Current account balance	4.6	4.8	3.3	1.0	−0.2
(in percentage of GDP)	4.4	3.1	1.9	0.5	−0.1
Capital account	−2.0	−4.4	−7.5	−2.1	3.0
Overall balance	2.6	0.4	−4.2	−1.1	2.8
Financing gap	0.0	0.0	4.3	3.4	0.8

	Actual 1998/99	Estimate 1999/2000	Projections		
			2000	2001	2002

(End-of-period, billions of US dollars)
Debt and reserves

Gross official foreign assets	25.7	27.8	29.2	31.1	33.6
(in months of imports)	6.7	6.5	6.3	6.1	6.0
Liquid reserves	20.3	25.0	26.5	28.4	31.7
(end-of-period, in months of imports)	5.3	5.8	5.7	5.5	5.6
(as percentage of short-term debt)	47.1	73.4	89.1	91.5	103.7
Debt–service ratio (per cent)[d]	39.1	34.8	29.9	27.3	35.0
Public debt (in percentage of GDP)	103.4	96.0	93.4	87.3	79.5
Of which: external	51.0	38.6	38.5	36.8	34.3

Notes:
n.a.   not available.
[a]   Fiscal years for 1998/99 and 1999/00 (fiscal year starts on 1 April) and calendar years for 2000 to 2002, with the exception of fiscal projections for 2000 which are based on the 9 month fiscal year from April to December.
[b]   From 2000 onwards, it includes financing gap.
[c]   Adjusted for transfers to IBRA.
[d]   In percentage of exports of goods and non-factor services.

Sources: Data from Indonesian authorities; IMF staff estimates and projections.

State bank restructuring is being implemented under the oversight of an interdepartmental restructuring committee. All state banks are required to prepare business plans with the help of international advisors, and to contract with international banks for their loan workouts. The Ministry of Finance is establishing a fully funded and staffed monitoring unit to ensure compliance of the state banks with their performance contracts. Henceforth, all state banks will be subject to an annual audit by international accounting firms, beginning with their end of 1999 positions. Progress is most advanced with Bank Mandiri. As a result, the bank's CAR has been raised to above 4 per cent, based on the December 1999 position estimated by an international account-ing firm.

As for private banks, Bank Indonesia (BI) is determined to ensure the soundness of the 73 A category banks. All owners and managers of these banks have been subject to fit and proper tests, and those who failed have been replaced. BI further required owners of banks whose capital fell below 4 per cent to raise capital to that level by 20 January 2000, and it took corrective actions against those banks whose owners failed to comply with the requirement. Banks whose business plans needed revision or correction to ensure compliance with the requirement to achieve CARs of at least 8 per cent by the end of 2001 have now submitted revised business plans, and these have been reviewed. All A category banks will be monitored on a quarterly basis to ensure they comply with their business plan, and BI will take appropriate corrective actions in all cases where these targets are not being achieved. Performance of the private banks jointly capitalized with the government will also be subject to quarterly monitoring by IBRA and BI, and any substantial deviations will be reported to the Ministry of Finance for appropriate resolution.

In terms of achieving greater financial transparency, the first audit of Bank Indonesia under the new central bank law, conducted by the Supreme Audit (Badan Pemeriksa Kevangan (BPK)) with the assistance of an international accounting firm, was completed and sent to parliament on 31 December 1999. In response, BI has adopted a time-bound programme of follow-up actions, aimed at addressing the issues raised by the audit, which will be implemented in cooperation with the BPK during 2000. The action plan covers a range of measures to clarify BI's financial position, improve the bank's internal controls and strengthen its supervision standards. Bank Indonesia is implementing a comprehensive master plan to upgrade bank supervision and comply with international regulatory norms by the end of 2001.

IBRA is crucial to the meeting of the objectives of restoring a sound banking system as well as promoting corporate restructuring and asset recovery to reduce the public debt. In this regard a comprehensive study, in collaboration with the World Bank, has been launched to develop a strengthened governance and oversight framework for IBRA. In the meantime, a number of steps have been take to strengthen IBRA and to make its operations more transparent: (a) the government has reaffirmed IBRA's status as the sole publicly funded entity in charge of asset recovery; (b) the president has issued an instruction clarifying that IBRA will report to his office on all policy issues; (c) IBRA's accounting policies are being amended on the basis of advice from international auditors; (d) the first audited accounts of IBRA's operations, covering its position as of December 1999, were publicized in April 2000, to be followed by regular quarterly and annual audited financial statements; and (e) an Ombudsman's office has been established within IBRA to respond to all inquiries from the public.

The authorities are adopting a comprehensive approach to achieve and maintain the soundness of the overall financial sector. Bank Indonesia will provide the IMF with monthly bank by bank data, beginning with the end of December 1999. The board of BI has approved a master strategy for enhancing bank supervision. The strategy will guide the implementation of the reforms necessary to bring supervisory and examination activities up to international standards, consistent with the Basle Committee's Core Principles, and ensure that technical assistance projects on bank supervision are effectively coordinated. It is anticipated that BI will maintain substantial on-site supervisory presence at each state bank. Similar master plans for the oversight of the non-bank financial sector, pension funds, insurance companies and finance companies, and securities markets by the Ministry of Finance, with the assistance of the World Bank and Asian Development Bank, were developed in March 2000.

The government has also issued bonds for bank recapitalization and is taking steps to develop a government bond market.

Corporate sector Corporate restructuring also needs to move ahead with much greater momentum in order to restart credit flows that are needed to sustain the recovery. This will require changing the incentive structure faced by corporate debtors and strengthening the institutional structure for corporate restructuring. The government intends to do this by giving new political leadership and direction to the corporate restructuring strategy, improving the implementation of the bankruptcy law, enhancing the governance framework of the judiciary, instructing IBRA to intensify implementation of its sequenced strategy towards its corporate debtors and strengthening procedures for non IBRA led restructuring.

The government has developed a strategy to give fresh momentum to corporate restructuring with the following key elements: (a) ensuring that IBRA plays an active role in the workout process with the ability to engage in various forms of debt restructuring; (b) for non-IBRA-led cases, establishing a procedure under which the government may direct cases to the Jakarta Initiative Task Force (JITF), and may refer to the attorney-general for the initiation of bankruptcy proceedings against those debtors that refuse to negotiate in good faith in accordance with the principles and timetables established under the new JITF mediation procedures; (c) strengthening the insolvency system; and (d) more generally, improving the corporate governance framework and subjecting companies to greater market discipline. In accordance with a presidential decree issued on 28 December 1999, the FSPC has been established to oversee bank and corporate restructuring, as mentioned previously.

It is essential for IBRA, as a major creditor to the corporate sector, to be able to engage in a full range of commercially acceptable methods of debt restructuring, including debt for equity conversions and, where appropriate, debt reduction. To that end, the FSPC has announced a set of policies and procedures for IBRA that specify the conditions under which debt and debt service reduction decisions can be taken. Efforts are also under way to allow IBRA to make more effective use of the insolvency system. Specifically, in cases where debtors fail to enter into good faith negotiations with IBRA in accordance with the timetable agreed upon with the debtors, IBRA will, where appropriate, file insolvency petitions in the Commercial Court.

The government has also announced measures to strengthen procedures for restructuring through the JITF's collective negotiating framework. The FSPC will be able to direct cases that cannot expeditiously be led by IBRA because, for example, IBRA is a minority creditor, for restructuring under the JITF. IBRA will take steps to ensure that it participates in the Jakarta Initiative framework when such participation is necessary for effective restructuring. The FSPC will be responsible for ensuring adequate coordination between IBRA and the JITF. These measures recognize that the JITF has a critical role to play in accelerating the pace of corporate restructuring.

A new governance framework for IBRA, including an independent governing body, was established at the end of June 2000. Steps have been taken to improve IBRA's transparency. IBRA has commenced regular publication of its activities, which includes monthly reports of sales and collection activities, progress in loan restructuring, and disposal of industrial assets, in addition to quarterly financial reports by the BTO (banks taken over). The government recognizes that a key incentive for debtors to enter into negotiations with their creditors has been ineffective, namely the threat that creditors will initiate bankruptcy proceedings, including rehabilitation proceedings against recalcitrant debtors. A primary problem has been the capacity of the judiciary to implement the insolvency law. To this end, a number of measures are being implemented to strengthen the judiciary.

Reform and privatization of state-owned enterprises   The government has also been reviewing the privatization schedule of the master plan for state enterprise reform and privatization. The government anticipated privatization revenue amounting to Rp8·6 trillion during 1999/2000. The government prepared a privatization plan for financial year (FY) 2000, designed to yield Rp5·9 trillion. The programme focuses upon enterprises, including small enterprises, operating in competitive markets where there is no compelling case for public ownership. The government is also preparing a liquidation plan for loss making and heavily indebted enterprises that have no prospect of achieving commercial viability. Among the larger enterprises the two publicly listed enterprises PT Telkom and PT Indosat are strong candidates for further rapid privatization.

The government does not plan to establish holding companies for public enterprises, believing that such arrangements would dampen competition and slow privatization. Indeed, where appropriate, the government will dispose of state-owned monopolies and encourage effective competition. Plans for restructuring Pertamina and Perusahaan Listrik Negasa (PLN) are under consideration. A strategy to improve the performance of other state monopolies, including ports, airports, telecommunications and toll roads, was prepared in March 2000 with assistance from the Asian Development Bank and the World Bank. State-owned enterprises are increasingly being required to adhere to the same standards of corporate governance as are required for listed companies.

Energy sector   The government remains committed to continuing and accelerating initiatives to resolve deep-seated problems that are impairing the performance of the electric power and oil/gas sectors. In the oil and gas sector, for example, the government has committed itself to the following actions: replacing existing laws with a modern legal framework; restructuring and reforming Pertamina; ensuring that fiscal terms and regulation for exploration and production remain internationally competitive; allowing domestic product prices to reflect international market levels; and establishing a coherent and sound policy framework for promoting efficient and environmentally sustainable patterns of domestic energy use.

Agricultural policy   The focus of the government in the agricultural sector is upon maintaining food security, and the promotion of efficient production, processing and marketing of agricultural products. Food security is made a key aim of the rice policy framework, by promoting competition in this sector. Accordingly, trade in all qualities of rice has been opened to general importers and exporters. The government is also preparing a strategy for a phased restructuring of the National Logistics Agency (BULOG), to follow up the recommendations of the recent special audit. This reform will aim at a more transparent accounting system and efficient operating structure for BULOG through a change in its legal status. Agricultural input policy will emphasize competitive, private market delivery of fertilizers and rural credit. With a return to normal agricultural conditions, the government proposes to revert as quickly as possible to meeting farmers' credit needs through the commercial banking system. From 1 April 2000 the working capital needs of farmers will be met by commercial banks only. Such banks will bear all the risks of non-repayment of principal and will be given full independence in making credit decisions. All lending quotas and targets will be eliminated. For sugar the government will pursue a policy of restructuring the domestic industry by consolidating the number of sugar factories on Java and promoting private sector led investment of Java in new capacity.

Small and medium enterprises   The government is committed to empowering small and medium enterprises (SMEs). However, it recognizes that many current SME support programmes have failed to meet the needs of the SME community. Consequently, the government has committed itself to re-evaluating government interventions so as to increase private sector involvement in SME support programmes. An action plan, completed in March 2000, provides for the following: (a) developing an institutional framework for SME policy implementation; (b) making business development services more responsive to SME needs; (c) expanding access to finance for SMEs; (d) streamlining government regulations affecting small and medium businesses; and (e) monitoring and evaluating government SME programmes.

The role of BI in funding and administering SME credit schemes has been eliminated, and SME credit schemes have been transferred to three banks, BRI, PT Mandani and BTN. These new credit lines were introduced on 1 April 2000 and are based on commercial principles with full risks of non-payment being borne by participating banks. Any interest rate subsidy is to be supported by adequate provisions in the budget. In addition, on 30 June 2000, Bank Indonesia announced a plan to phase out mandatory requirements on commercial bank lending to SMEs.

SMEs as well as larger firms need access to trade finance in order to compete in international markets. In response to this the government created a new institution, Bank Expor Indonesia (BEI), with the aim of expanding access to trade finance. On 31 March 2000, the government presented the Law on Bank Expor Indonesia to parliament, establishing BEI as an independent export credit agency for Indonesia.

Rebuilding economic institutions

There is widespread consensus in Indonesian society that key economic institutions need to be rebuilt or strengthened in order to command the trust of the people and allow the smooth implementation of the medium-term policy agenda. In this regard early priority has been given to the public sector,[13] the financial sector,[14] the judiciary and the institutions responsible for corporate governance.

The task of improving governance in fiscal management is vast and complex, and crucial to regaining public confidence as well as sustaining fiscal adjustment and public debt reduction. The tax system needs to be reformed to ensure that it is broad-based, non-distortionary, equitable and transparent. The governance of spending programmes needs to be greatly improved, and the allocation of funds redirected towards poverty alleviation to promote interregional equity and increase efficiency in the provision of public goods. Fiscal transparency needs to be enhanced by identifying and auditing off-budget activities and bringing them under the consolidated budget. A

Consultative Regional Autonomy Council was established in 2000 to oversee the implementation of fiscal decentralization.

The newly independent BI has a great responsibility to support the recovery of the economy by maintaining price stability, rebuilding banking supervision and ensuring a high level of disclosure of banking activities. Prudential supervision of the financial system needs to be carried out as quickly as possible to international standards. Effective oversight of BI will be exercised through regular reporting to parliament, as indicated previously.

Improving public confidence in the integrity of the judiciary and in the efficacy of the legal process is a vital objective of institutional reform and crucial to economic restructuring. A comprehensive agenda of legal and judicial reform with four key programmes is aimed at good governance in the legal system and administrative law reform; improved administration of justice; legal education, testing and discipline; and improved legislative capabilities. The programme includes measures to reduce the opportunities for corruption, by improving the transparency and speed of legal proceedings, while, at the same time, creating powerful disincentives for corrupt practices, the latter to include prosecution of the parties that engage in such practices.

The governance structure of other economic institutions is also being reviewed and improved to upgrade corporate governance. This includes adopting a new code of corporate governance, strengthening capital market regulation at the Securities and Exchange Commission (BAPEPAM), and improving the oversight of non-bank financial institutions at the Ministry of Finance.

Improved natural resource management
Indonesia's natural environment has continued to deteriorate during the crisis. Weak policy implementation and weak market institutions have combined to undermine Indonesia's base of natural resources. Natural resources still play a key role in the Indonesian economy, and there is a recognition of a need to implement policies and programmes that ensure their sustainable use for the benefit of present and future generations. The policy and institutional framework for natural resource management focuses on three key objectives. First, it aims to create consultation and stakeholder participation in decisions affecting natural resources, particularly in the formulation of new policies, and the location and selection of public investments. To ensure that these decisions are based on good information the government proposes to expand and improve environmental monitoring of Indonesia's air, water, forests and marine resources. Second, it will move towards a pricing structure for natural resources that better reflects their true value. Third, it will pay special attention to improving forest management and ensuring a sustainable production of goods and services from forest resources.

6   MEDIUM-TERM MACROECONOMIC POLICIES

Consistent with the medium-term strategy, medium-term macroeconomic policies are based on growth being in the 1–2 per cent range in 1999/2000, strengthening to the 3–4 per cent range during FY 2000 (see Table 4.2). Growth in the
final quarter of 1999, at 5·8 per cent, exceeded expectations, and this economic
recovery was sustained into the first quarter of 2000. It is now expected that
2000 growth will be at the top end of the target 3–4 per cent range. The mainte-
nance of low single-digit inflation is seen as a core outcome, and end of 2000
inflation is anticipated to be within the target 5–6 per cent range. Domestic
savings and investment, as a percentage of GDP, are anticipated to improve
steadily. The fiscal deficit, inclusive of settlement arrears, is anticipated to peak
in 2000 at around 5 per cent of GDP and to improve steadily thereafter. Public
debt, as a percentage of GDP, is anticipated to decline continuously. In terms of
external developments the current account surplus, as a percentage of GDP, is
anticipated to peak during 1999/2000 and to deteriorate thereafter, primarily
because of an expected recovery in imports. The capital account deficit is anticipated to peak in 2000 and to improve considerably thereafter, and indeed to
move back into surplus in 2002. Primarily because of this latter development,
the balance of payments is anticipated to show a considerable improvement by
2002, after the deterioration in 2000. The external reserve position, official and
liquid, is anticipated to strengthen continuously until 2002.

Underlying these medium-term macroeconomic outcomes are corresponding fiscal, monetary and external policies. These are now briefly discussed.

Fiscal Policy and the Social Safety Net

The target fiscal deficit for 1999/2000 was originally 3·75 per cent of GDP and,
inclusive of the settlement arrears, the budgetary financing need was estimated
at about 5 per cent of GDP. By mid-2000, however, the fiscal deficit for
1999/2000 was expected to be only 1·5 per cent of GDP, well below the target
level. The spending programme was achieved, and in fact there were some
spending shortfalls, while tax revenues – including those from higher oil
prices – were larger than expected. Inclusive of settlement arrears, the
budgetary financing need was reduced to 4·8 per cent of GDP, compared with
the original budget target of 5 per cent of GDP. This financing need is to be
met by privatization receipts, asset recovery and foreign financing.

There are clear principles underlying the operation of fiscal policy: first, to
strike a careful balance between supporting the economic recovery and starting
the process of reducing government debt; second, to continue to avoid domestic
bank financing; third, to initiate a range of structural tax reforms whose impact

will accrue over the medium term; fourth, to start the process of gradually reducing selected subsidies, while protecting small household users from their impact, and strengthening selected poverty alleviation programmes; and fifth, to begin to restore public sector wages, especially for the most senior officials, concurrently with administrative reform and stringent penalties for corruption.

There are three main elements to social spending: the social safety net (SSN), poverty alleviation programmes and selective fuel and energy subsidies. SSN programmes have the following principal components: the rice distribution (OPK) program, a health component, specific employment programmes, including one to enhance women's employment, a programme to provide funds directly to communities, scholarships for needy students and block grants for selected schools, and poverty alleviation.

Monetary and Exchange Rate Policies

Firm base money control, combined with a flexible exchange rate policy, have contributed to anchoring prices and strengthening the rupiah. Interest rates have also shown a considerable decline, and given the sharp decline in inflation there remains room to guide interest rates cautiously down further, as in the other Asian countries. Increases in base money are also designed to provide for the recovery of bank credit to the private sector, and is reviewed periodically to ensure that it remains fully supportive of economic recovery and is responsive to unanticipated capital inflows.

Balance of Payments and External Policies

The external current account surplus in 1999/2000 is projected to reach about US$5 billion, 3·1 per cent of GDP, because of the reduced fiscal expansion and stronger oil export prices. Liquid reserves are projected to be US$25 billion by the end of the fiscal year, or about six months of imports, and their coverage of short-term debt will improve to over 70 per cent.

With the onset of recovery and a strengthened currency, the current account surplus is expected to decline in 2000, consistent with a pattern experienced in the other Asian countries. Current projections point to the current account surplus falling to about US$2 billion in FY2000. Export volume growth is anticipated to strengthen, although this is expected to be outweighed by a recovery of imports, although the latter will still remain well below the pre-crisis level. In the capital account, private capital flows should improve, but new pressures are expected from at least two sources: (a) corporate reschedulings are likely to be associated with prepayments on account of arrears, and (b) banks are expected to make payments consistent with contractual obligations under the first exchange offer. Consequently, the government expected an external financing gap to emerge again in FY2000, of about US$4·3 billion, linked closely to the fiscal deficit. The government is confident, however, that the full amount of official external financing will be available.

7　SUMMARY AND CONCLUSIONS

Indonesia has experienced traumatic economic, political and social developments since the onset of the financial crisis in mid-1997. Many weaknesses existed in the country before the crisis, including reliance on capital inflows, particularly on a short-term basis; an overvalued exchange; a weak banking system; and the rapidly growing business interests of President Suharto and his family and close associates. However, these alone do not explain the depth of the crisis. Emphasis in this chapter has been placed upon policy mismanagement both domestically and, in particular, from the IMF as providing a major part of the explanation.

There are a number of key areas in which policy will need to be focused if a sustained recovery of the economy is to be possible. These include the attainment of political stability, the need to reform and recapitalize the banking system, restructuring of corporate sector debt, restarting the growth of exports and keeping the budget deficit within manageable limits. The government's medium-term economic strategy is aimed at tackling these issues, and some success has already been recorded. However, it is apparent that it will take many years before the country will be able to attain once more the high rates of economic growth achieved before the onset of the crisis.

NOTES

1. Such as Suharto's flirtation with the adoption of a proposed currency board in February 1998.
2. See, for example, Radelet (1999).
3. See Radelet (1999).
4. With the balance of US$7 billion owed by the government.
5. See Radelet and Sachs (1998).
6. See Radelet (1999).
7. It has been suggested that the measures involved in the IMF programme had been 'voluntarily proposed' by technocrats, especially in the Ministry of Finance in Indonesia, to take advantage of the programme in bringing about deregulation of the 'real' economy: that is, especially the abolition of state and private monopolies and other prerequisites of the Suharto family.
8. Furman and Stiglitz (1999) have shown that the higher interest rates did not have the effect on the exchange rate hoped for in the IMF programme.
9. Such as recapitalizing certain banks, restructuring the assets and liabilities of both the closed banks and those that remained open, and protecting depositors.
10. The IMF programme called for a long list of structural reforms throughout the Indonesian economy. While many of these reforms were likely to be beneficial to the economy in the

long run, and had been advocated by reformists within the government for many years, they were of less importance than the bank and debt restructuring to the immediate crisis. Debate on these reforms distracted urgent attention from the key issues. See Feldstein (1998) for a discussion.

11. The macroeconomic achievements included the reduction of inflation, the stabilization of the rupiah and the recovery of foreign exchange reserves. The financial sector had begun to stabilize, interest rates had fallen below pre-crisis levels, and bank restructuring and recapitalization had started.

12. See Table 4.2.

13. Fiscal management and civil service reform.

14. IBRA, the state-owned banks and the regulatory and supervisory institutions.

BIBLIOGRAPHY

Booth, A. (2000), 'The Indonesian crisis of 1997/99 and the way out: what are the lessons of history?', *Economic Papers*, 19(2), June, 21–43.

Cole, D. and B.F. Sale (1996), *Building a Modern Financial System: the Indonesian Experience*, Cambridge: Cambridge University Press.

Cole, D. and B.F. Sale (1999), 'Why has Indonesia's financial crisis been so bad?', *Bulletin of Indonesian Economic Studies*, 34(2), August.

Feldstein, M. (1998), 'Refocussing the IMF', *Foreign Affairs*, 77(2), March/April, 20–33.

Furman, M. and J. Stiglitz (1999), 'Economic crises: evidence and insights from East Asia', *Brookings Papers on Economic Activity*, 2, 1–114.

Gallup, J., S. Radelet and A. Warner (1998), 'Economic growth and the income of the poor', Harvard Institute for International Development, November.

Goldstein, M. and D. Weatherstone (1998), 'The Asian financial crisis', *International Economic Policy Briefs*, 98(1), Institute for International Economics, Washington.

Government of Indonesia (2000), 'Memorandum of Economic and Financial Policies', Jakarta, 20 January.

Government of Indonesia (2000), 'Memorandum of Economic and Financial Policies', Jakarta, 17 May.

Harvie, C. (2000), 'Financial crisis in Indonesia: the role of good governance', in Tran Van Hoa and C. Harvie (eds), *Causes and Impact of the Asian Financial Crisis*, London: Macmillan, pp. 95–130.

Harvie, C. (2000), 'Indonesia: the road from economic and social collapse', in Tran Van Hoa (ed.), *The Asia Crisis: the Cures, their Effectiveness and the Prospects After*, London: Macmillan, pp. 110–39.

Harvie, C. (2000), 'Indonesia: recovery from economic and social collapse', in R. Edwards, C. Nyland and M. Coulthard (eds), *Readings in International Business – an Asia Pacific Perspective*, Sydney: Prentice Hall, pp. 49–74.

Hill, H. (1999), *The Indonesian Economy in Crisis*, Singapore: Institute of Southeast Asian Studies.

MacIntyre, A. (1999), 'Political institutions and the economic crisis in Thailand and Indonesia', in H.W. Arndt and H. Hill (eds), *Southeast Asia's Economic Crisis: Origins, Lessons and the Way Forward*, Singapore: Institute of Southeast Asian Studies.

McLeod, R.H. (1998), 'Indonesia', in R.H. McLeod and R. Garnaut (eds), *East Asia in Crisis: from being a miracle to needing one*, London: Routledge, pp. 31–48.

Radelet, S. (1996), 'Measuring the real exchange rate and its relationship to exports: an application to Indonesia', Harvard Institute for International Development Discussion Paper no. 529, May.

Radelet, S. (1999), 'Indonesia: long road to recovery', Harvard Institute for International Development, March.

Radelet, S. and J. Sachs (1998), 'The onset of the East Asian financial crisis', Harvard Institute for International Development, March.

Radelet, S. and J. Sachs (1999), 'What have we learned so far from the Asian financial crisis', Harvard Institute for International Development, January.

World Bank (1997), 'Indonesia: sustaining high growth with equity', Country Department III, East Asia and Pacific Region, 30 May.

World Bank (1998), *World Development Indicators*, Washington DC: World Bank.

5. Malaysia's recovery: issues in economic management, trade policy, knowledge-based industries and globalization

Tran Van Hoa

1 INTRODUCTION

Malaysia is a modern growing Asian economy with a complex family of peoples and cultures and a melting pot of traditions stemming from the Malay Archipelago as well as from China, India and, in recent times, Portugal, Holland, Great Britain and Japan. Small Malayan kingdoms existed in the second or third centuries AD, when adventurers from India arrived and started what has become known as the Indian influence for more than 1000 years. Sumatran exiles founded Malacca (or Malega) in about 1400 AD and secured Chinese protection for the city-state. It later became a commercial and Islamic religious centre, but was captured by the Portuguese in 1511 and the Dutch in 1641, and lost its commercial status shortly after. The Minangkabau peoples from Sumatra migrated to Malaya during the late 17th century and brought with them a matrilineal culture. Also, in the 18th century, the Buginese from the island of Celebes invaded Malaya and established the sultanates of Selanggor and Johore (*Encyclopaedia Britannica*, Internet, June 2000).

In more recent times. the British founded the Straits Settlements – Malacca, Singapore, and Penang (or Pinang) Island – in the late 1800s, and the Chinese also began to migrate to Malaya in the late 19th century. During their rule in Malaya, the British invested heavily in the country, especially from the 1890s, developing in the process transport and rubber planting. This can be regarded as the setting of the stage for future economic developments of Malaysia in a way similar to that in Hong Kong at about the same time. In recent years for example, rubber, the main cash crop of Malaysia, has been grown primarily on small farms and accounts for one-quarter of the world's production. The birth of Malayan nationalism started only in 1946 with the emergence of the United Malaya National Organization (UMNO) after the British failed to organize Malaya into one state after World War II.

Since its independence from Great Britain in 1957, Malaya and then Malaysia (established finally in 1963 after many federation membership shifts) has again gone through numerous periods of external and internal turmoil. During this nascent period of its recent history, Malaysia (population: 22.083 million in 1998) like its neighbours, Singapore and Indonesia, has managed to exploit for better or for worse the links with its colonial and racially mixed past to embark on establishing its national sovereignty, a transformation from an almost feudal and colonial way of life to apparently broad-based democratic practices and law, political stability, economic development and prosperity, and a place in the global world. With its rich endowment of natural resources, its dedicated policies to attract foreign direct investment when the country needed it most or to reduce poverty among Malays and other indigenous people (one example is the New Economic Policy introduced in 1970, and its successors), its attractiveness for tourism (US$3910 million in revenue in 1995), and for all its development achievements in the past decades (for example, GNP at US$89·800 billion or US$4370 per head in 1996), Malaysia has come to be known as one of the economic 'tigers' in Asia, exerting, in spite of its small population and landmass (127 575 square miles, including inland water for both East and West Malaysia), a towering influence on the peninsula and sometimes beyond.

The real major modern economic crisis for Malaysia came shortly after July 1997, when it and the other economic 'tigers' of Asia came face to face with a sudden and substantial decline in the value of their currencies and massive capital flights. This so-called 'Asia crisis' has brought untold damage – economic, social and political – to Malaysia and necessitated drastic measures. Some of these measures are controversial, to say the least, as judged by the critiques at the time of the international economic and financial community.

After two years of soul-searching for the real causes and cures of the crisis, it is rather pleasing to many in the country, in the neighbouring region and in international organizations such as the Asian Development Bank (ADB), the International Monetary Fund (IMF) and the World Bank (WB) to observe that all the signs of an economic recovery in Malaysia seem to be appearing. This recovery to continuing and sustainable development and growth has however many aspects and issues that may promote or hamper it. These aspects and issues are related to international trade, investment, business, economic management and are within the context of globalization or regional economic integration (for example, the ASEAN and the Asia Pacific Economic Cooperation Forum). They are, in our view, pertinent and highly relevant to Malaysia during its economic recovery in the new millennium, and discussed briefly but critically below.

2 THE FUNDAMENTALS OF MALAYSIA'S DEVELOPMENT AND GROWTH: INTERNATIONAL TRADE

In its economic development and prosperity over the past three decades or so, Malaysia, besides its agriculture accounting for approximately one-fifth of GDP and employing about one-fourth of the workforce, can name a long list of other contributing factors, some internal and some external. Perhaps one of the most significant of these is international trade and foreign investment from its major trading partners, which include Japan, Singapore, the United States, the UK and Germany. And with foreign investment come know-how and technology transfer, the main ingredients for economic development and growth in developing economies. In this context, it is informative to have a closer look at the movement of Malaysia's international trade over the years in order to have a better understanding of the country's modernization process, its economic position, and the role and dynamics of its international trade sector.

Malaysia's international trade involves more than 100 tradable commodities according to the 1999 CEPII-CHELEM international trade databank. These commodities can be broadly classified into ten major groups. The historical patterns of trade for these groups between Malaysia and the rest of the world are shown in Figures 5.1 and 5.2 (Malaysia's exports to the world) and in Figures 5.3 and 5.4 (Malaysia's imports) over the 30-year period 1967–97. These ten major groups consist of construction products, basic metals, textiles, wood and paper, metal products, chemicals, mining, energy, agriculture and food products. The data for our charts are annual data and derived from France's 1999 CEPII-CHELEM harmonized international trade databases. These data have been standardized so that they are compatible for comparative purposes with all other countries' international trade statistics.

From Figures 5.1 and 5.2, we note that, during the early 1970s, Malaysia's exports to the world were concentrated on agriculture products (for example, in 1970, US$926·37 million or 54·45 per cent of total exports), basic metals (US$314·01 million or 18.45 per cent), food products (US$163·48 million or 9·61 per cent), energy (US$106·16 million or 6·36 per cent) and mining (US$66·41 million or 3·90 per cent). Since the early 1980s, however, metal products had taken a more important role in Malaysia's exports. The most explosive growth of exports of metal products started in fact in the late 1980s. In 1988, for example, this group of tradable commodities had taken over as the country's largest and most important exports (US$5939·77 million or 28·49 per cent, as compared to US$5788·16 million or 27·66 per cent for agricultural products). In 1997, exports of metal products stood at US$46 857·14 million or 51·26 per cent, almost eight times more than the second largest group of exports, energy (US$6184·76 million or 8·09 per cent), and more than nine

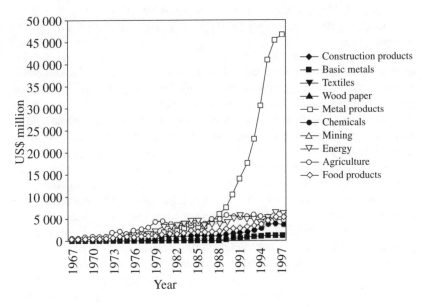

Figure 5.1   Malaysia's exports to the world (US$ millions)

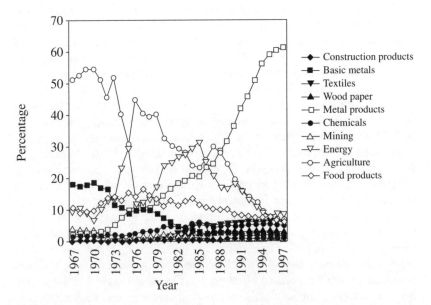

Figure 5.2   Malaysia's exports to the world (percentage)

times the third largest group of exports, food products (US$5059·15 million or 6·61 per cent).

From Figures 5.3 and 5.4, we note that, from the early 1970s, Malaysia's imports from the rest of the world had been centred chiefly on metal products, followed by chemicals, food products and basic metals. Since the late 1980s, however, the growth of imports of metal products had been explosive while that of chemicals, food products and basic metals had been moderate. An interesting observation from these charts is the appearance of textile imports as a significant item (ranked fourth in the list of all significant imported items) in the 1990s. As early as 1967, imports of metal products stood at US$261·54 million or 29·25 per cent of all imports, followed by agricultural products at US$145·19 million or 16·24 per cent, energy at US$139·76 million or 15·63 per cent, chemicals at US$69·56 million or 7·78 per cent, and then basic metals at US$48·91 million or 5·47 per cent. In 1997, however, imports of metal products reached US$43 600·61 million or 67·57 per cent, followed by chemicals at US$5295·95 million or 8·21 per cent, basic metals at US$4017·91 million or 6·23 per cent, agricultural products at US$1973·35 million or 3·06 per cent, and then energy at US$1836·37 million or 2·85 per cent. While imports of metal products had more than doubled during the 1967–97 period, imports of energy and agricultural products had substantially declined in importance in Malaysia's international trade, falling

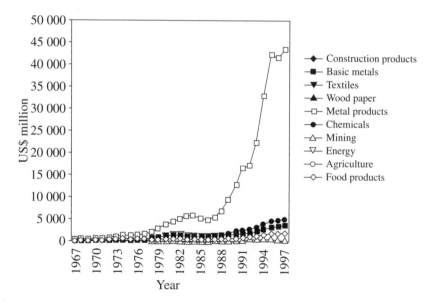

Figure 5.3   Malaysia's imports from the world

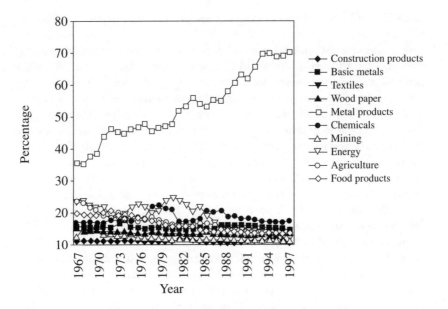

Figure 5.4   Malaysia's imports from the world (percentage)

from a prominent role of 31·97 per cent of total imports in 1967 to only 5·91 per cent in 1997.

In 1997, the trade balance in metal products stood in favour of Malaysia at US$3256·53 million, but the balance was in deficit at US$3013·34 million for basic metals and US$1441·29 for chemicals.

The above analysis of historical international data for Malaysia from Figures 5.1 to 5.4 seem to indicate that the country's foreign trade and its subsequent impact on development and growth in the past three decades had been closely linked to the single group 'metal products'. As metal products is the largest group of tradable commodities classified by CEPII-CHELEM and consists of about 23 items, this conclusion seems reasonable. However, a more detailed study of the data over the same period would reveal a different picture: Malaysia's international trade had been spearheaded mainly by a group of ten tradable commodities and only five of these are in the 'metal products' group. In 1997, the ranking in terms of the export value of these ten commodities (see Figures 5.5 and 5.6), in their descending order of importance is electronic components (27·12 per cent of all these exported commodities), computer equipment (22·59 per cent), consumer electronics (11·78 per cent), non-edible agricultural products (7·11 per cent), fats (6·98 per cent), telecommunications equipment (6·81 per cent), electrical apparatus (4·63 per cent), natural gas (4·63 per cent), crude oil (4·45 per cent) and wood articles (3·89 per cent).

In 1967, non-edible agricultural products were US$572·58 million, accounting for 81·97 per cent of the export value of the group of top ten exports, fats US$71·79 million or 10·28 per cent, crude oil US$27 million or 3·87 per cent, and wood articles US$20·12 million or 2·88 per cent. Electronic components started to improve modestly in 1973 with an export value of US$65·06 million or 2·63 per cent of the group's exports. Malaysia's natural gas supply and exports came on stream only in 1983 with a value of US$298·80 million or 2·81 per cent. Finally, exports of computer equipment emerged in 1989 with a value of US$317·33 million or 1·81 per cent of the group's exports at that time.

The above statistics indicate that, while Malaysia's traditional exports such as agriculture, wood and oil still play an important part in the country's international trade and hence economic development, its 'engines of growth' in recent years seem to be in the area of information technology (IT): electronic components, computer equipment, consumer electronics and telecommunications equipment. Since IT is a globalized industry with strong international competitiveness, especially in the Asian region, the success and sustainability of Malaysia's future development, growth and enhancement of the people's living standard will surely depend on its economic management and trade policy that are in tune with this kind of trade and finance environment in a modern world economy. The issues are more acute as a result of the damaging

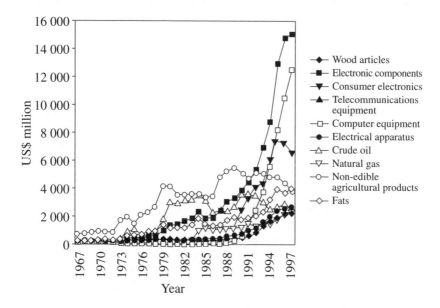

Figure 5.5   Malaysia's top ten exports

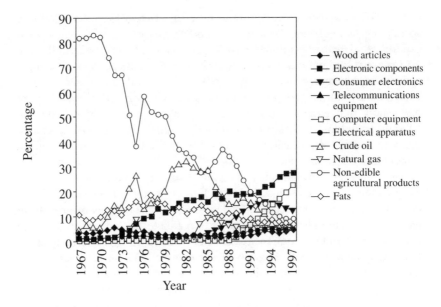

Figure 5.6   Malaysia's top ten exports (percentage)

impact of the Asian crisis on Malaysia and the controversial fiscal, monetary, financial and governance measures the government had taken to deal with it in 1998 and 1999.

3   MALAYSIA: RECENT TRENDS AND PROSPECTS

The economic and financial crisis that started in Thailand in July 1997 has stalled the long and hard-earned development and growth of many countries (developing and newly industrialized alike) in Asia, and produced untold economic, political and social damage to the 'miracle' economies of the 'economic tigers'. Of the five Asian economies most affected by the crisis (Indonesia, Malaysia, Philippines, Thailand, and Korea), Malaysia seems to have escaped to some significant extent the corporate collapse of Korea, the financial bankruptcy of Thailand, or the continuing social upheaval and ethnic unrest in Indonesia. There are signs, however, that a recovery in these crisis economies is well under way. As of June 2000, they are expected to grow by about 4·3 per cent on average in 2000 (Fischer, 1999; IMF, May 2000).

The more specific trends and prospects for our focus country, Malaysia, at the beginning of a new millennium and during the period of economic recovery from the aftermath of the Asian crisis, have been investigated by a number of international experts and organizations in the area. Some major aspects of these trends and prospects are summarized below.

According to a study by the Asian Development Bank (ADB) and also our estimates of economic trends for Malaysia (see Figure 5.7), the economy achieved a robust recovery in 1999, with real gross domestic product (GDP) expanding by 5·4 per cent after contracting by 7·5 per cent in 1998. In 1999, the manufacturing sector grew by 13·6 per cent, a significant increase in crude palm oil production pushed the agricultural sector growth to 3·8 per cent, and building output contraction lessened. Malaysia's exports also enjoyed a cost advantage due to the undervaluation of the ringgit, with a trade surplus achieved in both 1998 (owing to import compression) and 1999 (owing to export expansion). The overall balance of payments in 1999 was in surplus, with net international reserves of US$30·9 billion. Stronger economic growth also led to a slight decline in the rate of unemployment to 3 per cent of the labour force in 1999 from 3·2 per cent in 1998. Consumer price inflation, after reaching 5·3 per cent on average in 1998, fell steadily to 2·8 per cent on average in 1999. However, overall equity prices, as measured by the Kuala Lumpur Composite Index, rose by 39 per cent in 1999. In addition, most of the positive signs of economic growth came from greater external demand for

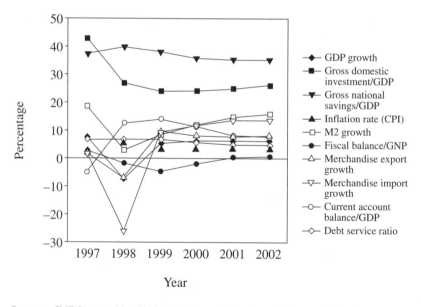

Sources: IMF, Internet, May 2000; Bank Negara Malaysia; author's own estimates.

Figure 5.7 Malaysia's main economic indicators, 1997–2002

manufactured goods and a rise in consumer confidence, as reflected in increased passenger car sales, sales tax receipts and imports of consumer goods (ADB, Malaysia, Internet, May 2000).

The ADB study also goes on to predict that Malaysia's GDP growth is likely to accelerate in 2000 as private consumption strengthens, reducing excess industrial capacity and providing more incentives to fixed investment.

> Purchasing power will recover further as asset values increase and unemployment eases, while fixed investment will pick up because of increased bank lending. These positive trends will, however, be partially offset as public consumption expands more slowly to bring down the level of fiscal deficit. Also the rate of increase in real GDP growth is likely to moderate in 2001 and 2002 (our estimates) as the recovery from recession ends. Inflation is likely to pick up slightly because of stronger domestic demand, rising real wages, and a recovery in non-oil commodity prices, but it will remain substantially below its 1998 level. The trade surplus is likely to narrow, as an expected improvement in export performance on the back of stronger world trade growth is offset by faster import growth, because of the import-dependent nature of exports and a higher demand for capital goods. Malaysia's dependence on trade-related service imports and increased outflows of profits and dividend payments will likely widen services and income deficits, in turn causing the current account surplus to narrow. The external debt position is expected to remain manageable, and Malaysia should not experience any problem in meeting its debt obligation. (ADB, Malaysia, Internet, May 2000)

The trends and prospects (predictions) of Malaysia during the period of economic recovery as assessed above indicate essentially that there is partially a direct accounting or short-term linkage between the various economic and financial activities (that is, they are part of a national accounting framework. For example, GDP = C + I. If C goes up, I must go down, given GDP). An example is that growth in private consumption will generate GDP growth, since private consumption is a component of GDP in a Keynesian or modern SNA (Systems of National Accounts) framework. As a result, the country should follow an ad hoc policy that will endeavour to maintain this consumption–GDP linkage and to achieve its expected outcomes (GDP growth). Judged from this perspective, the assessment is incomplete for appropriate economic policy formulation and implementation since it implicitly assumes that there is no fundamental simple (unidirectional) or instantaneous (circular or two-way) Granger causality (short- or long-term) between the various economic and financial activities. More importantly, the assessment also overlooks the underlying principle that drives the various activities and their interaction and that provides a long-term and coherent policy consistent with the macroeconomic as well as microeconomic structure and the Schumpeterian stages of development of the economy, its international trade make-up and its relationship to a global economy. These are the major issues to be discussed below.

4   MAJOR ISSUES IN THE RECOVERY

Major issues that are not exhaustive but nevertheless highly relevant to Malaysia's economic recovery can be grouped into the categories of economic management, international trade policy, development and growth, skilled labour and human resource development, and international competitiveness. These issues are more specific to Malaysia and cover only some aspects of the discussion (for example, labour standards, the environment, competition policy, investment rules, agricultural export subsidies and anti-dumping rules) between the Asia Pacific Economic Cooperation Forum (APEC) trade ministers at their meeting early in June 2000 in Darwin, Australia.

Economic Management

During the crisis, Malaysia had adopted an approach that has been described as controversial or even of the 1930 Depression type in minimizing the impact of its economic turmoil. This approach included the imposition, in September 1998, of controls on capital outflows from the country and a moratorium on the repatriation of portfolio capital. While the government of Malaysia claimed that this approach, followed by an expansionary fiscal and monetary policy, had the expected effect of blocking the internal contagion or further economic and financial damage of the crisis, many international experts have suggested that the effect was difficult to assess in any case. Their arguments are that the controls were imposed at the time that capital flows to the Asian region in general began to strengthen, and they were never tested against severe downward pressures (Fischer, 1999).

The fact that Malaysia's controls on capital outflows and the restrictions on the repatriation of portfolio investment were substantially relaxed during the country's strong economic rebound in 1999 shows that the approach was only a stop-gap short-term measure taken during an emergency when everything else seemed inadequate. In addition, the controls and restrictions could be used, as many had feared, to engineer a delay of the reforms of the financial sector or the corporate restructuring in Malaysia. This state of affairs would be in contrast to the international consensus on the need for financial sector and governance reforms around the world as a result of the Asian crisis. First deputy managing director of the IMF, Stanley Fischer, stated even more unequivocally that the controls adopted by Malaysia in 1998 are not a good way to operate in the international financial system, particularly for a country that is anxious to attract foreign investors to its shores (ibid.).

From this perspective, a long-term economic policy for Malaysia has to be prices-based. This requirement is more consistent with the rules of modern international economic relations and also of such institutions as the World Trade Organization or the APEC forum.

International Trade Policy

As we have discussed earlier, Malaysia's success in its development and growth over 30 years could be said to depend on its growing trade with the rest of the world and its attractive facilities and profits for foreign investors. Know-how and technology transfer have been the direct benefits of this trade and investment in the country. More importantly, the patterns and dynamics of Malaysia's trade have been observed to have substantially changed over this period, from an almost agricultural base in 1967 to an essentially IT base in 1997 and, unexpectedly or by policy design, beyond. The implications of our findings are important and wide-ranging for trade and investment policy formulation and implementation for the country. First, an IT base is a global base with borderless commerce and communications. Second, it is also a price-based system in which the principles of least costs and maximum profits are upheld across all boundaries. Third, Malaysia's economic, trade and investment policy, to be appropriate and credible, has to be designed and implemented on this assessment of its economic activities. Finally, foreign investment is also a price-based system: capital goes where its rates of return are the most profitable, *ceteris paribus*.

In this context, it is easy to see that a trade policy that is based on a closed economy concept is inappropriate. Why should other trading countries sit idle without invoking trade retaliation when a country makes a gain in trade (for example, by dumping its tradable commodities) for its own benefit and at the expense of these trading countries? It is also easy to see that a trade policy that is based on a fixed exchange rate regime can have serious drawbacks. The most relevant example of drawbacks is in the form of international competitiveness where cost advantages can be won or lost as a result of currency appreciation or devaluation in other trading countries while the country in focus maintains its fixed exchange rate regime. The experiences of the crisis economies in Asia in the last three years have provided good lessons in this respect.

Development and Growth

In the longer term, the retention of capital controls and the fixed exchange rate regime will increase the inefficiency in resource allocation not only in the country in focus but also in other trading countries in the global context. This will in turn have a negative impact on economic development and growth. In Malaysia, it has been noted that the number of foreign investment applications has fallen steadily since the imposition of capital controls in September 1998. This seems to indicate that foreign investors have found investment in Malaysia unattractive, or that other destinations of investment have offered better deals. The implications are serious for a country that wants to shift from low-cost, labour-intensive manufactured goods to high-technology, knowledge-based high value-added products.

As our discussion earlier has indicated, the shift has been substantial and successfully built up over many years. To say the least, the present monetary and fiscal policy in Malaysia, however, has not been helpful to this hard-won shift.

Skilled Labour and Human Resource Development

In its quest to change to an IT society and to develop knowledge-based industries, Malaysia has found itself in short supply of the required skilled labour, and its labour competitiveness is lacking when compared with most ASEAN countries, especially during its economic recovery (ADB, Internet, May 2000). To many, the results are not surprising. During the Asian crisis, the adverse impact on primary and secondary education in Malaysia had been mild but that on tertiary education had been severe. School estimates in Malaysia indicate that in 1998 there were 112 000 applications for the 42 220 places available at the country's ten public universities. Under these circumstances, local tertiary education costs have reportedly increased by 30 per cent, beyond the reach of most lower middle-income families. The situation has also been aggravated by the government's restrictive demand management programmes that, in 1998, made an across-the-board cut of 18 per cent in all categories of expenditure (including school construction, teacher training programmes and educational management information systems).

Given the shortage of skilled labour and the bottlenecks in tertiary education, there have been calls for the Malaysian government to induce private sector participation in providing vocational training, higher education and appropriate skills development programmes. The participation of the private sector also offers the opportunity to increase competitiveness that could improve labour standards in the country.

International Competitiveness

In a globalized economy where trade and investment are ultimately liberalized for the benefit of all trading countries (the so-called World Trade Organization *raison d'être* or requirements), competitiveness is a main determinant of success or failure. International competitiveness includes labour, trade and finance in our context. Above, we have discussed aspects of labour competitiveness in Malaysia as compared to other ASEAN economies. In order to continue its path of vigorous development and growth in the 21st century, however, Malaysia has to sort out urgently its skilled labour shortage problems. This is necessary not only to rectify a local issue in human capital development and formation but also to compete with other ASEAN countries for a better share of the world trade, investment and income.

Trade competitiveness involves not only the quality of the tradable products but also their prices on the world market. While the quality issue is related to skilled labour in high-technology industries by which most of Malaysia's major exports were produced (see the trends in Figures 5.5 and 5.6), the price issue is directly related to the exchange rate regime the country is adopting. Whether trade competitiveness exists or not may depend simply on the fluctuations of the trading countries' currencies. A fixed exchange rate regime is in this context highly inappropriate and irresponsible, with undesirable consequences in applications.

REFERENCES

Asian Development Bank (2000), 'Asian Development Outlook', Internet, May.
CEPII-CHELEM (1999), International Trade Databases, CEPII, Paris.
Encyclopaedia Britannica (2000), 'Malaysia', Internet, June.
Fischer, S. (1999), 'The Road to a Sustainable Recovery in Asia', paper presented at the World Economic Forum, Singapore, 18 October 1999, reported on Internet, May 2000.
International Monetary Fund (2000), 'World Economic Outlook', Internet, May.

6. The Philippines' economic recovery: trends, issues and strategies for balanced growth

Ma. Rebecca Valenzuela

1 INTRODUCTION

The financial turmoil that engulfed the Asian region in 1997 is now an old tale. Three years on, the region has bounced back and, by standard measures, is once again the world's fastest growing region (World Bank, 2000). Notwithstanding the abrupt reversal of negative economic trends, the crisis continues to leave indelible marks on the lives of people in the affected economies of the region. Trends such as depressed living standards, increased incidence of poverty and a rise in ethnic conflicts – the social legacies of the crisis – will take a while longer to reverse, in spite of the combined resources of local and international governments and assistance agencies to minimize such impacts. But getting the individual economies back on a solid growth path remains the top priority in the hope that it not only offers a strong foundation for further growth but, more importantly, the 'trickle down' effect will pull many out of their depressed economic state and equip them with a greater capacity to participate, once again, in a dynamic growth process.

As one of the crisis-affected economies, the Philippines has come out of the malaise with relatively little damage. Certainly, capital outflow increased dramatically, unemployment levels soared and prices increased in record magnitudes, but the numbers are generally considered not as bad as elsewhere. Consequently, short-term policy responses have not been as harsh and crippling, and the social backlash has been milder. Analysts have attributed this to sound fundamentals which resulted from years of economic and structural reform (Valenzuela, 2000; Milo, 1999; Intal *et al.*, 1998). The country's previous experiences with similar financial crises in the past are also seen to have equipped the country with a greater capacity to manage and contain the impact of this regional crisis (World Bank, East Asia Pacific Region, 1999). Whatever the case, it would be foolish for the government to rely on this good fortune for recovery. Much work needs to be done to ensure that the recovery efforts are made to rest on firm ground and to adopt sensible growth strategies that will enable the economy to pursue sustainable long-term growth. Rapidly developing trends in globalization, increased competition and the political reality in the Philippines will make this a very, very difficult, though not impossible, undertaking. A balanced growth strategy, prudent macroeconomic management and a strong political will will all be important and crucial elements for the Philippines' long-term recovery.

This chapter will provide an update on the latest economic developments in the Philippines' recovery efforts, provide a glimpse of the lingering social impact of the crisis, propose a balanced growth strategy – which simultaneously supports exports and the agricultural sector – and discuss the major issues in the implementation of this strategy.

2 THE ASIAN CRISIS: OUTCOMES AND RECENT TRENDS AND PROSPECTS

The Philippine peso was subjected to heavy speculation shortly after the collapse of the Thai baht in April 1997. To defend the local currency, the country's central bank tripled domestic interest rates in a series of steps between May and June that year. At the same time, there was heavy intervention in the foreign exchange to keep the exchange rate stable. In the end, these efforts could not be sustained and the peso was allowed to devalue in mid-July.

The high interest rates needed to defend the peso against the US dollar raised the cost of borrowing. As a result, higher commodity prices and a deterioration of corporate balance sheets affected consumption and investment expenditures, respectively. Sharp declines in share and property markets further eroded consumer and investor confidence. Interest rates have been restored to pre-crisis levels since, but the improved investment climate failed to impress capital. The decline in investment rate continued in 1999, though activity in this area picked up in early 2000. Such a sluggish response is widely interpreted as an expression of dissatisfaction among investors with the current slow pace of economic and political reforms (Asian Development Bank, 2000).

Previous episodes of peso devaluation in the Philippines have caused a dramatic rise in prices across the board (Intal *et al.*, 1998). In contrast, the effect was quite subdued in this round of devaluation. Inflation levels remained reasonable through the critical period – averaging 9·7 per cent in 1998 and reducing to 6·6 per cent in 1999 – despite the adverse impact of the exchange rate depreciation and climactic shocks (see Figure 6.1). Several factors contribute to offset the impact of the peso's depreciation. The inflation outcome reflects the strong supply of agricultural products as well as modest

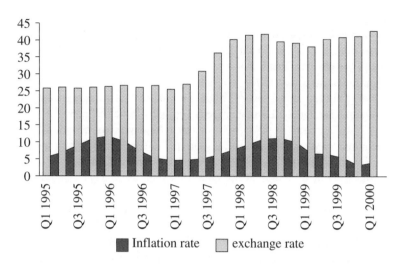

Figure 6.1   Inflation rate and peso–US$ exchange rate, 1995–2000

domestic demand and a relatively stable exchange rate. Weak aggregate demand and low world commodity prices – particularly for petroleum products – are also partly responsible. In addition, domestic manufacturers chose to run down their inventories and deferred price increases to be able to compete with cheap imports, whose entry was facilitated by a more liberalized trade environment (Milo, 1999).

The economic slowdown and the decline in share and property values took their toll on the banking sector. The main indicator here is the volume of non-performing loans (NPLs) relative to the total loans of commercials banks. The increased cost of borrowing simply impaired the ability of both corporate and individual borrowers to service their debts. As a result, NPLs rose from 3·4 per cent prior to the crisis to 4·7 per cent at the end of 1997, to 10·4 per cent in 1998 and to 14·6 per cent in 1999, before receding to 12·5 per cent in the first quarter of 2000. Interest rates have since been restored to pre-crisis levels, but credit growth is weighed down by borrowers' unwillingness to make commitments in a climate of general overcapacity and insufficient demand. Low credit growth continued in the early months of 2000, reflecting only a slow recovery of the private sector.

All other sectors of the economy suffered a similar backlash in the wake of the Asian crisis. The construction and manufacturing sectors of the economy felt the immediate setback with the sudden crunch in credit flows and the surge in capital outflows. This effected a negative growth rate of 1·9 per cent for the entire industrial sector in 1998. Depressed consumer and investor confidence could only muster a 0·5 per cent growth for the industrial sector in 1999. For a sector that consistently posted growth rates of at least 6·2 per cent in the years immediately preceding the crisis, this sluggish performance is very disappointing, even though first quarter 2000 figures indicate a bullish performance in the months ahead.

Poor industrial performance resulted from weak consumer demand for non-food manufactured items, severe contraction in the construction sector caused by overcapacity and NPLs that impeded growth in bank financing for new projects. Slow growth in industry has been symptomatic of economic performance in recent years. The industrial share in GDP has shrunk from more than 40 per cent two decades ago to around 35 per cent in 1998, in contrast to strong industrial growth in neighbouring countries such as Malaysia and Thailand (Milo, 1999).

A debilitating drought that set in in late 1997 depressed the rural economy and compounded the effects of the financial crisis on the agricultural sector. With substantially reduced levels of production, increased farm prices and a hostile rural credit environment, the agricultural sector shrank by 6·6 per cent in 1998 owing to the twin effects of the crisis and the drought. Fortunately, the drought was short-lived and there was abundant rainfall in 1999. The favourable weather conditions invigorated the agricultural sector, which grew by 6·6 per cent that year. Figures for early 2000, however, pointed to an imminent slowdown for the sector. (See Table 6.1.)

The services sector managed to expand in the midst of the financial crisis, even though growth rates show a slowdown of production activities in 1998 and 1999. In this sector, which absorbs more than 45 per cent of the country's 30 million workforce, the expansion was led by consistent, strong growth in the Transport, Communication and Storage subsector which overshadowed the sluggish recovery of the financial and real estate subsectors. On the services side, remittances from some five million Filipinos living and working abroad proved a far more stable resource inflow than other inflows such as portfolio or bank loans.

On the demand side, personal consumption expenditure declined significantly between 1997 and 1998, and has since remained subdued. Gross capital formation declined by as much as 20 per cent of GDP (in 1998) as high interest rates, tight financing and the uncertain economic environment discouraged investment spending. And, as mentioned, the negative growth in investment levels remained throughout 1999, though first quarter 2000 performance holds some promise of a positive growth in the coming months.

The external sector nonetheless provided much of the dynamism that was lacking in the domestic market in 1998. The Philippines' export growth remained remarkably robust during the crisis, notwithstanding declining regional demand and weak semiconductor prices, factors that have depressed export performance in most countries of the region. This has resulted in

Table 6.1 Growth of real GDP by industrial origin and by expenditure type, and other macroeconomic indicators, 1995–2000 (per cent)

	1995	1996	1997	1998	1999	1997 Q1	Q2	Q3	Q4	1998 Q1	Q2	Q3	Q4	1999 Q1	Q2	Q3	Q4	2000 Q1
GNP	5·0	7·2	5·3	0·1	3·7	5·4	5·3	5·1	5·1	1·5	−0·05	0·7	−1·2	1·5	4·0	3·8	5·1	3·4
GDP	4·8	5·8	5·2	−0·5	3·2	5·5	5·6	4·9	4·7	1·1	−1·0	−0·1	−2·0	0·7	3·6	3·8	3·3	3·4
By industrial origin																		
Agriculture	0·8	4·3	2·8	−6·7	6·7	4·9	1·8	0·4	4·1	−3·8	−11·5	−3·1	−7·8	2·9	9·2	5·3	6·6	0·2
Industry	7·0	6·2	6·2	−1·9	0·9	5·1	7·6	6·4	5·6	0·2	−0·7	−2·0	−4·7	−3·6	0·6	2·5	3·8	4·8
Manufacturing	6·8	5·6	4·2	−1·1	1·6	2·3	5·3	4·3	4·7	2·0	−0·9	−1·5	−3·5	−1·0	0·9	2·4	3·7	5·8
Construction	6·6	10·9	16·4	−8·5	−1·6	21·3	18·5	18·1	7·6	−12·8	−5·1	−7·5	−8·5	−12·8	1·8	5·2	1·6	−0·7
Services	5·0	6·4	5·5	3·5	4·1	6·2	5·8	5·5	4·4	4·5	3·6	2·8	3·2	3·2	3·8	4·3	5·0	3·8
By expenditure share																		
Personal consumption	3·8	4·6	5·0	3·5	2·6	5·0	5·1	5·0	4·9	4·5	3·9	2·9	2·6	2·5	2·6	2·5	2·6	3·2
Government consumption	5·6	4·1	4·6	−2·1	5·3	4·5	7·3	6·2	0·4	−5·4	−2·4	−1·3	0·6	7·9	4·2	3·1	6·5	−1·9
Investment	3·7	13·3	11·6	−16·4	−1·7	14·9	7·1	9·3	15·0	−6·0	−18·2	−19·1	−22·3	−5·9	6·2	−0·6	−4·8	3·0
Merchandise exports	16·2	9·6	13·4	−0·3	3·6	8·6	15·2	15·0	14·8	10·6	−1·4	3·9	−14·4	−8·4	3·3	11·5	8·9	13·5
Merchandise imports	16·0	16·9	7·7	−15·4	−2·8	3·0	2·7	10·2	15·0	−2·3	−12·1	−13·1	−33·9	−16·8	0·1	1·5	6·6	4·4

Source: National Statistical Coordination Board (2000), Asian Development Bank (2000).

increased investor confidence. The remarkable performance of the export sector in 1998 and 1999, combined with a sluggish domestic demand for imports, effected a sharp improvement in the trade balance, soaring from a deficit of $19 million in 1998 to a surplus of more than $4 billion at the end of 1999. At the same time, the current account surplus widened from $1·3 billion to nearly $6 billion. These surpluses were driven primarily by the surge in the export of electronic goods. The surplus in the balance of payments resulted in a substantial increase in international reserves to nearly $15 billion, exceeding the pre-crisis level by more than $2 billion. While the external debt-to-GDP ratio increased to around 65 per cent mainly because of the peso's depreciation, the debt–service ratio was a comfortable 13 per cent (Asian Development Bank, 2000)

Employment Effects

During the second quarter of 1998, the rural economy suffered from an abrupt contraction of farm employment due to the prolonged dry spell brought about by the El Niño phenomenon. Crop production was drastically reduced and farm profits were severely slashed that year, resulting in a total contraction of the agricultural sector by 6·6 per cent, as mentioned earlier. Fortunately, the drought subsided quickly and favourable weather conditions returned in 1999, increasing employment levels in the agricultural sector significantly as farmers and part-time labourers returned to the fields. The quick recovery of the agricultural sector was in fact a main source of expansion for the economy in 1999. In early 2000, the continued ascent of employment levels in this sector (see Table 6.2) reflected the sector's absorption of the excess labour supply from the more urbanized sectors of the economy.

Urban workers suffered the brunt of the contraction of the industrial sector in the initial months of the crisis. The number of firms 'downsizing' or closing down in 1998 and 1999 was more than double that of 1997, and more than 60 per cent of these firms are in the National Capital Region, which includes Manila and its surrounding areas. The surge in lay-offs began in early 1998 and continued unabated until the end of the following year. In the industrial sector, the manufacturing and construction subsectors were the hardest hit, while the contraction in the services sector was widespread.

Official statistics from the Department of Labour and Employment show that the total number of displaced workers in both 1998 and 1999 was nearly three times as great as in 1997 (see Tables 6.3 and 6.4). This represents more than 150 000 laid off workers for each year, with half of them being laid off permanently. This figure even excludes those workers who had to adjust to pay cuts and/or reduced number of hours on the job. In the urban areas, those initially affected are the unskilled workers, who are the first to be laid off,

Table 6.2 Selected labour statistics, 1990–2000

Year	Total labour force (000s)	Unemployment rate (%)	Under employment rate (%)	Total number employed (000s)	Employment by sector		
					Agriculture (%)	Industry (%)	Services (%)
1990	24 244	8.3	22.4	22 212	46.7	15.1	38.2
1991	25 631	10.5	22.5	22 914	44.9	15.8	39.3
1992	26 290	9.8	20.0	23 696	45.3	16.1	38.6
1993	26 879	9.3	21.7	24 382	45.7	15.6	38.7
1994	27 654	9.5	21.4	25 032	45.1	15.8	39.1
1995	28 382	9.5	20.0	25 676	43.4	16.1	40.5
1996	29 733	8.6	20.9	27 186	42.8	16.3	40.9
1997	30 355	8.7	22.1	27 715	40.8	16.7	42.5
1998	31 056	10.1	21.8	27 911	39.2	16.4	44.4
1999	32 000	9.0	22.1	29 216	38.8	16.2	45.0
2000 Q1	32 103	9.3	21.2	28 892	39.5	15.3	45.2

Source: National Economic and Development Authority (2000) and National Statistical Coordination Boaod (2000).

*Table 6.3   Number of firms reporting difficulties due to economic problems,
            number of workers affected, 1996–9*

Year	Number of firms reporting			Number of workers affected		
	Total	Closure	Workforce reduction	Total	Permanent lay-off	Temporary lay-off
1996	1 076	347	724	80 701	47 008	29 487
1997	1 155	338	804	62 724	39 176	19 843
1998	3 072	642	2 310	155 198	76 726	50 744
1999	2 936	505	1 788	157 432	69 735	49 873

Source: Bureau of Labor and Employment Statistics.

followed by labouring families whose livelihoods depend entirely on daily wages, such as factory workers, construction workers, taxi drivers and casual labourers. Department of Labour and Employment (DOLE) data further show that the lay-offs in the city predominantly affected male workers who were mostly the main breadwinners in their respective households. The data also suggested that more than half of laid off workers lost full-time and permanent positions.

Overall, the positive effect of the rural sector recovery on employment levels had a dampening effect on a very steep rise in the national unemployment rate of 10.1 per cent in 1998 and was a significant pull-down factor in the 1999 rate, which stood at 9 per cent. But agriculture could only absorb so much of the excess labour supply from industry and services. Those who had been displaced moved to the more informal sectors of the urban economy to work where they could and for less money. There were also no jobs to absorb the new entrants to the labour force, which resulted in an increase in the number of underemployed workers in the economy of 400 000 between 1998 and 1999.

Latest figures for early 2000 indicated a loosening of this tight labour market situation, reflecting the slow recovery of the industrial sector. Increased demand for particular high-tech export products is creating new job opportunities and the recovery of most sectors will gradually push unemployment rates down. But even as the recovery of the industrial sector continues, closures, mergers and 'downsizing' will be commonplace as business enterprises seek ways to strengthen their position in the market place. Already in 1999, firm data showed that 50 per cent of firms cited organizational restructuring as a reason for the recent reduction in the size of their workforce, and there is no sign of a let-up in the foreseeable future.

Table 6.4   *Number of firms reporting difficulties due to economic problems, number of workers affected, by industry origin, 1996–9*

Industry	1996	1997	1998	1999
Agriculture	97	70	95	65
Industry	545	568	1254	846
Mining & quarrying	14	23	48	19
Manufacturing	508	505	1025	716
Construction	21	31	173	14
Utilities	2	9	8	97
Services	435	517	1723	1355
Transport	68	91	257	193
W & R trade	134	167	600	452
Finance	93	130	491	422
Personal services	140	129	375	288
All firms	1077	1155	3072	2266

Source: Bureau of Labour and Employment Statistics.

Household Adjustments

With the financial crisis, the total income of most households in the Philippines came under threat on two fronts: a reduction of job hours, or job loss altogether, and higher prices of most essentials, increasing the household financial and social insecurity of families across the country. A recent government survey provides a glimpse of the household effects of the crisis (see Table 6.5): about 20 per cent of families reported significantly reduced incomes due to the loss of jobs within the country, 5 per cent through the loss of jobs overseas, and 17 per cent through a reduction in wages. On the expenditure side, nine out of ten families reported being hit by higher prices of food and other basic commodities. The surveys also found that 60 per cent of families, mostly from the agricultural areas, reported being affected by the El Niño drought.

Indeed, there was a steady decline in personal consumption as a percentage of GDP in 1998 and this remained at a low 2·6 per cent of GDP in 1999. Whether this reflects the welfare of the poor or of the better off will not be known until more detailed expenditure data become available.[1] On the basis of national accounts data, though, it can be seen that households tended to forgo spending on durable and luxury-related goods. This implies that spending cuts were proportionately larger among the middle class and wealthy,

Table 6.5   Impact of the financial crisis on Filipino families

Income strata	No. of families reporting	Percentage of families affected				
		Higher prices	Job loss (local)	Job loss (migrant)	Reduced wages	Drought
Phillipines	13.5	96.6	20.3	4.9	17.0	62.9
Lowest 40%	5.5	95.7	17.9	3.7	15.2	76.0
Highest 60%	8.0	97.0	22.0	5.9	18.4	54.0

Source: National Statistics Office.

while the poor and those close to poor were better able to maintain basic spending. It is possible that the continued growth of work remittances may have helped to maintain such consumption. And while the sharp drop in agricultural output in the first half of 1998 and typhoon related damage in the fourth quarter hurt the rural poor, the recent rapid agricultural expansion has limited the effects of the crisis on the poor (World Bank, 2000).

The most common responses of households to the income and price effects were, in a broad sense, to change their eating patterns, to increase the working hours (for those who had jobs) and to ask for money or obtain credit from better-off relatives or friends. The type of coping mechanisms adopted naturally varied across households. As the budget share of food comprises between 80 and 90 per cent of the total budget of the poor household, a reduction in income implies large cuts in food consumption. This is achieved through switching to cheaper food or reducing meals from, say, three times a day to twice, or eating less food. In contrast, the higher-income households tend to cut back on luxuries and other non-necessities. Earning additional income from extra hours of work is another popular way to maintain the level of consumption in the context of the reduced purchasing power of the peso. For a significant number of households, the generosity and kindness of relatives and friends is a chosen alternative, as this serves as an informal credit market – one that is speedy, does not require credit checks and relies heavily on the social relationship of the transacting parties. There was a higher tendency for the poorer households to take their children out of school. In fact, the growth in school enrolment has slowed down significantly following the crisis. School enrolments increased by only by 0·9 per cent between the academic years 1997–8 and 1998–9, after growing at an average annual rate of 2·6 per cent during the previous five years. Others households were assisted by government transfers and/or moved to other towns in search of employment.

Because of all these developments, there is great fear of a rise in the incidence of poverty in the economy. The Asian Development Bank, for instance, foresees that poverty incidence in the Philippines will grow by 5 percentage points, from 32·3 in 1997. Recent estimates of self-rated poverty based on the Social Weather Station's December 1999 survey showed a picture of fluctuations in self-rated poverty without any clear trend. In December 1999, the estimate was 59 per cent, which compares with 63 per cent, 60 per cent and 62 per cent in October, June and March, respectively, of the same year. The various human development indicators are thus expected to take a turn for the worse (Intal *et al.*, 1998). Income distribution also appears to have worsened as a result of the crisis (Milo, 1999).

The ability of the government to offer assistance to the affected families was severely constrained by the enlarged amount of budget deficit. From a minimal surplus in the first half of 1997, the government posted a deficit of 2·3 billion pesos in the second half of the same year. This ballooned to 60 billion pesos in 1998 and to 112 billion pesos at the end of 1999. To contain the deficit, the government imposed a mandatory 25 per cent reserve requirement on all expenditures other than personnel and debt service and a 10 per cent deferment in the internal revenue allotment for local government units, in addition to suspending all tax subsidies of all government agencies and corporations. The social services sectors were eventually exempted from the mandatory reserves in July 1998. Expenditures on social services fell by around 10 per cent relative to the programmed levels in 1998, in contrast to economic services, for instance, which fell by 30 per cent. Although this reduction was less than that in other sectors, it has serious repercussions for the poor, especially given the government's historical underinvestment in the health and education sectors.

Summary

Overall, the recovery of the Philippine economy from the Asian financial crisis is well under way. While the macroeconomic situation continued to reflect the impact of the crisis, short-term policy responses have been well managed and the government's efforts to mitigate the social impact of the crisis have also been favourable. The task ahead is to ensure that the recovery effort rests on solid ground. To this end, much work needs to be done. The unemployment rate, underemployment rate and the number of non-performing loans continued to be high, and industrial activity, demand for credit, investment demand and foreign private capital inflows were all low. In addition, a greater effort is required to speed up the recovery process, as the pace of economic and structural reforms appears to be slow when compared to other crisis-affected countries (World Bank, 2000; Asian Development Bank, 2000). Concerns for the Philippines include reduced revenue, quality of public expenditures, delayed reforms in the banking and financial sectors, and slow progress in legislation required for capital market reforms and in the privatization programme. Many of the pending reforms are close to implementation, and are expected to boost investor confidence in the country when implemented. Measures to accelerate the implementation of reforms are critical to improve medium-term growth prospects, address the serious poverty problem and arrest further environmental degradation.

3   BALANCED GROWTH: PROMOTING EXPORTS AND INVESTING IN AGRICULTURE

More than anything else, the regional crisis has exposed the remaining structural weaknesses of the Philippine economy and highlighted its high degree of vulnerability to sudden shifts in external economic forces such as investor confidence, market sentiment and price changes. Much of the economic recovery has been addressed through continued reforms in the finance and corporate sector, as well as institution of changes in approaches to economic and social management of the economy. Economic recovery is clearly under way, despite the relatively slow pace of implementation of the strategies adopted. Full recovery is imminent and the focus now is on ensuring that the economic fundamentals of the country are indeed sufficiently strong for sustainable long-term growth. The following sections focus on two sectors of the economy that are considered crucial for this purpose: the export sector and the agricultural sector. These two sectors are deemed to offer the best chance for the long-term economic well-being of the Philippines. They also offer the best hopes for breaking free from the boom-and-bust growth cycle that has characterized its development in the past, and for finally being on the road to solid growth.

Increasing Export Competitiveness

In an era of increasing regional integration, globalization and intense market competition, the Philippine economy can look to exports to push its growth rates higher. In particular, manufactured exports from the Philippines exhibited an impressive annual growth rate of 36 per cent during the period 1991–7, and have proved very resilient during the crisis years to date. As the World Bank noted, the Philippines' export growth has outpaced that of its neighbours since 1995 and up to the present time. If the size of manufactured exports is taken in the context of those of other Asian countries, the achievement of this Philippine sector becomes even more remarkable because it is the smallest player in the region (see Figure 6.2).

A narrow range of products – electronics – has driven the outstanding export record of the Philippines in recent times, and within electronics, the

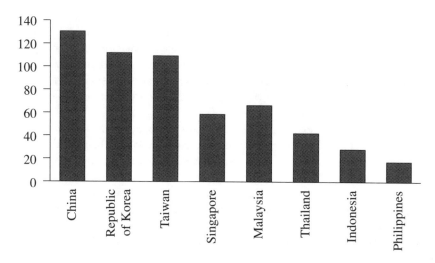

Source: World Bank, East Asia Pacific Region (1999).

Figure 6.2   Total value of manufactured exports, 1996 (US$ billions)

export of semiconductors accounted for 64 per cent of total export value in 1999. Other countries in the region export semiconductors, but export growth from the Philippines has been much faster. In particular, the Philippines has outpaced Malaysia and Singapore in the ranking stakes, in spite of their being more mature and longer term players. The two other main export products are input/output peripheral units and garments, but they make up only a small proportion of the total value of the major electronic products (about 18 per cent for peripherals, and about 12 per cent for garments).

Indications are that this stronghold of the Philippines in the export market of semiconductors and other electronic products will continue, and if this is so, it will definitely push overall growth rates higher. Already the flow of foreign direct investments to the industry is solid, with investor confidence in this sector having diminished little in spite of the regional crisis. This is mostly attributed to the cheap and plentiful technical labour that abounds in the country.

They are cheaper than Malaysia's and relatively skilled and English-speaking. There is also an abundance of engineers, whereas Malaysian companies have had to use (expensive) expatriate technical staff. Labour turnover rates are slower in the Philippines allowing for greater skill formation. Japanese investors regard the discipline, trainability and loyalty of Filipino workers very highly; some have rated the workforce as the best in the world. (World Bank, 2000)

A long-term trend of high growth rates in Philippines' exports is thus highly likely. However, it is prudent to expect that there will always be economic forces that will threaten such a comfortable position. For example, it is always possible that Malaysian exports will revive and other regional production sites may suddenly offer better incentives for foreign investors. The high technology market is also highly volatile and a sudden shift in sentiment is not a remote possibility.

It will thus be necessary for the Philippines to broaden its export base. High dependency on one export product is an inherently risky strategy for driving national exports, even if these products happen to be among the fastest growing and dynamic exports in the world. To drive this point further, it is noted that the more mature industrialized countries of the world, where the largest technology exports originate, have more diversified exports. In the United States, for example, high-tech exports accounted for 28 per cent of total value of exports in 1995, while the equivalent ratios for Japan and the United Kingdom are 27 per cent and 25 per cent, respectively (World Bank, 2000). In contrast, the equivalent figure for the Philippines is 84 per cent. Consequently, any downturn in the inflow of foreign direct investments or a technological shift that affects costs or production in the Philippines could be disastrous. Skill and technical requirements are also changing constantly. All industrializing countries are trying hard to attract electronics corporations, and keeping ahead of the rest will be a demanding task.

An equally important reason for diversifying the economy's export structure is the fact that the Philippines needs to retain its relative strength in the export of labour-intensive products. The export garment industry, for instance, is an activity in which the economy can harness the inherent advantage of low wages. However, this labour-intensive export has performed badly in recent years in spite of Philippine wages being lower than in Malaysia or Thailand (though higher than in China or Indonesia).[2] The recent performance of garment exports in non-quota markets, which face the most intense open competition from lower-wage countries like Bangladesh, China and Sri Lanka, has been even worse. This reinforces the situation that the upgrading of quality and technology among Philippine exporters is lagging (ibid.). Other labour-intensive products such as footwear, toys and leather goods have also performed poorly, with annual growth rates of less than 3 per cent during 1994–7. The most important resource-based export, processed foods, also shows a generally weak and cyclical growth.

To revive the competitiveness of these exports, the Philippines needs to formulate and implement strategies aimed specifically at improving skill, using advanced technology and strengthening marketing know-how in a range of manufacturing activities. The government appears fully aware of these needs and has mounted a comprehensive response, but, as noted, much of this response remains on paper. In addition, it is crucial for the government to provide a more equal playing field by levelling off incentive biases against certain types of export industries (mostly the labour-intensive ones) and against certain types of manufacturers (small and medium-size firms against the more highly favoured large, multinational operations). The boom-and-bust cycles that have long characterized Philippine growth have resulted mainly from the adoption of such policies. A total dismantling of protectionism in industry will be necessary to increase the competitiveness of the export products, and so trade and industry can grow and deepen as well.

Reinvigorating Agriculture: Back to Basics

The Philippines' agricultural sector is the other sector of the economy that needs reconsideration. A second look at this sector is important because the economy remains mainly agricultural, the sector provides employment to as much as 45 per cent of the Philippines' labour force, and the poorest citizens of the economy are largely dependent on agriculture. A vibrant and dynamic agricultural sector provides a solid foundation for the sustainable growth of industry, and consequently of the service sector. At this stage of the Philippines' development and industrialization, agriculture continues to play an important role for the economy. This was highlighted as recently as 1999, when the agricultural sector increased its total production by 6·6 per cent, making it a major factor in pulling the Philippines out of the doldrums of the regional crisis.

For many developing economies, agriculture is important for many reasons. First of all, it is the primary source of food products for its citizenry. In the Philippines, the 75 million-strong population depends on agriculture to meet their daily provision of rice, the dominant food crop and the country's staple food. Maize is also a major crop and is a staple food for some regions in the south. Root crops such as cassava and yam combine with fish, chicken and pork to comprise the other most common items in the menu of Philippine households. While self-sufficiency in food supply is always a goal of the government planners, there were periods when the country had to import rice to augment a shortfall in supply. Such shortfalls are the result of unfavourable weather conditions. Longer periods of low supply (the late 1970s, for instance) resulted from a mix of unfavourable policies which stymied productivity and growth in the agricultural sector.

The sheer size of the sector also makes it a good provider of jobs for people in the rural economy. Rice cultivation, in particular, is labour-intensive relative to other major crops. And while farm work is often seasonal and casual, the agricultural sector also gives rise to many rural non-farm activities that provide work opportunities for casual farm labourers during the off season, and also for rural women.

On the demand side, the agricultural population is a rich market for both farm and non-farm products. Rural communities consume a significant proportion of their local produce; otherwise they engage in agricultural product trading between communities – say for fish and other livestock – to meet their other food needs. The sector also serves as a market for the products of the more industrial sector, though the strength of this backward linkage depends on the standard of living of the rural households. The extent to which the rural population depends on products from the industrial sector is directly linked to the type of income distribution current in the economy. If income distribution is highly uneven, the large majority of the rural population will be poor. Their expenditure basket will necessarily be limited to food and other basic necessities, and their demand for industrial products will be low, or zero, as a result. However, if there is a greater degree of equality in the distribution of income, living standards for rural families will be higher and this can increase demand for products from the modern sector. If a large rural market exists, local industries can continue to grow after the urban sector market has been saturated, until such time as the industries are better able to compete in the foreign market.

Finally, a dynamic and vibrant agricultural sector can also be a rich source of savings and investment capital, necessary to accelerate the country's overall economic growth. It is common for developing countries to import capital in the form of aid or private investment to speed up the rate of capital accumulation and hence the growth of the economy, as in South Korea, where foreign aid was drawn upon to provide capital. Home-grown capital, however, is still preferred as this does not bring with it the risk of capital flight in times of difficulties. Capital comes from invested savings and savings from income, and an agricultural sector which is thriving and growing will lend itself easily to capital accumulation in the economy. Another factor is foreign exchange. Agricultural products sold overseas can serve as the principal source of foreign exchange. The agricultural sector's ability to supply foreign exchange enables the economy to import capital equipment and intermediate goods necessary for its continued growth. The fact is that the industrial sector has to maintain these important backward and forward linkages to agriculture, as any weakening of these linkages can spell trouble for the industrial sector – and the economy for that matter.

The 30-year period between 1950 and 1980 appears to be the strongest growth period for the agricultural sector in the Philippines (see Table 6.6).[3] Annual growth in agricultural output averaged 4·9 per cent, with production dominated by rice and corn (for the food crops) and coconut and sugar (for the export crops). Increases in agricultural output in the early years were due to an increase in the amount of land being cultivated, which subsequently gave way to more intensive use of land. Later productivity increases reflected

Table 6.6   Industry shares of GDP

	1950	1961	1965	1971	1980	1985	1990	1999
Agriculture	36.5	34.2	33.6	28.9	23.4	24.6	22.5	20.0
Industry	26.1	26.3	27.0	30.3	40.6	35.0	35.8	34.5
Manufacturing	13.5	17.5	17.5	23.6	27.6	25.2	25.4	24.5
Services	37.4	39.6	39.8	40.8	26.0	40.4	41.7	45.5

Source: NSCB, *Philippine Statistic Yearbook.*

the use of superior technology (for example, use of fertilizers and of high-yield varieties) and the government's massive investment in farm irrigation. The growth of agriculture in the 1980s and the 1990s remained positive, but has slowed down significantly. The country's leading export products have lost their competitiveness, not only because of the decline in world commodity prices, but more because of an overvalued exchange rate regime and heavy price intervention in agricultural output and fertilizer prices. The economy's agricultural sector growth in the 1990s averaged only 1·5 per cent per year, but it is believed that it holds the key to the nation's chronic problems of poverty and inequality.

The next question to address is how to reinvigorate the Philippines' agricultural sector. There are several approaches, but the main elements to this problem's solutions are well known. Already a floating exchange rate is in place, which is an improvement on the case where the peso was so overvalued. The sharply depreciated value of the peso should make the economy's export products (including agricultural products) very competitive in the world market. Other tried-and-tested agricultural push measures include the removal of all vestiges of trade protectionism, a massive investment in rural infrastructure, investment in agricultural research and development, increasing agricultural incentives (such as subsidies for water and credit) and adopting superior technology. These have worked for the Philippines before and no doubt they will work again if employed.

All these measures will stimulate activity in the Philippines' agricultural sector and, if well managed, will result in a strong economic revival for the rural economy. In the context of all these efforts, the most important measure that will have to be applied is to ensure that the gains derived from the reinvigorated agricultural sector are spread widely across the rural population. First and foremost, increased growth rates must immediately be translated into increased incomes for the mass base population in agriculture. One essential step towards this is the removal of factor price distortions which are biased towards use of capital instead of labour. Agricultural production methods that are more labour-intensive are the surest way of ensuring a broad rural participation in the growth process. Another essential step towards greater participation in rural growth is to ensure that there is wide and more equitable access to the infrastructure and incentive packages for those that desire to participate. Access to credit, irrigated water, subsidies for fertilizer, electricity and other important infrastructure facilities must not be just limited to large producers, but be broadened to include small-scale farm operators.

Broad participation in the growth process implies that the highly inequitable distribution of productive assets will have to be addressed more seriously. Specifically, vigorous efforts to implement land reform effectively must continually be pursued. Policy makers should keep going with land reform, no matter how difficult the institutional and political obstacles. In addition, a more equitable access to educational opportunities should also be provided, particularly for children of poorer rural households. After all, a solid thrust towards human development in the form of basic education and health care and so on facilitates economic and industrial expansion.

An agricultural growth process that has a wide income base will lift many of the rural poor above the poverty line and raise the general standard of living in the rural areas. This will result in a rural consumption that favours labour-intensive, locally produced goods, rather than capital-intensive products and imported goods. This could also provide the much-needed stimulus to the growth of non-agricultural income, which could generate significant employment multiplier effects on the local, regional and national economies. These spillover effects include vast improvements in the productivity of private investment, reduced fertility levels through the effect on labour allocation and educational investment decisions, further development of intangible 'social capital' (in the form of social networks, peer group effects, role models and so on), and mitigate erosion in the quality of life in urban areas through its effect on rural–urban migration decisions. In Taiwan, public investment in rural areas appears to have induced such externalities, thereby contributing to the country's broadly based pattern of economic growth during the last three decades (Park and Johnston, 1995). Improved living standards in the rural areas will also address the regional growth imbalances in the Philippines that have characterized growth in the last 30 years.

4 CONCLUSIONS

The Philippines is showing encouraging signs of economic recovery from the regional crisis, despite the slow pace of infrastructure reform. A full recovery is imminent and the focus now is on ensuring that the recovery efforts are founded on firm ground. The medium and long-term strategies that the government employs to push growth rates higher will require two basic elements: promotion of Philippine export products and reinvigoration of the agricultural sector.

Improved growth prospects are contingent on several factors. First, continuing prudent macroeconomic management is required, along with progress in reforms. The government expects that budgetary deficits will continue at least until 2001. These deficits may be necessary to impart the needed boost to the economy in an environment of flagging aggregate demand, and to maintain vital social sector expenditures. However, care must be taken to ensure that financing these deficits does not push up interest rates and crowd out much-needed private investment. Second, strong export growth momentum must continue. However, because the export basket is composed of a narrow range of products – electronics, transport equipment, machinery, garments and textiles – it is sensitive to shifts in market sentiment and price volatility. Diversification of the export basket and encouraging small and medium-size enterprises in areas where the Philippines has a comparative advantage will help maintain export dynamism and will ensure future export growth. Finally, a continued favourable regional environment is necessary for recovery.

Complementing the push for exports should be efforts at invigorating the agricultural sector. This sector continues to play a crucial role in the economic development of the Philippines, and its level of industrialization is such that industry continues to depend on agriculture for some support. The intricate linkages that bind non-agricultural growth to agricultural sector dynamism will have to be strengthened. And there is the simple exercise of looking at the past, and not committing the same policy mistakes. An invigorated agricultural sector is also seen as a key element in addressing the chronic problems of poverty and inequality in the economy.

Overall, the main objective of the exercise is to ensure a wide participation in the recovery and growth process. It is important to ensure that the fruits of development are immediately translated into increased incomes for the mass base, particularly the poor sections of the rural economy. Ensuring this gives rise to many positive externalities that can feed on to even higher rates of growth for the whole economy.

NOTES

1. The Family Income and Expenditure Survey in the Philippines is conducted every three years. One was conducted in 1997, and the next one is in 2000. Results of the latter will not be analysable until at least six months into 2001.
2. The annual rate of growth of garment exports from the Philippines in 1990–95 was 7.7 per cent, compared with 11.5 per cent for Malaysia, 12.3 per cent for Thailand, 15.7 per cent for Indonesia, and 20.1 per cent in China.
3. See Bautista (1995) and David *et al.* (1987) for a detailed discussion of agricultural growth in the Philippines.

BIBLIOGRAPHY

Alburo, F.A. (1999), 'The Philippines and the Asian Crisis: Has it turned the corner?', in F.G. Adams and W.E. James (eds), *Public Policies in East Asian Development*, New York: Praeger.

Asian Development Bank (2000), *Asian Development Outlook 2000*, Oxford: Oxford University Press.

Balisacan, A (1999), 'Growth, Poverty and Inequality in the Philippines', in G. Ranis, S.C. Hu and Y.-P. Chu (eds), *The Political Economy of Comparative Development into the 21st Century*, Cheltenham, UK and Lyme, US: Edward Elgar.

Bautista, R.M (1995), 'Rapid Agricultural Growth is Not Enough: The Philippines, 1965–80', in J.H. Mellor (ed.), *Agriculture on the Road to Industrialisation*, Baltimore: Johns Hopkins University Press.

Bureau of Labor and Employment Statitics (2000), http://www.bles.gov.ph/.

David, C.C., R. Barker and A. Palacpac (1987), 'Philippines', *Productivity Measurement and Analysis: Asian Agriculture*, Tokyo: Asian Productivity Organization.

Intal, P., M. Milo, C. Reyes and L. Basilio (1998), 'The Philippines', in R.H. McLeod and R. Garnaut (eds), *East Asia in Crisis: From being a miracle to needing one*, London: Routledge.

Milo, M. (1999), 'Contagion Effects of the Asian Crisis, Policy Responses and their Social Implications', Discussion Paper Series no. 99–32, Philippine Institute of Development Studies.

National Economic and Development Authority (2000), http://www.neda.gov.ph/.

National Statistical Coordination Board (2000), http://www.nscb.gov.ph/.

National Statistical Office (2000), http://www.census.gov.ph/.

Park, A. and B. Johnston (1995), 'Rural Development and Dynamic Externalities in Taiwan's Structural Transformation', *Economic Development and Cultural Change*, 44, 181–208.

Valenzuela, M.R. (2000), 'Asian Crisis and the Philippines: Counting the Social Costs', in Tran Van Hoa (ed.), *The Social Impact of the Asia Crisis*, London: Macmillan.

World Bank (2000), http://wbln0018.worldbank.org/eap/.

World Bank, East Asia Pacific Region, Poverty Reduction and Economic Management Sector Unit (1999), 'Philippines: The Challenge of Economic Recovery', World Bank.

PART II

Major Transition Economies in Asia

7. Vietnam: economic recovery and social issues

The Dzung Nguyen

1 INTRODUCTION

Contrary to many other transition economies, Vietnam was able to attain a spectacular economic growth, macroeconomic stability and a remarkable improvement of living standards of its population during the period 1991 to 1996. However, since then this growth has been steadily slowing down. The tendency was exaggerated during the recent Asian financial crisis, halving Korea's annual GDP growth from 9·5 per cent in 1995 to 4·8 per cent in 1998/99. Signals of the country's economic recovery came in late 1999, later than in other Asian economies, and became stronger in the first half of 2000. But the recovery appears to be a long and slow process and the country has to revise its growth targets. The slowdown has unveiled the volatility of Vietnam's recent social achievements and stressed the urgent need to address its crucial social issues, including widespread poverty, unsustainable development, increasing inequality, growing unemployment pressures, access to and quality of social services, and the lack of an equitable social protection system.

This chapter argues that the underlying driving force of the development in Vietnam was and remains the process of economic reform – often called 'doi moi' (renovation) – which the country has embarked upon since 1986. The reform has dramatically reshaped the country's social sector and changed the way social issues are tackled, from the 'support-led' pattern to the 'growth-mediated' one. Therefore, being also influenced by the performance of the global economy and the economic recovery in the other Asian economies, the pattern of Vietnam's recovery could largely be defined by its measures to deepen the current reform process, particularly in critical areas such as non-state sector development, SOE (state-owned enterprise) reform, public administration, and banking and finance. This is also found to be the key to mitigating the negative social impact of the slowdown and the crisis on the social sectors and to addressing effectively social issues in the long run.

Section 2 provides an overview of Vietnam's recent economic performance and analyses major factors influencing its recovery. Section 3 reviews the country's major social issues, existing problems, the impact of the slowdown and recovery, and discusses potential solutions before summarizing them in Section 4. The information used in the chapter is based on government statistics and data collected by international agencies operating in Vietnam, particularly the World Bank and UNDP (United Nations Development Programme).

2 VIETNAM'S ECONOMIC RECOVERY

Since it embarked upon the reform process in 1986, Vietnam has followed a unique growth path, which produced impressive gains in terms of rapid growth, increasing political stability and rapid improvement of social welfare. First, its annual GDP growth rates were accelerated over seven consecutive years, 1991–7, and averaged 8·5 per cent – the highest level the country had ever achieved – with an average annual growth rate of exports of about over 25 per cent and doubled agricultural production. The size of the economy expanded by 76·6 per cent in the seven years from 1990 to 1997. The reform process is characterized by a dramatic shift in the ownership structure of the economy. The non-state sector, particularly the household economy, exhibited steady growth and became dominant in agriculture and services. Currently it provides about 60 per cent of the country's GDP and 85 per cent of its total employment, including the non-state industry. Contrary to the other transition economies, Vietnam's state sector recovered quickly after its collapse in the late 1980s, owing to the abolition of direct production subsidies and the raising of interest rates. This sector then obtained higher annual growth rates than those in the non-state sector in the following years. As a result, there were two dramatic shifts in economic structure taking place in the country.

On the one hand, the services sector has overtaken agriculture and become the largest sector of the economy since 1992, despite the fact that the latter grew stably and turned the country from a net food importer for decades into the world's third largest rice exporter. On the other hand, the external sector, in general, and exports, in particular, has become the leading sector of the economy with an average growth rate of exports topping 25 per cent per annum. On average, exports and imports totalled about 80 per cent of GDP in 1995–7, a high figure for a populous country (80 million people in 1999), indicating its opening up to international markets.

Second, major macroeconomic balances were re-established in the early 1990s and well maintained afterwards. In particular, hyperinflation in the late 1980s was brought down to two digits in the period 1989–95 and to one digit in the following years. As a result, the government was able to increase rapidly its revenues after 1991 and restore its investment and social expenditures in 1994, after severe and painful cuts since the start of the reform. Real investment more than doubled, from about 12 per cent of GDP in the period 1984–92 to 28 per cent in 1996, owing to a fivefold increase of domestic savings, from 3 per cent of GDP to about 17 per cent, and to the dramatic growth of foreign investment inflows to about 8 per cent of GDP in 1996 (World Bank, 1997).

Finally, the majority of Vietnamese people were able to benefit quickly from this growth and stability. According to the Living Standard Measurement Surveys (LSMS) which were conducted by the National General Statistical Office with the assistance of the World Bank, the UNDP and SIDA (Swedish International Development Agency), in the periods 1992/93 and 1997/98, Vietnam's living standards, measured in terms of household expenditures, had improved by nearly 43 per cent across all social groups and socioecological regions in just five years, mainly owing to strong agricultural growth and an equitable distribution of income and social services. As estimated by the World Bank, the poverty rate in Vietnam was reduced from 70 per cent in the 1970s and 1980s to 57 per cent in 1992/93 and further to 37 per cent in 1997/98. These achievements are in sharp contrast to the performance of many transition economies and other low-income developing countries, which also carried out similar policy reforms.

Since 1996/97 however, the tendency of accelerating growth has been reversed. As shown in Table 7.1, the country's economic growth slowed markedly, from 9·5 per cent – the highest growth rate – in 1995 to 9·3 per cent in 1996 and further to 8·1 per cent in 1997. This slowing-down tendency was further exaggerated during the period of the Asian financial crisis in 1997/99. According to government statistics, the annual growth rate decreased by nearly one-third, to 5·8 per cent in 1998 and then to 4·8 per cent in 1999: the lowest level since 1988. This is confirmed by the World Bank estimates, which appeared even more pessimistic: the country's real GDP growth rate was estimated at 4 per cent in both 1998 and 1999.

In general, the slowdown has affected all economic and ownership sectors, but in quite different ways. In 1998, agriculture recorded its lowest growth since 1992, largely the result of severe droughts and typhoons. Bumper crops helped agriculture to show again strong growth (5 per cent) and absorb the continuing stagnation in the other sectors of the economy in 1999. Both rice production and exports achieved record levels, 31 million tons and 4·5 million tons, respectively. However, at current prices, agricultural growth was less impressive, owing to a sharp drop in both the international and domestic prices of agricultural products. However, growth in the industry and services sectors continued its downward tendency. The services sector was depressed most, with its growth rate being reduced nearly three times from 7·1 per cent in 1997 to 2·3 per cent in 1999. The industry sector performed a little bit better, although construction recorded a negative growth in two consecutive years,

Table 7.1 Vietnam: major macroeconomic indicators, 1995–9

Growth rates	1995	1996	1997	1998	1999 (est.)
GDP	9·5	9·3	8·2	5·8	4·8
Incl. economic sectors:					
Agriculture	5·1	4·4	4·3	3·5	5·2
Industry & construction	13·6	14·5	12·6	8·3	7·7
Services	9·8	8·8	7·1	5·1	2·3
Incl. ownership sectors:					
State sector	11·1	11·3	9·7	5·6	4·3
Non-state sector	7·6	7·9	7·1	5·9	5·1
Private	10·7	14·4	9·8	7·9	6·2
Foreign investment	10·8	19·4	20·8	19·1	13·4
Export	34·4	33·2	26·6	1·9	20·1
Import	40·0	36·6	4·0	–0·8	–0·6
Investment (per cent of GDP)	27·3	27·9	27·6	23·6	21·0
Savings (per cent of GDP)	17·0	16·7	20·1	17·0	18·0
FDI disbursed (US$ mn)	2 230	1 980	2 000	800	600
Inflation rate (CPI)	12·7	4·4	4·3	9·2	0·1

Source: 'Vietnam Economy – Basic Data; Statistics' (http://vneconomy.com.vn/vn/csdl/thong_ke/tke2–2.htm) May 2000.

1998 and 1999. This was largely due to the performance of the non-state sector and foreign investment, which accounted for about 53 per cent and 31 per cent of industrial output, respectively.

During the pre-crisis period, the non-state sector was sluggish behind the state sector. During the crisis, however, this non-state sector, coping with the changing and more competitive environment faster and better, had overtaken the state-owned sector in terms of growth rates. In 1998 and 1999, the former grew by 5·9 per cent and 5·1 per cent, respectively, compared with the latter's growth rates of 5·6 per cent and 4·3 per cent, which were its lowest growth rates since 1986.

As expected, Vietnam's economic slowdown and the Asian crisis have produced dramatic effects on the external sector of the economy. The foreign investment sector appeared to play an increasing role in the economy owing to its expanding production capacity (with investment amounts committed in past years but coming into operation in the crisis period) and the slowed-down growth of the domestic sector. In fact, the share of the foreign investment sector in the country's GDP quickly increased from 9 per cent in 1997 to nearly 12 per cent in 1999, at the expense of the state-owned and household sectors, the shares of which decreased by 1 per cent each, to 39 per cent and 33 per cent, respectively.

Foreign trade was also negatively affected by the regional crisis. In 1998, exports increased by only 1·9 per cent while imports dropped by 4·5 per cent. In 1999, exports were able to restore their fast growth at 20 per cent, owing to the country's diversification to new markets (for example, Vietnam's exports to the European and US markets increased by 25 per cent in 1997/98, making their shares in Vietnam's exports increase from 32·9 per cent in 1997 to 38·1 per cent in 1998) as well as the early recovery of the Asian economies. Imports, however, continued their negative growth, which was in sharp contrast to the steady growth which averaged 44·7 per cent in the period 1993–6.

While the fall in imports was partly influenced by the government import restrictions, the negative growths of imports and the construction sector during the crisis period were largely attributed to falling investment, which was expected to produce serious negative impacts on the country's economic growth and employment in the future. Total investment as a share of GDP declined from about 28 per cent in 1997 to 21 per cent in 1999, largely as the result of a sharp decrease in foreign direct investment (FDI). The fall affected almost all components, including SOE and ODA (Official Development Assistance)-funded public investments. However, FDI suffered the largest decline. With averages of US$2 billion per annum in the years 1995–7, FDI inflows fell to US$800 million in 1998, and to around US$600 million in 1999, largely because of the decrease in FDI from East Asia and Japan as a result of the regional crisis. The downward tendency of investment, particularly FDI, had in fact started as early as 1996, indicating the country's still restrained business opportunities and evaporating comparative advantages as compared with the neighbouring countries. Clearly, the Asian crisis has also exacerbated this tendency and FDI inflows are likely to be down in the near future, as indicated by the low level of new FDI commitments in 1998/99.

In spite of the worsening conditions, the government of Vietnam was able to maintain macroeconomic stability, and avoid serious balance distortions and financial or banking crises, largely by giving priority to stability over growth. After a burst of inflation in 1998, the inflation rate was 0·1 per cent in 1999, thanks to a sharp decline in food prices in late 1999, while non-food prices remained relatively stable. Despite the government's efforts to stimulate demand by expanding public investment and reducing taxes and bank interest rates, Vietnam's aggregated demand remained depressed and confidence among business people was weak over the whole period.

Signals of Vietnam's recovery appeared only in late 1999, becoming stronger in early 2000 with production and consumption being gradually revitalized quarter by quarter. According to the National General Statistical Office

(GSO) and the government's report to the May session of the National Assembly on Vietnam's socioeconomic development, the country's growth was revitalized in the first half of 2000, when GDP increased by 6·2 per cent compared with the same period in 1999 (growth rate was 5·6 per cent and 6·6 per cent in the first and second quarters, respectively). Growth also improved in all economic sectors and major industries. Agricultural production increased by 4 per cent owing to the record spring harvest, totalling 16·7 million tonnes (an increase of one-third compared with the same period in 1999). Industry and construction grew by 14·7 per cent, the highest level in the same period in the four years 1996 to 1999, as a result of the government's import restrictions and demand stimulation policies. In particular, the state sector increased by 12·5 per cent compared with its growth rate of 4·3 per cent in the first quarter of 1999, while the non-state and foreign investment sectors posted 18·6 per cent and 13 per cent, compared with 5·8 per cent and 17·6 per cent, respectively. The services sector grew by 5·6 per cent, partly restoring its past growth rates. Exports increased by 26·2 per cent, to US$6427 million, while imports arrested their negative tendency and grew by 33·8 per cent, to US$7157, compared with the same period in 1999. However, both domestic investment and FDI were still in deep stagnation. The threat of deflation grew despite the volume of retailed trade increasing by 7·6 per cent, compared with 5·1 per cent in the same period of 1999. It was the first time that the consumer price index fell, compared with the end of the previous year: the index fell by 1·1 per cent, mainly because of a continuing decline in food products of 2·3 per cent, and particularly of rice and other cereals (by 7·6 per cent), which negatively affected the income of agricultural workers.

The above development forced the government to reconsider its long-term projections and accept slower but more sustainable growth. The government predicted that in 2000 the growth rate would be about 6·0 per cent. Other sources also agreed that Vietnam would still be able to maintain a reasonably strong growth in the period 2000 to 2002, but this would be lower than that achieved prior to the Asian crisis and the government's projections. In partic-ular, the various projections made by the Asian Development Bank, the Economic Intelligent Unit, the Institute of Developing Economics of Japan's External Trade Organization and the International Monetary Fund indicated in 1999 that the country's economic growth would be about 5 per cent and 6·7 per cent in 2000 and 2001, while inflation would rise to 6·2 per cent and 10 per cent, and current account deficits to 2·9 per cent and 4·4 per cent, respec-tively. Annual growth of exports and imports would be 13·8 per cent and 15 per cent in 2000 and 20·6 per cent and 22·9 per cent in 2001, respectively (ICSEAD, 2000b, p.10). Recent projections gave a brighter perspective. For example, the forecast based on the ESCAP's Economic and Financial Survey of Asia and the Pacific in May 2000 foresees Vietnam's growth at about 5·8 per cent in 2000 and 6 per cent in 2001–2, assuming a rapid economic recovery with a stable macroeconomic environment in the region. But the country's inflation would increase to 6·5 per cent in 2000, 7·6 per cent in 2001 and 8·9 per cent in 2002. However, the recovery would depend largely on a number of factors, many of which already influenced the country's recent developments.

In the short run, Vietnam's recovery is tied up closely with the performance of the global market, and particularly the recovery of other Asian economies, owing to its thorough opening to international trade and investment since the early 1990s. First, existing data indicate that, in 1991 to 1997, the annual growth of exports, the leading sector of the economy, of 2·5–3 per cent would result in a 1 per cent growth of GDP. Second, FDI is a major source of capital and technology in the capital-scarce economy. So FDI contributed about 32 per cent of the total capital investment in 1997. Third, Asian economies were and remain the country's biggest foreign trade partners and investors, which in total accounted for 47 per cent of total exports and 70 per cent of total FDI in 1997. The recovery of other Asian economies is expected to restore their capabilities for imports and overseas investment. Moreover, it also fosters the process of transferring labour-intensive technologies in, for example, textiles and consumer good production, in which more developed countries cease to enjoy comparative advantages, to less developed countries such as Vietnam. Finally, the crisis has shown evidence of a strong linkage between the Vietnamese economy and external markets. However, while Vietnam was able to maintain relatively strong growth, the crisis in other Asian economies produced a slower but longer negative impact on Vietnam's economy. Table 7.2 shows that the economy was still in deep stagnation in 1999, while the five Asian economies, which were in trouble in 1997 and 1998, had already reversed the tendency of negative growth. This is specially true of Korea, Malaysia and Thailand.

However, the link appears not to be straightforward and Vietnam's recovery

Table 7.2 Vietman's recovery compared with five Asian economies in trouble, 1996–9

		GDP growth rate (per cent)				
	Vietnam Korea	Malaysia		Thailand	Philippines	Indonesia
1996	9·34	6·75	10·00	5·93	5·85	7·80
1997	8·15	5·01	7·54	−1·75	5·16	4·71
1998	5·80	−5·84	−7·50	−10·36	−0·54	−13·20
1999	4·50	8·50	4·50	4·00	3·00	0·00

Source: ICSEAD (2000a).

may be affected by a number of other conflicting external factors. On the one hand, the recent Asian crisis has seriously weakened the import and investment ability of Asian countries, especially those in trouble, such as Korea, Thailand and Malaysia. Indeed, their imports from Vietnam had already decreased by 5 per cent in 1997 and 20 per cent in 1998, reducing the share of the Asian economies in Vietnam's exports by 6 per cent. On the other hand, the competitiveness between the trading partners has increased during the crisis as the other Asian countries undertook bold measures to devalue their currencies and strengthen their banking and finance sector. Compared with these, Vietnam's adopted measures appeared much more moderate (for example, in 1997/98, Vietnam's currency was devalued only by 17 per cent, while other currencies were devalued by 35–45 per cent on average). Moreover, Vietnam is more vulnerable to the downward tendency and fluctuations of international prices for its commodities such as crude oil, rice, coffee, rubber and coal, which comprise three-fifths of Vietnam's exports. Therefore Vietnam's ability to participate effectively in the broader process of economic globalization would play a vital role in the country's recovery and further growth. The country's recent export market diversification, the signing of the Vietnam–US trade agreement in July 2000, and efforts to join the World Trade Organization (WTO) are the right steps in this direction.

In the long run, Vietnam's recovery and further development would be principally influenced by the country's own efforts to realize its huge potentials for growth. Despite a weak infrastructure and scarce capital resources, the country possesses a 36 million well-educated and hard-working labour force and considerable natural resources. Since 1986, the reform programme of doi moi has been the driving force of growth. In fact, Vietnam's pre-reform economy in the 1970s and late 1980s was characterized by chronic socioeconomic crises which were further blown up in 1980–86 by the government's unsuccessful attempts to maintain the centrally planned system. The first reform measures, which took place in 1987, were the elimination of the government's centralized compulsory plan and the liberation of domestic trade, but the turning point was the abolition of cooperatives and an equitable reallocation of land to peasants in 1998. Initial effects on growth, however, were quickly upset by macroeconomic distortions, which were addressed only in 1989–93 by bold measures of market liberalization. These measures include foreign trade liberalization and FDI promotion since 1989, price liberalization and exchange rate reforms in 1989, raising real interest rates to positive levels in 1990 and their gradual liberalization afterwards, and the establishment of a two-tiered banking system and its opening for the private sector in 1990–92). Other measures include macroeconomic stabilization maintaining restricted monetary, wage and fiscal policies since 1989, including the elimination of direct production and consumption subsidies through the budget in 1989, cuts in government expenditures in real terms in 1989–93 and the termination of financing budget deficits by bank credits in 1991. When incentives were established at the micro level and macroeconomic stability restabilized in the early 1990s, growth quickly accelerated from 4·3 per cent per annum in 1986–90 to 8·5 per cent in 1991–7, despite the collapse of the Soviet bloc, Vietnam's former (and almost exclusive) trade partner and source of official development assistance (ODA).

However, growth has slowed down since the mid-1990s in spite of growing FDI inflows and incremental reform efforts, which largely focused on strengthening market institutions such as the decentralization of budget management (1995), further promotion of FDI and integration of Vietnam into the international economy, and enacting new tax regimes (1997/98). It is argued that the slowdown tendency is due to the sluggish progress of the reform in some critical areas such as state-owned enterprises, public administration and banking and finance, which, to some extent, are the bottleneck of Vietnam's current reform strategy that emphasizes the 'leading role of the state sector' and state control. Thus scarce resources were increasingly used in favour of the state sector or capital-intensive projects. In 1995–8, the share of the state-owned sector in total capital investment increased from 35 per cent in 1995 to 54 per cent in 1998, at the expense of the private sector and the foreign investment sector.

Contrary to other transition economies, Vietnam's state sector did expand during the transition. Its share of GDP grew from 30·9 per cent in 1980 to 40·1 per cent in 1998, although the number of SOEs decreased from 12 000 to 7000 during this period. Vietnam's current SOE reform places its emphasis on equitization instead of privatization, but it has progressed slowly because of conflicts of interest and the lack of appropriate policies. Thus a large number of SOEs remained inefficient but continued to receive financial support in terms of credits from state-owned banks. This practice has weakened both Vietnam's SOEs and banking sector, making them vulnerable to adverse external changes. According to government sources, in 1998, the banks' bad debt rate was between 14 and 28 per cent. In contrast, the non-state sector received no government subsidies and very limited credit from the banking and financial system. In spite of this, it was able to benefit quickly from the enabling environment created by the reform and partially offset the lack of competitiveness and efficiency in the state-owned sector. Currently, this sector is faced by growing challenges due to the exhaustion of resources for extensive growth and increasing competition from neighbouring countries. As recognized by Prime Minister Phan Van Khai at the government's Donor Conference on 15 June 1998,

Vietnam's financial and monetary systems have many shortcomings. The Government's management apparatus has not improved and is engaged in corrupt activities. Useful lessons must be drawn from the regional crisis. These include the need to create a level playing field [for all sectors], the encouragement of the entrepreneurial spirit, and the improvement of the competitiveness of Vietnamese goods.

In addition, an adjustment of some current macroeconomic policies on a long-term basis is also needed. This concerns foreign trade and investment, exchange rates and finance management. The current import restriction policy has helped the country to maintain stable trade and budget balances and offset the impact of its weakened competitiveness in the crisis situation of 1997–9. In the long run, however, the policy undermines incentives for strengthening the competitiveness of the domestic production and constrains the country's efforts to expand its bilateral and multilateral economic cooperation. Furthermore, given the country's lack of both necessary foreign currency reserves and an efficient banking system, particularly the inter-bank foreign exchange market, the current overvaluation of Vietnam's national currency creates increasing pressures on the current account balance. To some extent, the slowdown and the Asian crisis may represent an opportunity for the country to rethink its reform strategy, which is largely crisis-driven. Clearly, Vietnam's quick recovery and further growth are unthinkable without addressing the bottleneck. So, in the long run, Vietnam's economic recovery largely depends on how speedily the country would be able to deepen its current reform process and also how rapidly it can be fully integrated into the increasingly competitive global economy.

In short, in the early 1990s, Vietnam had attained remarkable economic growth. However, since the mid-1990s, growth has been slowed down by the slow progress of the current reforms in a number of critical areas. The tendency of the slowdown was exaggerated during the recent Asian crisis. This can give the country a vivid and invaluable lesson. Vietnam is still able to maintain a relatively strong growth and stable macroeconomic balances, and the quick recovery of the other Asian economies has already produced a positive influence on the performance of the country's economy early in 2000. Vietnam's full recovery and further development will be a long process, which will be largely influenced by the country's ability to deepen the reform in some critical areas such as state-owned enterprises, banking and finance, and public administration, and to foster its integration in the global economy.

3   VIETNAM'S RECOVERY AND SOCIAL ISSUES

The slowdown has had a profound impact on the country's social sectors. As stated in the government's Country Report to the Social Summit in Copenhagen in 1995, 'there exists a close relationship between economic

growth and social development. Economic growth creates the essential conditions necessary for social development while the latter is the ultimate goal and
the driving force of economic growth'. The continuing transition from a
centrally planned system to a market-oriented economy has also reinforced the
pronounced linkage by involving a dramatic shift of social development from
'support-led' patterns to 'growth-mediated' ones. In the pre-reform period, by
giving a high priority to social support through an extended system of highly
subsidized but fairly distributed social services, often at the expense of
growth, Vietnam was able to attain rather high levels of literacy (about 85 per
cent), life expectancy at birth (65 years) and nearly full employment despite
its annual per capita GDP being as low as US$180–200 in the mid-1980s.
Since the start of doi moi, the emphasis has been placed on a shared economic
growth, which is expected to benefit the majority of people while providing
social protection for those who cannot participate in the growth through selective public expenditure programmes. So, after 1989, the system of subsidized
social services was gradually replaced by the user-pay system. Public expenditures for social expenditures were cut in real terms in four consecutive years,
1989–93, before being restored and increasing as public revenues grew in the
following years. The strategy has resulted in an impressive improvement of
human welfare in terms of living standards, human resources development and
employment. However, in the late 1990s, the slowdown started to threaten
these achievements by affecting the income basis of the poor, increasing
unemployment and underemployment, and reducing public funding for social
services. When there is a lack of effective social protection, continuing slowdown can result in extremely high social costs.

**Poverty still Widespread and Recent Achievements in Living Standards
still Unsustainable**

A rapid improvement in the living standard of a large number of people represents a distinguishing feature of Vietnam's recent development since it
embarked upon the reform process. At the macro level, the solid increase of
per capita GDP (at 1994 constant prices) by 76 per cent since 1986 (see Figure
7.1) indicates an expanding general opulence of goods and services. This is
due to both the high GDP growth rates and a sharp drop in population growth,
from 2·2 per cent per annum in the 1980s to 1·65 per cent in the 1990s.
However, Vietnam is still a very impoverished country with per capita GDP
only at US$330 equivalent in 1998.

This tendency is also confirmed by the data on household expenditure,
collected through Vietnam Living Standard Surveys (VLSS) in 1992/93 and
1997/98. In the period, the average per capita living expenditure of
Vietnamese households at 1998 prices increased 1.43 times from 1.9 million

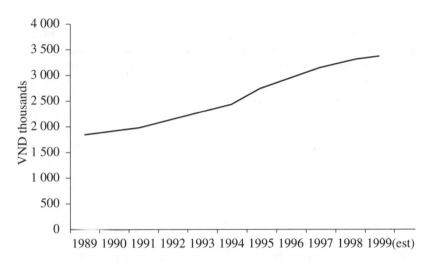

Source:　World Bank (1999a).

Figure 7.1　Vietnam: GDP per capita, 1989–99 (VND thousands)

VND to 2.8 million VND. The remarkable improvement is observed in all expenditure quintiles of the population (see Table 7.3), leading to a sharp reduction in absolute poverty. As a result, according to estimates using internationally comparable standards, the percentage of the Vietnamese who cannot afford basic foods was nearly halved, dropping from 24·9 per cent to 15 per cent in this period. When basic non-food needs were included, the percentage fell from 58·1 per cent to 37·4 per cent, representing an unprecedented achievement in such a short period, compared with international findings. This fall was largely attributed to both the high and shared economic growth and the country's market liberation and stabilization, which shifted the entitlement exchange relations in favour of the rural sector in the 1990s. Agriculture also played an important role, despite the fact that its share in GDP steadily decreased. Agriculture provides a livelihood for rural dwellers, who comprise 80 per cent of the population but 90 per cent of the poor in Vietnam. Most of them were able to benefit from steady agricultural growth and the 72 per cent rise in prices of food products, while prices of the non-food items increased by only 22 per cent.

Vietnam is still faced with a number of challenges to sustain the past achievements in the future, when the above-mentioned positive tendencies might be reversed. First, the poverty rates are still very high and a large portion of the non-poor remains just above the poverty line and, thus, easy to move downwards as a result of various economic and natural irregularities and the

Table 7.3   *Vietnam: household per capita expenditure, by quintile, 1992–8 (VND 000s, 1998 prices)*

	1992–3	1997–8	Changes (per cent)
Poorest	854	1 099	129
Less poor	1 233	1 632	132
Middle	1 582	2 125	134
Less rich	2 098	2 929	140
Richest	3 911	6 032	154
Total	1 936	2 764	143

Source: GSO (2000, p.269).

lack of an effective social protection system, especially in the huge rural and informal sectors. Second, the slowdown seriously constrains efforts to create non-agricultural livelihood opportunities, which is most crucial for further poverty eradication and improvement of the existing living standard, given the increasing difficulty which the rural sector has to deal with in order to maintain the past agricultural growth rates. Finally, Vietnam's further integration into the global economy might challenge certain groups of the population because of the low competitiveness of the goods and services it offers on the markets. In this respect, the peasantry is particularly vulnerable to price volatility. In fact, despite the fact that their production increased by 6 per cent in 1999, their income fell because of the sharp fall in agricultural prices (by about 10 per cent) in late 1999 and early 2000.

Increasing Inequality

Equality is always a sensitive issue in Vietnam's social policy. A number of recent studies, particularly the VLSS, also revealed that in general inequality has started to increase, slightly, among the population groups and geographical regions. The Gini coefficient slightly increased from 0·33 in 1993 to 0·35 in 1998. However, gaps between the population groups and geographical regions persistently expanded. Table 7.3 shows that, while all expenditure quintiles were able to improve their living standard, the rich were better off much more than the poor. So the gap in the living standards between the richest and the poorest increased from 4·6 times in 1992/93 to 5·5 times in 1997/98.

The tendency of increasing gaps is more striking between geographical areas (see Table 7.4). Surprisingly, the Mekong River Delta and Central

Table 7.4   Vietnam: household per capita expenditure, by region, 1992–8 (VND 000, 1998 prices)

	1992–3	1997–8	Changes (per cent)
Rural/urban			
Rural	1 669	2 166	130
Urban	3 013	4 829	160
Region			
Mekong River	2 129	2 536	119
Central Highlands	1 537	1 942	126
South Central	2 026	2 641	130
Northern Uplands	1 442	1 920	133
Northern Central	1 486	2 197	148
Red River Delta	1 866	2 938	157
Southeast	2 801	5 019	179

Source: GSO (2000, p.269).

Highlands – the largest producers of rice and cash crops for the market – experienced the smallest improvement of living standards in 1992–8. The Northern Uplands, Central Highlands and the Northern Central Coast remained the poorest regions, where about half of the population still suffer from poverty. However, the increasing gaps are largely attributed to the rapidly growing gaps between the rural and urban areas. The urban–rural gap in welfare-related expenditures expanded from 1·8 times in 1992/93 to 2·2 times in 1997/98. While the poverty rate dropped nearly three times from 25 per cent to 9 per cent in the urban areas in 1992–8, it was reduced only by one-third from 66 per cent to 45 per cent in the rural areas. With 90 per cent of the poor living in the rural areas, poverty in Vietnam is largely a rural phenomenon, although acute poverty does exist in pockets in the urban areas.

It is the persistent poverty and starvation among ethnic minorities that represents the most serious challenge to equity concerns in Vietnam. There are 53 ethnic minorities, most of whom live in remote and mountainous areas and are able to enjoy a very limited participation in the national economic and social life because of physical and cultural isolation, limited livelihood opportunities, excessive risk and environmental unsustainability. As a result, although ethnic minorities comprise only 15 per cent of the total population, they account for nearly 30 per cent of the total poor. They are also particularly stricken by chronic hunger and starvation, which affect 2–3 per cent of the total population (200 000 Vietnamese), despite the fact that the country has become one of the world's largest rice exporters since the mid-1990s. These signal increasing market failures and deficiency in the existing entitlement exchange system, which obviously are exaggerated by the slowdown resulting from the Asia crisis.

Increasing Unemployment Pressure

In Vietnam, the slowdown has produced a large negative impact on employment, not so much through labour lay-offs as through diminishing job opportunities and slower employment creation. According to the annual labour and employment surveys conducted by the Ministry of Labour, Invalids and Social Affairs (MOLISA) in Vietnam, open urban unemployment went up from about 6 per cent of the total working age population in 1996/97 to 6·8 per cent in 1998 and 7·4 per cent in 1999, and became a serious concern, especially in big cities. However, the figures did not reflect disguised unemployment, which has spread widely. Another MOLISA study of 2214 enterprises in mid-1998 revealed that 9 per cent of their workforce (60 000 persons) did not have any job to do and, for the SOEs covered by the study, the percentage was more than 25 per cent. This indicates that, without the creation of at least 100 000 new job places per annum to absorb the backlog in a ten-year timeframe, the SOEs' reform and economic restructuring would further inflate urban unemployment. In the rural areas, underemployment also increased from 24 per cent to 29 per cent, while open unemployment also rose from 1 per cent to 2·5 per cent in the period. This occurs especially in the Red River Delta area, where the population density is particularly high.

The increasing unemployment and underemployment can also be attributed to the rapid growth of the labour force, 3·3 per cent per annum, as a consequence of the post-war child boom in the 1970s and slow employment generation compared with the growth of GDP. Vietnam's growth pattern in the 1990s is characterized by its low employment elasticity: on average, a 4 per cent GDP growth generates only a 1 per cent increase in employment. This result is largely due to the constrained development of the non-state sector, particularly the household economy and small enterprises, which tend to utilize more labour-intensive technology, in contrast to the state sector. In the 1990s, the non-state sector was able to absorb most of the 1·2–1·3 million new entrants into the labour market every year and turned into the largest source of employment and livelihood of the people. Given a slower growth of the economy and, consequently, the urban sector, and limited prospects of further employment expansion in agriculture, future job creation would largely rely on non-agricultural employment generation in the rural areas. It has been estimated that, in 2000, the urban unemployment rate will increase to 14 per cent if the growth of GDP continues to be sluggish, at 5 per cent per annum, and the rural underemployment rate is maintained at about 25 per cent. A 7 per cent GDP growth would help to reduce the urban unemployment rate by 11 per cent. Alternatively, the unemployment rate would go down to 8 per cent if there was a remarkable shift in favour of labour-intensive technology. Obviously, the latter is unthinkable without strong measures for non-state sector promotion and SOE reform.

Unequitable Access to Social Services and their Low Quality

Access of the population to social services also changed dramatically in the 1990s (see Table 7.5). In education, after the start of the reform, enrolment in all levels of education, except the primary one, showed an unusual downward tendency, while dropout rates increased. An improvement was achieved only in 1993, reaching the 1985 level in 1994/95. In general, access to education in Vietnam is comparable to that in countries with much higher GDP per capita. In fact, universal primary education was attained in most provinces; secondary education enrolment grew fast and achieved a 78 per cent age group at the lower secondary and 33 per cent at the upper secondary levels; and enrolment in higher education doubled over the previous five years, while the number of students in vocational, technical and tertiary education almost reached one million. The major issue of the Vietnamese education system is its slow response to the demand of the labour market. According to recent government statistics, about 88 per cent of the total labour force were unskilled workers, and every fifth member of the skilled labour force has not received any formal technical or secondary vocational training. Moreover, about one-third of the trained workers did not have the necessary basic work skills, even according to Vietnam's standards. Thus, in spite of Vietnam's abundant human resources and the high level of education attained, its economy has suffered from a lack of skilled workers. This is largely due to the fact that upper secondary education, vocational training, and technical and tertiary education remain restricted for the absolute majority of young people: in the 1990s, only 6–9 per cent of those aged 15–24 had a chance to enrol in the formal educational and training institutions and the remainder had to rely on on-the-job training and their ability to learn from work experience. Second, the quality of education and training also remain a problem because of a lack of qualifications and incentives among teaching staff, outdated teaching methodology and content (especially in higher education) and the sector's inefficient management and coordination capacity (MOET, UNDP *et al.*, 1992).

In the health sector, Vietnam has also attained remarkable achievements, compared with its level of economic development, particularly in terms of infant mortality rate, maternal mortality rate, 95 per cent full immunization among children, malaria and TB control and 55 per cent fertility reduction

Table 7.5 *Vietnam: access to social services and some Human Resource Development (HRD) indicators, 1980–98*

	Unit	1980	1985	1990	1995	1998
Access Indicators						
School gross enrolment		n.a.	63	64	75	81
primary education	% of age group	108	102	104	112	109
lower sec. education	% of age group	42	42	43	62	78
upper sec. education	% of age group	n.a.	16	13	21	33
Physicians per 100 000 people		24	32	35	41	44
Assistant, nurses & midwives per 100 000 people		n.a.	n.a.	195	146	145
Beds per 100 000 people		370	352	312	269	265
Output indicators						
Life expectancy at birth	males/females	64/68[1]	64/68	63/68[2]	64/69[2]	65/70[3]
Infant mortality rate	per 1000 births	54.8[4]	46.0[5]	42.2[6]	45.1[7]	37[7]
Under-five mortality	per 1000 births	82.1[4]	68.7[5]	55.4[6]	61.6[7]	n.a.
Child malnutrition	per cent	n.a.	n.a.	n.a.	43	39
Annual population growth	per cent	2.23[8]	2.23[8]	1.65[9]	1.65[9]	1.65[9]
Adult literacy rate	per cent: males/females	91/78[1]	n.a.	93/84[2]	n.a.	94/86[3]

Notes:
1. For 1979, based on 1979 census.
2. For 1989, based on 1989 census.
3. For 1999, based on 1999 census.
4. For 1979–83.
5. For 1984–8.
6. For 1989–93.
7. For 1996. 8. For 1980–85.
9. For 1990–99.
n.a. not available.

Sources: United Nations in Vietnam (1999), World Bank (1999a), GSO (1997).

(compared with 1995–7). However, child malnutrition and the abortion rate are still among the highest in the world. Public health facilities show a downward tendency in terms of the steadily decreasing number of hospital beds, medical assistants, nurses and midwives per 100 000 people, and the deterioration of the commune-based health care centre system. The emerging private sector has provided increasing alternatives, especially in supplying pharmaceutical products and in the urban areas. However, because of the limited coverage of the health insurance system, for an identical service, there occurred striking inequality in access to health services: the poorest quintile has to pay 45 per cent of its non-food expenditure per capita per visit to a public hospital, while the richest quintile pays only 4 per cent. As a result, high-quality services are often not accessible for the poor. Second, the interregional disparities in health status, especially between the urban and rural areas, populous deltas and remote mountainous areas, are significant and increasing. So infant mortality in the Central Highlands is over twice that of the Southeast and Red River regions. Almost half the births in the Central Coast and Central Highlands are not attended by health personnel, compared with 12–18 per cent in the Southeast and the Red River areas.

Financing remains a major common issue among social services. In the 1990s, the introduction of the user pays system dramatically changed the way education and health services were financed. Currently, the government plays a quite limited role in their financing (45 per cent for education and even less for health), while still dominating in service delivery. (See Figure 7.2.) However, the slowdown does have a negative impact on the various sectors by undermining the sources of government revenue, especially the SOE, export–import and FDI sectors – their major sources. Under these pressures, the share of state revenue in GDP steadily decreased from 25 per cent in the mid-1990s to 22 per cent in 1997 and about 20–21 per cent afterwards. As a response, the government had to cut back both current and capital expenditures, including expenditures for the social sector in 1998 in both nominal and real terms, leading to the need for greater mobilization of resources from the population. Given the already heavy burden of these expenditures on the household budget and increasing pressure on the sources of income, this may constrain access and their family members' access to the social services, including the basic ones.

On the other hand, the slowdown has also affected private spending on social services because of its strong positive relationship with public spending on education and health. The slowdown has also affected different localities differently. The existing budget mechanism often reinforces interprovincial revenue disparities. Therefore, while none of the provinces in the country is expected to escape the consequences of the reduction in growth, certain localities, particularly the poor ones, are more adversely affected by the negative

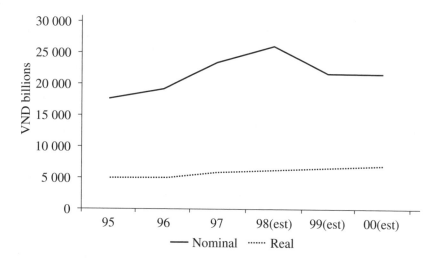

Source: Government of Vietnam (1998).

Figure 7.2 *Vietnam: total government expenditures for education, health and social protection, 1995–2000 (VND billions)*

impact of the slowdown and the crisis than others. In addition, intrasectoral reallocations are also important in view of the existing bias in public expenditures towards non-basic education and non-basic health. On average, expenditure for primary education and communal health centres, to which the poor can gain access most readily, comprises only 44 per cent and 6 per cent of the total public expenditures for eduction and health, respectively. Reduction of the bias would help to cope with the financial constraints. In other words, to respond to the slowdown, there is an urgent demand for a more equitable and pro-poor mechanism of financing the social sectors. At the national level, there is also the need to protect annual allocations and actual spending on basic social services during the time of reduced state revenue. For this purpose, the reallocation of external debt service expenditure towards basic social services should be an alternative to be seriously considered by the government and donor community.

Lack of an Equitable Social Protection System

The natural disasters and crisis of 1998–9 revealed the weakness of Vietnam's recent social protection system, the development of which is lagging behind current economic reform. The pre-reform nationwide formal social protection system covered only state employees and their families, mainly in the urban areas, while cooperatives were responsible for their members, leaving others without formal protection. Major reform steps taken included the establishment of a special fund to help retrenched (laid off) state employees in the early 1990s, the adoption of the Labour Code followed by the establishment of the national social insurance and health insurance agencies in the mid-1990s, and the establishment of a number of poverty-related public expenditure programmes in the 1990s. The recently introduced social protection system is characterized by four specific features: (a) strong concern about equality at the expense of selectivity and efficiency; (b) the dominating role of the government in funding, management and delivery; (c) strong differentiation between the state and non-state sectors, rural and urban areas in terms of target groups, benefits, coverage, funding sources and institutional aspects; and (d) dependence on residence status: delivery of social services is based on people's residence status.

The system constitutes four major elements: social insurance, a guarantee fund for regular relief to assist non-working and unprotected members of society such as the disabled, orphans and lonely elderly, a contingency fund for emergency relief to people affected by pre-harvest starvation and natural disasters, and public poverty-related expenditure programmes focusing on the various target groups.

Social insurance
The existing social insurance comprises compulsory social insurance, voluntary social insurance and health insurance, and provides five major benefits: retirement pensions, survivors benefits, work accidents and industrial diseases benefits, sickness benefits and paid maternity leave for up to two births. There is a limited provision for longer-term illness and no unemployment benefit. The system is financed on the pay-as-you-go principle. The social insurance fund is derived from the contribution of workers (5 per cent of basic salary), employers (15 per cent of basic salary), and the government contribution to cover payments for those who retired before 1995.

The slowdown and recovery have revealed a number of problems facing the system. First, it lacks the unemployment insurance and insurance against fluctuations in crops and prices to protect workers and peasantry, respectively, from market volatility. Moreover, there are no invalidity benefits for most people, no sole parent allowances and no family benefits to protect their income base. Second, it has very limited coverage. Theoretically, the social insurance covers 11 per cent of the total workforce, who work in the formal sector. However, actual membership is only a small fraction of the number, as many appear to be classified as temporary employees. On the other hand, the health insurance covers only 13 per cent of the total population. So, in general, beneficiaries of the social and health insurance are workers in the formal sector, who tend to have higher income than the rest of the population. Third, the system appears financially unviable because of the widespread non-compliance with legal contribution obligations (this concerns over one million workers) the low retirement pension ages (55 for women, 60 for men, and even lower for some categories of workers) and generous pensions for those who have relatively short contribution periods. Thus the system's current cash surplus is due to the young age structure of the workforce and the expansion of its schemes. Finally, the system offers low benefits that hardly meet actual needs since the contributions are based on the basic salary, which covers only a small part of actual incomes. In view of the recent crises, the government and donor countries are working together to develop an effective system to protect peasants' and workers' income from natural disasters and market volatility.

The social guarantee fund for regular relief
The social guarantee fund for regular relief is designed to protect the living standard of a small group of people who cannot work, are in extreme poverty and do not have other family members to assist them, such as lonely elderly, the seriously disabled and orphans. This group does not include a large group of the disabled who have already received disability pensions from the government as former civil or military employees. Recently, the fund has also been used to fund the following assistance: (a) providing temporary benefits for a small group of homeless people and children in extreme circumstances; (b) covering school costs and medical insurance fees for some from priority target groups such as the poor and their families; (c) covering the operation costs of local vocational training and employment promotion centres, and (d) funding some activities to deal with medical–social problem groups such as HIV/AIDS cases, prostitutes and drug addicts.

The lack of funding represents the major problem of the fund. First, owing to budget constraints, the fund is able to provide support only for a very small fraction of those who are eligible (for example, lonely elderly: about 50 per cent, orphans: 25 per cent). The number of the beneficiaries, especially the disabled, was largely cut back as a response to the increasing number of applicants and reducing government revenue in 1998/99. Second, it can afford only very low benefits, well below the national food poverty line.

The contingency fund for pre-harvest starvation and disaster relief
This fund serves as a reserve for the government provision of aid in case of natural disasters and supplementary food aid (by cash or in kind) for the very poor people stricken by starvation in the pre-harvest periods. The fund is provided by both the central budget and local resources.

The main problem facing the fund is its funding mechanism. The localities which are prone to natural disasters and starvation tend to be poor and, thus, it is very difficult to raise the required local funds. On the other hand, this fund is often used for other purposes when the ostensible need for it is not anticipated. There is no mechanism for reallocation of the fund to a disaster-stricken area from other areas. Second, aid is often provided according to availability of funds and tends to cover only a very small part of the losses households have suffered (for example, a standard payment of US$100 equivalent per death) and their need for assistance. In 1998–9, the fund was able to provide immediate food aid for only 16 per cent of those requiring it and 54 per cent of the total number of cases suffered from pre-harvest starvation.

Poverty-related public expenditure programmes

These programmes aim to help specially selected people, such as the poorest, ethnic minorities, and poor women and children, to maintain their minimal living standards and get out of the crisis situations they have been trapped in, such as poverty, illiteracy and disease. They originated in the local initiatives started in 1992. In 1998, the government established the National Programme for Hunger Eradication and Poverty Reduction (HEPR), National Target Programme (NTP) and the Programme for Poor Commune Development, which were public expenditure programmes combining development and relief purposes. To some extent, the NTP is a part of the existing broader safety net for the vulnerable in Vietnam (van de Valle, 1998).

The programmes include both relief and development activities in nine areas: (a) commune infrastructure, particularly in the 1715 communes faced with extreme difficulties, (b) agricultural and off-farm production and employment, (c) credit, (d) health care, (e) education, (f) extension (agricultural services), (g) managerial training, (h) sedentarization (permanent residence in agricultural production areas) and internal migration, and (i) assistance for ethnic minorities faced with extreme difficulties. In 1999, at least VND 600 billion were committed to the programme for direct benefits of the poor people and communes, although no commitment about the total programme funds has yet been made.

The major concern regarding the programmes is their financial sustainability and their capacity to develop necessary supporting pro-poor macroeconomic policies and implement them in a transparent and selective manner with active participation of the people. The credit element, which is the largest programme element and provides credit for the poor at a preferential interest rate lower than the market rates, is particularly unsustainable. On the other hand, the pressure of budget deficits in the case of a prolonged slowdown and increasing demand for more investment in the economic and infrastructure sectors may rechannel necessary funds from the programmes.

As a result, when compared with other low-income countries, Vietnam has developed a fairly extensive system of social protection which, however, is still far from meeting the demands of its population in the emerging market-oriented economy. In spite of the recent efforts, the design of the system, the level of spending and the quality of the services remain inadequate compared with the demand. A viable solution to the social welfare crisis has yet to be found because the economic impetus of market reform often directly contradicts the government's strong concerns about equality and its commitment to protect the weak.

4   CONCLUSIONS

In the 1990s, Vietnam made remarkable progress in improving its living standards and addressing a number of social issues. This was mainly attributed to the current economic reform which soon generated rapid economic growth and created conditions for more equitable distribution of benefits from it. However, the slow progress of the reform in some critical areas such as non-state sector development, SOE reform, public administration and the banking and finance sector has slowed growth since the mid-1990s. Exaggerated by the negative impact of the Asian crisis in 1997–9, this trend was worsened by the country's major social issues, namely poverty and unsustainability of poverty reduction achievements, inequality, social services and social protection. Under these circumstances, even with its strong concern about equity and equality when growth is slower, the government finds it difficult to sustain disproportionate allocation of public expenditure to help the poor and address the social issues.

Thus it is necessary for the country to further deepen the current reform process in the critical areas. Concerning the social issues, there are four major policy options in the government agenda. The first is to protect the livelihood and further improve the living standard of the population, especially the working poor, by non-agricultural employment generation through the non-state sector development and labour-intensive public works. The second strategy is to further develop social safety nets, especially measures to protect income of the peasants and workers during crises, including relief and other short-term measures. The third strategy is to ensure minimal necessary funds and the more effective utilization of the scarce resources by more pro-poor intra- and intersectoral allocation of public expenditure for the social sector, including a reallocation from richer regions to poorer ones. Redefining the role of the government and promoting the active participation of the community and the private sector are crucial for this strategy. The fourth strategy is to improve direction and efficiency of the social services through further decentralization, promotion of participatory approaches and creation of appropriate incentive systems.

BIBLIOGRAPHY

Dreze, Jean and Amartya Sen (1989), *Hunger and Public Action*, Oxford: Clarendon Press.

Government of S.R.Vietnam (1998), 'Monitoring the 20/20 Initiative. Basic Social Services in Vietnam: An Analysis of State Public and Donor Expenditures', The Country's Report on Basic Social Services in Vietnam to the International Conference on 20/20 in Hanoi, 10/1998, Hanoi: The Government of Vietnam.

Government of S.R.Vietnam (1999), 'Government's Country Report on the Implementation of Commitment made at the World Summit for Social Development' (draft).

GSO (1997), *Social Indicators in Vietnam 1990–95*, Hanoi: Statistical Publishing House.

GSO (2000), *Vietnam Living Standards Survey 1997–1998*, Hanoi: Statistical Publishing House.

ICSEAD (2000a), *East Asian Economic Perspectives (EAEP)*, Kitakyushu Japan, International Centre for the Study of East Asian Development (ICSEAD).

ICSEAD (2000b), *East Asian Economic Perspectives (EAEP): Recent Trends and Prospects for Major Asian Economies (Special Issue)*, Kitakyushu Japan, International Centre for the Study of East Asian Development (ICSEAD).

MOET, UNDP *et al.* (1992), Vietnam Education and Human Resources Sector Analysis (Synthesis Report). Hanoi, Ministry of Education and Training of Vietnam, United Nations Development Program–United Nations Education, Science and Culture Organisation.

Nguyen, The Dzung (1999), 'Capacity Assesment for the National Target Program for Hunger Eradication and Poverty Reducation', Report to the UNDP, Hanoi.

Nguyen, The Dzung, Mark Rix, Matt Ngui and Nguyen Phuoc Binh Thanh (1998), 'The Role of Australian Higher Education and Vocational Training Institutions in Vietnam's Human Resource Development', occasional paper, The Centre for Research Policy, University of Wollongong.

Preston, David (1999), 'Safety Net in Vietnam' (Report to ILO and UNDP, draft).

United Nations in Vietnam (1999), *Looking Ahead: A Common Country Assessment*, Hanoi: UNDP.

Vu, Tuan Anh (1999), 'Socio-economic impacts of the Asian financial crisis in Vietnam', paper presented to the Joint NWRCEAS-CCSEAS Conference on 'Emerging Southeast Asia Identities in an Era of Volatile Globalization', 22–4 October, Vancouver.

vom de Nalle, D. (1998), *Protecting the Poor in Vietnam's Emerging Market*, World Bank.

World Bank (1997), *Vietnam: Deepening Reform for Growth. An Economic Report.* Washington, DC: World Bank.

World Bank (1999a), 'Vietnam Development Report 2000: Attacking Poverty' (A draft report of the Government-Donor-NGO working group for discussion), Hanoi: World Bank.

World Bank (1999b), 'Vietnam: Preparing for Take-off? – How Vietnam Can Participate Fully in the East Asian Recovery' (an Informal Economic Report of the World Bank to the Consultative Group Meeting for Vietnam, 14–15 December, Hanoi), Hanoi: The World Bank.

8. China: aspects of trade and investment in a globalized economy

Yanyun Zhao and Jinping Li

1   INTRODUCTION

China's trade and investment have two significant characteristics: the services trade share in total trade is very small, and direct investment abroad is relatively small compared to total foreign direct investment (FDI). The export of services accounted for 13 per cent in China's total exports, and direct investment abroad was only 6·25 per cent of FDI in 1998. Therefore trade in this chapter refers to trade of goods, and investment refers to FDI.

The rest of this chapter consists of three parts. Section 2 describes the general situation of exports and FDI in China. In section 3, exports and FDI after the Southeast Asian Financial Crisis are analysed. Section 4 provides a quantitative analysis of China's trade and investment by constructing and estimating a cointegration and error-correction model to scrutinize the influence of exports and FDI on the growth of GDP in China.

2   THE GENERAL SITUATION OF TRADE AND INVESTMENT IN CHINA

The General Situation of Trade in China

The year 1978 represents an important line of demarcation in China's foreign trade, which can be seen from increases in exports and imports in Figure 8.1. (See also Appendixes.) For quite a long period after the foundation of the People's Republic of China (PRC) in 1949, China, under a closed-door policy, regarded foreign trade as complementary to domestic production. The purpose of trade was mainly to adjust the domestic economy's surplus and deficiency, and not to take advantage of specialization of the internationalized world. At that time, China's foreign trade system was characterized by a unified planning and centralized management. Consequently, the scale and growth of trade in China were both restricted during the 22-year period 1955–77. Annual exports were kept under US$10 billion, increasing from US$1·41 billion to

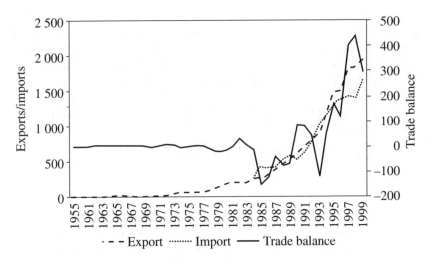

Figure 8.1   Trade of China (US$ millions)

US$7·59 billion, at an average growth rate of about 8·0 per cent. China's imports increased from US$1·73 billion to US$7·21 billion, at an average growth rate of 6·7 per cent. The country's trade balance was kept almost at the zero level during this period. China's share in world exports decreased from 1·23 per cent in 1953 to 0·75 per cent in 1978, and its ranking dropped from the 17th to 32nd, correspondingly. This shows that the exports of China grew much more slowly than those of other countries.

Since 1978, China has adopted an opening up of the economy as one of her fundamental policies, and rapidly merged into the world economy. China has established a good trade relationship with more than 200 countries or regions all over the world. In this post-1978 period, China's foreign trade has been established mainly to save productive factors as much as possible through using international specialization according to the theory of comparative advantage, and to accelerate its technological development by introducing advanced technology, apart from adjusting the domestic economy's surplus and deficiency. Corresponding to the change of purposes and policies, the foreign trade system has been greatly reformed since 1979. First, the trade management system was transformed from mandatory planning to macro management by economic means including customs, taxes and foreign exchange rates, and so on. Second, the trade mode combining industry and trade has replaced the monopolized operation of state-owned foreign trade companies, and the trade agency system has been gradually improved. Third, all commodities, except a small number of essential products that must be managed in a unified or centralized manner, can be traded freely.

In addition, the Chinese government has been progressively improving the incentive system for exports. As a result, the exports of China were expanded rapidly from US$9·79 billion to US$194·93 billion during 1978–99, growing by 15·3 per cent annually. Imports also increased, from US$10·89 billion to US$165·72 billion, growing by 13·8 per cent annually in the same period. China's trade balance is no longer at the zero level. In the 1980s, it was mostly in deficit, but in the 1990s it was in surplus (except in 1993). Meanwhile, China's export share increased gradually, and her ranking in exports kept rising. At the time of writing in 2000, China's export share has exceeded 3 per cent and China has become one of the ten largest exporting countries in the world since 1997.

The trade structure of China has been greatly improved since 1978 (as shown in Table 8.1). The exports of primary goods accounted for about half of

Table 8.1   Trade structure of China, 1980–98

| | Exports | | Imports | |
	Primary goods (%)	Manufactured goods (%)	Primary goods (%)	Manufactured goods (%)
1980	50·30	49·70	34·77	65·23
1981	46·57	53·43	36·54	63·46
1982	45·02	54·98	39·59	60·41
1983	43·28	56·72	27·15	72·85
1984	45·66	54·34	19·00	81·00
1985	50·56	49·44	12·52	87·48
1986	36·43	63·57	13·17	86·83
1987	33·55	66·45	16·00	84·00
1988	30·32	69·68	18·21	81·79
1989	28·70	71·30	19·87	80·13
1990	25·59	74·41	18·47	81·53
1991	22·47	77·53	16·98	83·02
1992	20·02	79·98	16·45	83·55
1993	18·17	81·83	13·67	86·33
1994	16·29	83·71	14·26	85·74
1995	14·44	85·56	18·49	81·51
1996	14·52	85·48	18·32	81·68
1997	13·10	86·90	20·10	79·90
1998	11·21	88·79	16·37	83·68

Source: *China Statistical Yearbook*, 1999.

total exports before 1985, while it accounted for only 11·21 per cent in 1998. On the contrary, the proportion of exported manufactured goods to total exports rose from 49·70 per cent in 1980 to 88·79 per cent in 1998.

The General Situation of Investment in China

Under its closed-door policy, China thought that financial income and expenditure should always be balanced, and there should be no external and internal debt. Except for a borrowing of RMB53·68 billion from the former USSR government in the early 1950s, China did not use any other foreign capital before 1978. However, after 1978, China began to adopt use of foreign capital, including loans from foreign governments, multilateral financial organizations and foreign commercial banks, as well as direct investment. Before 1992, over half of China's foreign capital was from foreign loans but, after 1992, FDI accounted for over 70 per cent of China's foreign capital (see Figure 8.2).

It is obvious from the figure that the year 1992 is a turning point for China's utilization of FDI. The inflow of FDI was less than US$5 billion during 1982–91. After Deng Xiaoping's southern inspection in 1992, the inflow of FDI increased sharply. The inflows of FDI in 1992 and 1993 were both more than twice that in the previous year, and China became the second biggest country in the world (after only the United States) to attract FDI. The inflow of FDI in 1999 was US$40·4 billion, almost ten times more than that in 1982.

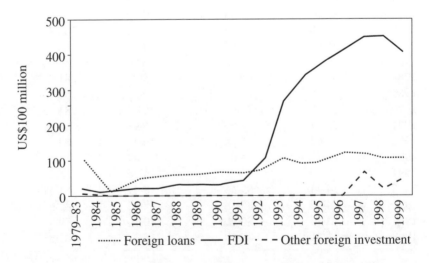

Figure 8.2   China's use of foreign capital

3 EXPORTS AND INVESTMENT AFTER THE SOUTHEAST ASIAN FINANCIAL CRISIS

China's Exports after the Southeast Asian Financial Crisis

From Figure 8.3, we find that the exports of China have a steady growth trend,[1] with significant seasonal and even monthly fluctuations. Getting rid of the trend by the ordinary least squares-fitted value and the monthly fluctuations by the moving average method from the original data according to our economic model, we can derive the cyclical fluctuation index of exports of China, shown in Figure 8.4. According to this index, we find that China's exports were kept at the average level from 1994 to the mid-1996. After that time, the export index increased successively, and reached its height in September 1997. Since then, the negative influence of the Southeast Asian Financial Crisis began to emerge, and the export index of China decreased continuously, reaching a trough at the end of 1998.

Two important factors led to the fall in the export cyclical index. First, over 20 per cent of China's exports were to the crisis-affected countries, including Japan, Korea and Southeast Asian countries, but the growth rates of all of these were negative in 1998 (see Table 8.2). As a result, the domestic demand of these countries for Chinese goods was reduced. Second, the currencies of the crisis countries were devalued substantially in 1997, and their exchange rates were still kept at the low levels in 1998, while the RMB remained stable and even appreciated slightly (see Table 8.2). Therefore the prices of China's

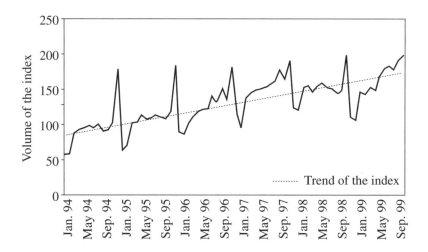

Figure 8.3   Monthly exports of China, 1994–9

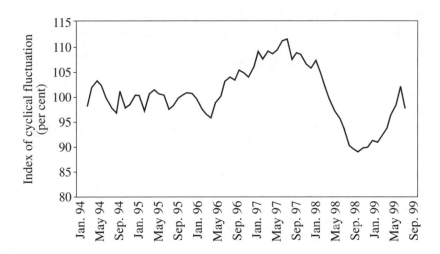

Figure 8.4   Cyclical fluctuation of China's exports, 1994–9

exported goods increased relatively and the exports of China lost their competitiveness in the international market to some extent.

Nevertheless, we are very glad to note that China's exports in 1999 began to step out of the trough, although it had not yet recovered to the average level. The improvement resulted from the same two factors. On the one hand, the economies of the crisis-hit countries began to grow positively in 1999, and, on the other hand, the currencies of Japan, Korea and Indonesia appreciated substantially. In addition, the exports of China appeared to have a strong growth trend in the first quarter of 2000; the growth rates in January, February and March relative to the same months of the previous year were respectively 50·8 per cent, 43·2 per cent and 30·1 per cent. These data appear to reveal that the exports of China have been walking out of the shadow of the crisis.

China's FDI after the Southeast Asian Financial Crisis

China's stable development can be seen in foreign direct investment inflows (shown in Figure 8.5); that is, there is no significant speeding up or slowing down trend in the inflow of FDI.[2] However, we note that the growth rates of the FDI inflow were negative in most quarters from 1998. This reveals that the Southeast Asian Financial Crisis has had some unfavourable impact on the attractiveness of FDI to China.

The slowdown of the growth rate of FDI inflows resulted mainly from the structure of investment countries. Over 85 per cent of the FDI stocks were from the Asian countries, and about 70 per cent of the FDI inflows came from

Table 8.2 GDP growth rate and exchange rate of crisis countries and China

	GDP growth rate (1995 = 100)			Exchange rate (national currency/US$, end of period)			
	1996	1997	1998	1996	1997	1998	1999
China	n.a.	n.a.	n.a.	8·2982	8·2798	8·2787	8·2795
Indonesia	107·8	112·9	97·6	2383	4650	8025	7085
Japan	104·0	104·9	103·5	116·00	129·95	115·60	102·2
Korea	106·8	112·1	105·6	844·20	1695·00	1204·00	1138·40
Malaysia	108·6	117·0	n.a.	2·5290	3·8919	3·8000	3·8000
Philippines	105·8	111·3	110·8	26·288	39·975	39·059	40·313
Thailand	105·5	105·1	94·4	25·610	47·247	36·691	37·520

Source: IMF, *International Financial Statistics*, March 2000.

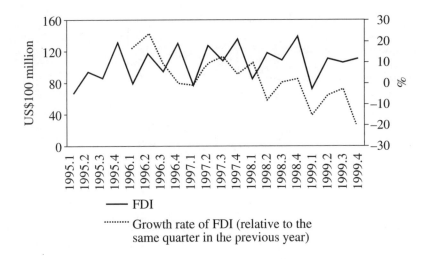

— FDI

········ Growth rate of FDI (relative to the
same quarter in the previous year)

Figure 8.5   FDI and its growth rate

these countries in recent years. In comparison, FDI from the United States and
European countries accounted for only 10 per cent of total FDI stocks. The
financial situation of many companies of the crisis countries has deteriorated
owing to the shock of the financial crisis, which has greatly restricted FDI
from flowing into China. Moreover, the devaluation of the currencies of the
crisis countries has increased the acquisition and merger of the companies of
those countries by companies from the United States and European countries.
All this has the effect of making FDI into China less attractive. Of course, the
fact that the domestic economy of China has been enduring some slackening
of growth is also an important cause of the decline in the growth rate of FDI
inflows.

4   THE COINTEGRATION AND ERROR CORRECTION
MODEL FOR GDP, EXPORTS, FDI AND GDI

In this section, a quantitative approach is undertaken to study China's trade
and investment issues in recent years. The approach makes use of cointegration and error correction analysis fitted to China's trade and investment data.
First, a model is established to test the influence of exports and FDI on GDP
growth. The dependent variable is gross domestic product (GDP), and the
independent variables include exports (EXP), FDI and gross domestic investment (GDI).

In the testing procedure, we first test for the presence of unit roots and,

Table 8.3   Results of the ADF test

Variables	Test type (c, t, l)	t-statistic	Cricial value
log(GDP)	(c,0,1)	−1·6884	−3·9228**
log(EXP)	(c,0,0)	−1·0055	−3·9228**
log(FDI)	(c,0,2)	−0·7569	−3·9635**
log(GDI)	(c,0,1)	−1·2370	−3·9228**
log(GDP)	(c,0,3)	−3·6877	−3·1222*
log(EXP)	(c,0,0)	−4·0536	−3·9635**
log(FDI)	(c,0,1)	−3·1264	−3·0818*
log(GDI)	(c,0,6)	−6·0972	−4·3260**

Notes:
1. *c*, *t* and *l* denote respectively the constant, trend and lag.
2. ** and * denote respectively the critical value at the 1 per cent and 5 per cent levels.

Sources: *China Statistical Yearbook* (1999); *China Foreign Economic Statistical Yearbook* (1998); The People's Bank of China, *Quarterly Statistical Bulletin* (2000, p.1).

second, cointegration. After calculating the logarithms of these four series, we test for unit roots using the augmented Dickey-Fuller (ADF) method (see Table 8.3). From our testing results, all four series in our model have unit roots.

The next step is to test for the presence of cointegration between GDP and EXP, FDI, and GDI using the Engle–Granger two-step method. First, the static regression is obtained as:

$$\log (GDP) \quad 0·5701\log(EXP) \quad 0·2363\log(FDI) \quad 0·8276\log(GDI) \quad ECM_t$$
$$\quad\quad (4·5954) \quad\quad\quad (−16·4534) \quad\quad\quad (8·8766)$$
$$R^2 \quad 0·9960 \quad \text{Adjusted } R^2 \quad 0·9954 \quad F \quad 1705·09$$

Second, the ADF test is applied to ECM_t, and the result is shown in Table 8.4.

It can be concluded that EMC_t is stationary because $t = −3·6746 < −2·7275$. Therefore we can also conclude that a cointegration relationship exists among these four variables and (1, −0·5701, 0·2363, −0·8276) is an integration vector. The cointegration and error correction model can be reported as in Table 8.5.

Table 8.4   Result of the ADF test applied to EMC_t

Variables	Test type (c, t, l)	t-statistic	Cricial value
EMC_t	(0,0,1)	−3·6746	−2·7275**

Table 8.5   Cointegration and error correction model

Dependent variable	$\log(GDP)_t$ Coefficient	t-statistic
ECM_t	–0·2249	–1·762•
$\log(GDP)_{t-1}$	0·3589	4·297•••
$\log(EXP)_t$	0·2512	3·187•••
$\log(FDI)_{t-1}$	0·0701	2·241••
$\log(GDI)_t$	0·2748	4·810•••
R^2 0·9123	Adjusted R^2 0·8804	
D.W. 1·9111	F 28·6004	

Note: *, ** and ** denote respectively the critical values at the 0.1, 0.05 and 0.01 significant levels.

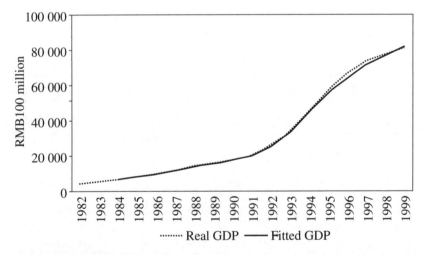

Figure 8.6   Real GDP and fitted GDP

The estimated R^2 of the model is higher than 90 per cent, which reveals that the model fits the actual data quite well; the estimated DW value is 1·9111, which reveals that there is no autocorrelation among the residuals; and the estimated F-statistic is larger than its critical value, which reveals that the model is totally significant. Calculating the fitted value for GDP, we find that the fitted values and the original values tally very closely (shown in Figure 8.6).

The results of the cointegration and error correction model as reported above reveal the following:

1. The growth of GDP is significantly influenced by the GDP growth of the previous year; that is, China's GDP growth has a strong inertia.
2. The growth of both exports and of FDI has a positive influence on the growth of GDP, and the influence of exports is greater, which shows that exports are an important engine for Chinese economic growth.
3. The growth of FDI has a lagged influence on the growth of GDP, and it can be concluded that a certain part of FDI is in fact formed by accumulation, which means that FDI is conducive to Chinese technological improvement if China can absorb technology contained inside the assets of FDI.
4. China's domestic fixed investment has a greater impact on GDP growth than FDI, which reveals that China's economic growth depends more on domestic investment.

As a large and populous country, self-reliance is persistent and an inevitable choice for China, and this can be verified by the findings from the estimated regression model. Meanwhile, the model shows us that China should utilize international markets and foreign capital to motivate its economic growth, which requires China to adopt and strengthen an aggressive approach to exports and to attract FDI.

The most important problem for China to overcome in order to expand exports is the country's low productivity, which leads to a disadvantage in the quality–price ratio. Consequently, a critical means to expand China's exports is to improve productivity, which would require China to accomplish two important missions: to achieve technological innovation, and to improve enterprise management.

The main problems for China as an attractive place for foreign investment are two-fold. The first is that infrastructure, including road and telecommunications, is not well developed. The second is that there exist some restrictions on the ability of foreign investors to acquire control of domestic companies. Therefore China should improve its infrastructure and further reduce its protectionism policy in order to attract more FDI. China is carrying out the West Region Exploitation in its national economic development programme and also preparing to enter the World Trade Organization. These developments should provide a good opportunity for China to achieve more effectively the two important goals mentioned above.

NOTES

1. The regression model between exports and time is

$$Exports = 86 + 1.30T$$
$$(15.4) \quad (9.8)$$

2. The regression model between FDI and time is

$$FDI = 95 \cdot 1 \quad + \quad 1 \cdot 02T$$
$$(9 \cdot 3) \qquad (1 \cdot 2)$$

The t-stastic of independent variable T is not significant, which reveals that there is no significant trend for FDI flows.

BIBLIOGRAPHY

Bayoumi, Tamim and Gabrielle Lipworth (1998), 'Japanese foreign direct investment and regional trade', *Journal of Asian Economics*, 9 (4), 581–607.

Dunning, John H. (ed.) (1974), *Economic Analysis and the Multinational Enterprise*, London: Allen & Unwin.

Kunrong, Shen (1999), 'The foreign direct investment and the growth of economy in China', *Management World* (Beijing), 5, 22–33.

Xiaojuan, Jiang (1999), 'The transformation of the introduction of foreign capital and the model of economic growth', *Management World* (Beijing), 2, 7–15.

Table 8A.1 China's trade, 1955–99

Year	Trade volume	Export	Import	Trade balance	Year	Trade volume	Export	Import	Trade balance
1955	31·4	14·1	17·3	–3·2	1980	381·4	181·2	200·2	–19·0
1960	38·1	18·6	19·5	–0·9	1981	440·3	220·1	220·2	–0·1
1961	29·4	14·9	14·5	0·4	1982	416·1	223·2	192·9	30·4
1962	26·6	14·9	11·7	3·2	1983	436·2	222·3	213·9	8·4
1963	29·2	16·5	12·7	3·8	1984	535·5	261·4	274·1	–12·7
1964	34·7	19·2	15·5	3·7	1985	696·0	273·5	422·5	–149·0
1965	42·5	22·3	20·2	2·1	1086	738·5	309·4	429·1	–119·7
1966	46·2	23·7	22·5	1·2	1987	826·5	394·4	432·1	–37·7
1967	41·6	21·4	20·2	1·2	1988	1027·9	475·2	552·7	–77·5
1968	40·5	21·0	19·5	1·5	1989	1116·8	525·4	591·4	–66·0
1969	40·3	22·0	18·3	3·7	1990	1154·4	620·9	533·5	87·5
1970	45·9	22·6	23·3	–0·7	1991	1356·3	718·4	637·9	80·5
1971	48·4	26·4	22·0	4·4	1992	1655·3	849·4	805·9	43·5
1972	63·0	34·4	28·6	5·8	1993	1957·0	917·4	1039·6	–122·2
1973	109·8	58·2	51·6	6·6	1994	2366·2	1210·1	1156·1	54·0
1974	145·7	69·5	76·2	–6·7	1995	2808·6	1487·8	1320·8	167·0
1975	147·5	72·6	74·9	–2·3	1996	2898·8	1510·5	1388·3	122·2
1976	134·3	68·5	65·8	2·7	1997	3250·6	1827·0	1423·6	403·4
1977	148·0	75·9	72·1	3·8	1998	3239·3	1837·6	1401·7	435·9
1978	206·4	97·5	108·9	–11·4	1999	3606·49	1949·31	1657·18	291·13
1979	293·3	136·6	156·7	–20·1					

Data sources: China Foreign Economic Statistical Yearbook (1998); China Statistical Yearbook (1999).

Table 8A.2 *Utilization of foreign capital in China, 1979–99*

	Total	Foreign loans	FDI	Other foreign investment		Total	Foreign loans	FDI	Other foreign investment
1979–83	144·38	117·55	18·02	8·81	1992	192·02	79·11	110·07	2·84
1984	27·05	12·86	12·58	1·61	1993	389·6	111·89	275·15	2·56
1985	46·47	26·88	16·61	2·98	1994	432·13	92·67	337·67	1·79
1986	72·58	50·14	18·74	3·70	1995	481·33	103·27	375·21	2·85
1987	84·52	58·05	23·14	3·33	1996	548·04	126·69	417·25	4·10
1988	102·26	64·87	31·94	5·45	1997	644·08	120·21	452·57	71·30
1989	100·59	62·86	33·92	3·81	1998	585·57	110·00	454·63	20·94
1990	102·89	65·34	34·87	2·68	1999	563·00	109·00	404·00	50·00
1991	115·54	68·88	43·66	3·00					

Data source: *China Statistical Yearbook* (1999).

Table 8A.3 *China's monthly exports, January 1994–December 1999*

Date	Exports	Date	Exports	Date	Exports	Date	Exports	Date	Exports	Date	Exports
Jan. 94	57·2	Jan. 95	65·0	Jan. 96	91·7	Jan. 97	116·5	Jan. 98	127·8	Jan. 99	113·7
Feb. 94	59·6	Feb. 95	71·2	Feb. 96	86·7	Feb. 97	98·1	Feb. 98	122·8	Feb. 99	109·9
Mar. 94	87·3	Mar. 95	102·4	Mar. 96	104·1	Mar. 97	140·8	Mar. 98	154·3	Mar. 99	148·1
Apr. 94	94·1	Apr. 95	102·8	Apr. 96	113·9	Apr. 97	147·8	Apr. 98	159·6	Apr. 99	147·8
May 94	94·5	May 95	114·9	May 96	121·5	May 97	151·6	May 98	149·2	May 99	155·2
Jun. 94	98·6	Jun. 95	109·6	Jun. 96	122·4	Jun. 97	153·6	Jun. 98	156·1	Jun. 99	153·1
Jul. 94	96·2	Jul. 95	111·3	Jul. 96	123·9	Jul. 97	155·3	Jul. 98	161·6	Jul. 99	173·2
Aug. 94	100·4	Aug. 95	115·8	Aug. 96	141·2	Aug. 97	160·2	Aug. 98	155·6	Aug. 99	183·2
Sep. 94	92·1	Sep. 95	112·9	Sep. 96	134·2	Sep. 97	165·5	Sep. 98	154·8	Sep. 99	185·7
Oct. 94	94·1	Oct. 95	109·7	Oct. 96	152·2	Oct. 97	178·1	Oct. 98	147·3	Oct. 99	182·3
Nov. 94	103·1	Nov. 95	120·5	Nov. 96	136·2	Nov. 97	167·5	Nov. 98	151·3	Nov. 99	194·8
Dec. 94	179·2	Dec. 95	184·7	Dec. 96	183·3	Dec. 97	191·9	Dec. 98	200·1	Dec. 99	202·4

Data source: The People's Bank of China, *Quarterly Statistical Bulletin* (1996, p.1, 2000, p.1).

Table 8A.4   Quarterly FDI in China, 1995–9

	FDI		FDI		FDI
1995·1	67·9	1997·1	78·3	1999·1	73·4
1995·2	94·9	1997·2	128·9	1999·2	112·3
1995·3	86·8	1997·3	108·2	1999·3	106·6
1995·4	131·2	1997·4	137·4	1999·4	111·7
1996·1	79·3	1998·1	86·0		
1996·2	117·4	1998·2	118·5		
1996·3	95·5	1998·3	109·1		
1996·4	131·3	1998·4	141·0		

9. Can China sustain fast economic growth? A perspective from transition and development

Mei Wen

1 INTRODUCTION

China has attracted worldwide attention during the past two decades with an average annual GDP growth rate of 9·95 per cent. However, after a soft landing of the economy from 1995 to 1997,[1] a lasting expansionary fiscal policy which started in 1998 has not yet stimulated a new round increase of non-state investment and an expansion of domestic consumption. The modest decrease of the GDP growth rate from 12·6 per cent in 1994, 10·5 per cent in 1995, to 9·6 per cent in 1996, 8·8 per cent in 1997 and to 7·8 per cent in 1998 has caused many worries to the Chinese government and global economists. Krugman (1994) once pointed out that even a modest slowing in China's growth will change the geopolitical outlook substantially. Furthermore, many optimists have turned to pessimists after the soft landing from 1995 to 1997. Hence there are wide concerns about whether China can sustain its fast growth. What will China's growth perspective be?

To address this issue, we need to review the determinants of China's economic growth in the past two decades. In interpreting China's economic development, many economists regard the high growth as indicating the success of its piecemeal economic reform characterized by management decentralization, market formation, gradually strengthened competition, opening of the economy, financial source shift and ownership diversification.[2] Yet some economists such as Sachs and Woo (1997) attribute China's fast growth to her initial conditions as an agrarian society with a low industrialization level and the scope for China to catch up with the Western developed market economies. If China's growth is a convergence towards developed economies, slowing down of the economy is inevitable after China has been growing with a growth rate far above the average of the growth rate of OECD countries. In addition, economists who thought that

China's piecemeal economic reforms were successful are realizing that further economic reforms are much more difficult than the reforms. Therefore, whether the current reforms such as further SOE reform, financial system reform and land management reform can be as successful as earlier reforms in terms of promoting economic growth is also of great concern to many.

Krugman guesses (1994) that some, but not all, of the efficiency in China's growth, was obtained because of the turn towards the market. This gain represents a one-time recovery. However, the rest represents a sustainable trend. If his guess is correct, it will be interesting to find out whether fast growth can last, as the turn towards the market has not finished yet and the per capita GDP of China is still far below the average of the OECD countries. This chapter will examine China's economic growth in the light of both transition and development, and try to present a picture of China's growth perspective.

The chapter is organized as follows. Section 2 provides a review of China's economic growth. Section 3 examines China's plan for further economic reforms and economic growth. Section 4 identifies key issues in sustaining China's economic growth. A summary and conclusion are presented briefly in section 5.

2   CHINA'S ECONOMIC GROWTH IN RETROSPECT FROM TRANSITION AND DEVELOPMENT

Economic Growth during the past 21 Years

China has experienced fast economic growth since 1978. With an average growth rate of 1·3 per cent in population, its annual per capita GDP grew at 8·49 per cent on average. Although important initiatives of the economic reform were launched simultaneously in urban and rural industries, agriculture, foreign trade and investment at the end of 1978, each sector of the economy performed differently over past 20 years.

As the national general account divides the economy into three large sectors, the growth rate of national GDP and the growth rate of the GDP of each sector can be shown as in Figure 9.1. From the figure, we can make the following observations. First, the primary industry grew very fast from 1981 to 1984, then grew steadily by around 4 per cent from 1985 to 1997. Second, the secondary industry grew at more than 10 per cent during most of the years in the reform period, but at 8·2 per cent in 1979, 1·9 per cent in 1981, 5·6 per cent in 1982, 3·8 per cent in 1989 and 3·2 per cent in 1990. The secondary industry is the main force behind national GDP growth since 1985. Third, the

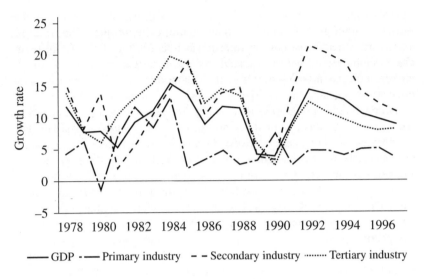

— GDP ·—· Primary industry   – – Secondary industry ········· Tertiary industry

Source: Calculated from *Statistical Yearbook of China* (1998).

Figure 9.1   Growth rate of gross domestic product

tertiary industry experienced the highest growth rate among the three sectors
from 1981 to 1989. It was outperformed by the secondary industry from 1990
to 1997, although this sector grew much faster than the primary industry
during this period.

What forces have generated the differences in growth rates among these
three sectors: differences in reform policies, differences in adopting advanced
technology, differences in investments, sector-specific factors or some other
factors? Below we shall review the literature to see what are the determinants
of the GDP growth for each of the three sectors.

Determinants of Economic Growth

There are three ways to increase production: an increase in inputs, institutional innovation and technology progress. Strictly speaking, the extent to
which the GDP growth of each sector in China can be attributed to each of
these factors is hard to establish, as all three approaches can be adopted
simultaneously. However, there are quantitative studies that try to figure out
what factors, by and large, contribute to the growth, especially in primary
industry.

Agriculture

Agricultural reforms in China consist of price reform, institutional reform and market orientation reform. Price reform was intended to reduce the unreasonable price difference between agricultural and industrial products by increasing prices of agricultural products in order to stimulate agricultural production. Price reform includes an increase of quota prices for grain, oil crops, cotton, sugar crops and pork; an increase of the premium paid for above quota delivery of grain and oil crops; price subsidies to urban households after the rise in retail prices of agricultural products; formation of contract prices after mandatory quotas for cotton and grain were abolished in 1984 and 1985, respectively, and replaced by procurement contract; formation of market prices after farmers were allowed to sell their products above quotas in the free market in the late 1970s. Market prices were higher than the state procurement prices, even measured with the above quota premium.

Institutional reform was mainly meant to shift the production management form from a production team to a Household Responsibility System (HRS hereafter). After a long period of collective production in agriculture in the form of production teams, a small number of production teams, first secretly and later with the blessing of the local government, tried the system of contracting land, other resources and output quotas to individual households at the end of 1978. The central government conceded this HRS but restricted it to the poor regions after these teams brought in yields much higher than those of other teams a year later. Full official acceptance of HRS was endorsed in late 1981, when 45 per cent of the production teams had already been dismantled. By the end of 1983, 98 per cent of the production teams had adopted HRS. As return to peasants in the former production teams was not directly related to the efforts they put into production, HRS is an important institution reform regarded as a mechanism to raise farmers' incentives.

At the beginning of the economic reform, the government intended to reduce its intervention in agricultural production by increasing grain imports, cutting down grain procurement quotas, reducing the number of products included in agricultural planning, and loosening restrictions on private interregional trade in agricultural products. To reduce government intervention in agricultural production is to increase the efficiency of resource allocation and to allow the market to coordinate resource allocation according to individual households' and regional comparative advantage. Having observed the effect of HRS on agricultural production reflected in the fast growth of agricultural GDP from 1981 to 1984, the government declared that there would no longer be any mandatory production plans in agriculture, and that obligatory procurement quotas were to be replaced by contracts between the state and the farmers at the beginning of 1985. However, after production grew at a slower rate and grain output declined in 1985, the voluntary procurement contract was made mandatory again. During the period 1985–91, administrative intervention in market and production increased. In 1992, the market price of grain was wholly determined by the market. Owing to the decline in grain output in 1994, the price of grain increased by 46 per cent. Later on, in 1998, the government ruled that grain could only be purchased by the state from farmers, following another drop in grain output in 1997.

In addition to the above-mentioned reforms, there was a change in lease length of arable land under the HRS. When the HRS was first utilized, the collectively owned arable land was leased to agricultural households for up to 15 years. Fifteen years later, farmers were allowed to renew their lease of the land for up to 30 years. The government tried to encourage farmers to make long-term investments by lengthening the lease period.

Did the above-mentioned agricultural reforms drive agricultural growth? According to earlier empirical studies, HRS had significant positive effects on agricultural production (Lin, 1992; Wen, 1993; Wu, 1995). It is the most important factor that contributed to the fast agricultural GDP growth from 1981 to 1984, and total factor productivity (TFP hereafter) increased. The changes in state procurement prices and market prices also had a positive impact on output growth by encouraging expansion of production, change of cropping intensity and crop pattern (Lin, 1992). However, the shift of production organization form from production team to HRS is a once only change. As it had been realized nationwide by 1984, the growth rate of agricultural GDP from 1985 to 1997 was relatively stable and varied around a rate of 4 per cent in most of the 13 years. These studies reached the consensus that the TFP increase from 1981 to 1984 was mainly due to an increase in technical efficiency, that is, more output produced with the same or fewer inputs. In addition, Wu (1995) found that technological progress dominated technical efficiency changes as the main source of TFP growth from 1986 to 1991. In fact, investment in agricultural fixed assets grew steadily from 1985 to 1998, as shown in the increase in the number of major productive fixed assets in Table 9.1.

Industry

Compared with agricultural reform, industrial reforms are more complex. They consist of management system reforms within state-owned enterprises (SOE hereafter), price reforms and market formation, entry and increase of non-state domestic components in many industries, reforms for encouraging foreign investments, reform of banking industry and financial source shift, and related urban housing system reform and establishment of a social security system. Here we shall discuss market formation, reforms in SOEs and introduction and development of the non-state sector, while leaving discussions on other relevant reforms to later sections.

Table 9.1   China: number of major productive fixed assets per 100 rural households (end of year)

Year	Motor vehicles	Large and medium tractors	Mini and walking tractors (motorized ploughs)	Motorized threshing machines	Carts with rubber tyres	Handcarts with rubber tyres	Pumps
1984	0·09	0·32	20·00	1·11	5·83	40·64	1·48
1985	0·25	0·35	2·17	1·91	5·49	36·86	1·69
1986	0·19	0·43	3·10	1·82	6·52	41·82	2·07
1987	0·28	0·40	3·75	2·15	7·05	41·36	2·48
1988	0·35	0·48	4·33	2·24	7·56	41·32	3·89
1989	0·28	0·47	4·84	2·61	7·68	41·18	3·81
1990	0·28	0·45	5·30	3·55	7·89	40·17	3·86
1991	0·24	0·51	6·61	3·85	8·24	35·21	4·73
1992	0·28	0·55	7·25	4·16	8·67	35·07	5·48
1993	0·33	0·64	8·40	5·57	9·60	41·71	8·54
1994	0·40	0·79	8·77	5·15	9·32	40·68	7·90
1995	0·51	0·77	9·93	6·33	9·29	40·27	9·07
1996	0·78	0·99	12·46	6·87	8·78	37·57	10·97
1997	0·82	1·39	14·26	7·41	8·83	37·38	12·12
1998	1·01	1·22	14·34	8·58	8·52	88·45	13·73

Source: *Statistical Yearbook of China* (various years).

Industrial reforms in China typically reflect the experimental character of China's economic reform and the gradual shift from central planning to a market system. Owing to a lack of direct knowledge on how the market would work in the economy, free markets were first allowed for trading agricultural products and small industrial commodities. Early success of agricultural reform and fast development of collective enterprises amplified the immature market with abundant agricultural products and light industrial products. Then, progressively, most final industrial goods were opened to market competition. However, the supply of intermediate goods continued to be planned because of the ideology of socialism that dictated the state ownership of capital goods and land. The 'dual track' price system introduced in 1984 allowed state firms to deal with non-state, marketized firms with the purpose of protecting SOEs.[3] The two tracks started to merge into one track: the market in 1992 and most intermediate goods were opened to market competition. In 1996, fewer than 10 per cent of commodity categories were under government control. Over 90 per cent of retail prices and 80 per cent of agricultural and producer goods prices (as a proportion of output value) were determined by the market. The relatively well formed product market and gradually strengthened market competition were regarded as key factors in China's rapid increase in industrial output and diversification of consumption goods (see Naughton, 1994; Wen *et al.*, 1998, for example). Many economists also take formation of the product market as a key factor that has made China's transition more successful, at least in the short run, than other transitional economies, since the market provides a ground for enterprises with different ownership types to compete with each other. Nevertheless, the development of the market and the increase in market competition were based on successful agricultural reforms, and the simultaneous introduction of other economic forms outside the state sector and the reforms within SOEs proceeded in parallel.

Before the economic reform, SOEs were the main industrial production units, which in total produced 78 per cent of gross industrial output in 1978. Furthermore, they were not only the administrative units fulfilling central production plans but also in charge of providing social welfare for their workers. The three-stage SOE reforms summarized in Table 9.2 started by changing SOEs from administrative units to economic entities by gradually increasing enterprises' autonomy in production decision making.

The absolute size of state-planned output has been frozen since the economic reform. Any further incremental growth in the state sector was to occur in the portion of their outputs sold in the market. SOEs became able to retain some funds to rebuild their capital or to serve as the firm's activity fund, and were required to remit to the government only the profit in excess of these retained funds. Later, various taxes replaced the remittance requirement. With the development of the marketed components of the state sector, production decisions of SOEs have been gradually and partially decentralized to the firm level. SOEs were exposed to full product market competition in 1992, when the 'dual track' prices merged into market prices with incomplete enterprise autonomy. Although the contract system was attended to increase the production incentives within SOEs, it could not stop more and more SOEs making losses under market competition. In 1990 and 1991, the ratio of total loss of loss-making SOEs to the total profit of SOEs was around 0·9. The ratio reached 0·96 in 1995, 1·92 in 1996 and 1·94 in 1997. As the total loss of SOEs was almost twice as much as the total profit SOEs made in 1997, people had to ponder how successful the reforms within the state sector had been.

Evaluations on TFP change of the SOEs are controversial. While many studies indicate that there is a modest increase in TFP of SOEs up to 1994, some other studies indicate that there is no TFP or even negative TFP growth within the state sector.[4]

From 1978 to 1997, China's gross industrial output value grew with an average annual growth rate of 15 per cent. Although state-owned industry

Table 9.2   Three-stage reform of state-owned enterprises

Management system	Time period	Objectives	Main contents	Related reforms
The managers' responsibility system	1978 to 1986	To transfer SOEs from administrative units to independent management and accounting economic identities	To gradually expand enterprises' decision-making power in production planning, raw material purchasing, product marketing, allocation of retained funds, determination of wages and bonus, cross-region and cross-industry cooperation, employee recruitment and appointment of middle-level managers, disposal of redundant assets and exporting	Price reform: the 'dual track' pricing system introduced in 1984. Taxation reform: to change the tax and profit remittance system to 'tax for profit' system
The contract system	1987 to 1992	To strengthen the linkage between responsibility, autonomy and incentives of SOEs' managers	To contract SOEs out in various forms for three to five years to guarantee sufficient autonomy to contractors. There were five main types of contracts varying with enterprises' performance situations. See Duncan and Huang (1998) for detailed description	Price reform: the 'dual track' prices merged into market prices in 1992. Regulations on wages and bonus
The modern enterprise system	1993 to present	To solve inefficiency problems caused by unclearly defined property rights, unclear divided responsibilities, to intertwine administrative function and economic management of SOEs	To further expand SOEs' autonomy, strengthen monitoring by floating some well-performing SOEs and make SOEs operate under stronger market competition; to 'grab the big' by giving pre-selected and well performing large SOEs preferential policies in bank lending and support in management and R&D to reduce production cost; and to 'let go the small' by allowing lease, sale, merger or bankruptcy of small SOEs	Urban housing reform: urban housing is changed to semi-commercial and commercial channel. Social safety net reform: workers laid off from SOEs can enjoy some unemployment benefit. Taxation reform: taxation items changed to be levied separately by central and local governments

Source: Summarized from Duncan and Huang (1998), Xu and Wen (1996) and Dong Tang (1992).

grew by 7·8 per cent annually during this period, other economic components grew much faster. As a long legitimated enterprise form, collectives produced only 22 per cent of gross industry output in 1978. However, the collectively owned industry expanded, with a 19 per cent annual growth rate during this period. By 1997, it contributed 38 per cent to gross industrial output value, while the SOEs' share dropped to 26 per cent. Collectives were able to expand so fast mainly because of the legitimacy of their existence. While the constitution did not provide legal grounds for the existence of medium and large-sized domestic private firms, collectives provided a good channel for youth employment in the urban area and for absorbing surplus labour from the agricultural sector. Up to 1997, 13·27 million people were employed in the collective industrial sector. Owing to the state ownership of most banks, collectives have been given both policy and financial preference in their fast development, compared with domestic individuals and private firms. Although earlier studies show that collectives were less efficient than SOEs in the earlier years of economic reform, many convincing studies demonstrated that collectives have been more efficient in terms of technical efficiency and TFP than SOEs since the second half of the 1980s.[5] However, Jin and Qian (1998) demonstrated that TVEs (town and village enterprises) do not increase rural income, given the levels of non-farm employment and local public goods provision, indicating possible inefficiency of TVEs as compared to private enterprises.

Although individuals have never disappeared from China's economy, they were not recorded in Chinese industrial statistics in 1978 owing to their small size (in terms of total output value of the sector) and lack of legitimacy under the constitution compared with SOEs and collectives. However, individuals developed like wildfire in the 1980s when people described the situation as 'the whole country jumped into the business world and picked up some business'. From 1981 to 1988, the gross industrial output value of the individual sector grew at an average annual growth rate of 87 per cent. Most individual businesses were located in the industrial retail sector and in service industries. This is the main reason why the growth rate of the tertiary industry was higher than that of primary and secondary industries in most of these years. Fast development of individuals provided an outlet of self-employment for people who could not get into SOEs and collectives or who were not satisfied with their situations in SOEs or collectives. Compared with the domestic private firms, the form of individuals was more feasible owing to capital constraint on domestic private economic agents. Although individuals were now contributing 18 per cent to the total gross industrial output value in 1997, individual businesses were usually small in size.

China opened its economy to foreign trade and created special economic zones in the southern parts of China. The policy of special economic zones attracted worldwide attention. Together with the policy of allowing the duty-free import of inputs for export processing contracts, the adoption of the *Coastal Development Strategy* in 1987–8 promoted the export-oriented sector and foreign investment. After further openness policies were released in late 1992 and several economic laws were discussed, foreign investment was stimulated to a new level. In fact, the total yearly investment in fixed capital of economic units related to foreign ownership or overseas Chinese ownership was less than 1 per cent of the total investment in fixed assets before 1993. However, the yearly investment in fixed capital relating to foreign and overseas Chinese ownership increased to 8 per cent in 1993, and 16 per cent in 1994 and 1995. According to the *Guiding List of Industries for Investment by Foreign Businessmen* (issued on 20 June 1995 by the Ministry of Foreign Trade and Economic Cooperation, amended in December 1997), foreign investors were encouraged to enter the broad areas of China's economy. Since 1996, the power of inland provinces, autonomous regions, cities under independent planning authorities, relevant departments of the state council and other departments to examine and approve projects designed to absorb foreign direct investment has been increased. These authorities are now authorized to approve projects up to US$30 million, compared to US$10 million previously.

This further facilitates the processing of foreign direct investment. Foreign financial institutions are now permitted. Large amounts of foreign investment to China from 1993 have brought capital resources, advanced technology and modern management knowledge into China and promoted export-oriented production. More importantly, recent empirical studies show that foreign invested enterprises, especially Sino-foreign and Sino-overseas Chinese joint ventures, are technically more efficient than SOEs and collectives under present market conditions and other institutional settings.[6] With China's attempt to join the World Trade Organization, the environment for a new wave of foreign investment has been forming and foreign investment will be further encouraged.[7]

Since empirical studies show that on average foreign invested enterprises were more technically efficient than collectives and SOEs, and collectives were more efficient than SOEs in recent years, there is an efficiency gain from ownership diversification. Steady growth of industrial investment has been another source of China's industrial growth. (See Table 9.3, which shows that industrial investment by collectives has grown at the highest rate on average since 1988, while investment by SOEs has increased with the second highest speed.) On the one hand, gradually strengthened market competition may force all kinds of enterprises to improve their TFP. On the other hand, many studies point out that there are heavy efficiency losses generated by misallocation of domestic capital. Bai *et al.* (1997) argue that, as most SOEs were not maximizing their profits, an increase in TFP of SOEs

Table 9.3 Growth rate of investment in fixed assets, by different ownership group (percentage)

	1988	1989	1990	1991	1992	1993	1994	1995	1996	1997	1998
Total	25·4	–7·2	2·4	23·9	44·4	61·8	30·4	17·5	14·8	8·8	13·9
State-owned units	23·3	–7·0	6·3	24·4	48·1	44·1	21·3	13·3	10·6	9·0	17·4
Collectively owned units	30·1	–19·9	–7·1	31·7	94·8	70·5	19·1	19·2	11·3	5·5	8·9
Individuals	28·4	1·0	–3·0	18·1	3·3	20·8	33·5	29·9	25·4	6·8	9·2
Others							99·4	21·3	23·7	13·0	11·6

Source: *Statistical Yearbook of China* (1999).

Table 9.4 Share in total investment in fixed assets, by different economic components, versus ownership group share in gross industrial output value

	1987	1988	1989	1990	1991	1992	1993	1994	1995	1996	1997
State-owned units	*0·63*	*0·61*	*0·61*	*0·65*	*0·66*	*0·67*	*0·61*	*0·56*	*0·54*	*0·52*	*0·52*
	0·58	0·57	0·56	0·55	0·53	0·48	0·43	0·34	0·33	0·28	0·26
Collectively owned units	*0·15*	*0·16*	*0·14*	*0·12*	*0·13*	*0·17*	*0·18*	*0·16*	*0·16*	*0·16*	*0·15*
	0·35	0·36	0·36	0·36	0·36	0·38	0·38	0·41	0·36	0·39	0·38
Individuals	*0·22*	*0·23*	*0·25*	*0·23*	*0·21*	*0·16*	*0·12*	*0·12*	*0·13*	*0·14*	*0·14*
	0·04	0·04	0·05	0·05	0·06	0·07	0·08	0·12	0·15	0·15	0·18
Others							*0·09*	*0·16*	*0·17*	*0·18*	*0·19*
							0·10	0·14	0·17	0·17	0·18

Note: The italic figures are shares in total investment in fixed assets. The roman figures are shares of gross industrial output value.

Source: Shares in total investment in fixed assets by different economic components are calculated from *China Statistical Yearbook of Investment in Fixed Assets* (1950–95, 1997, 1998). Shares of different economic components in gross industrial output value are calculated from *Statistical Yearbook of China* (1988–98).

would cause greater distortion in capital allocation, lower profits and economic efficiency. As shown in Table 9.4, SOEs which contribute to less than one-third of total gross industrial output value are absorbing most domestic capital and making more than half of total investment in fixed assets with their high initial capital stock compared with other domestic ownership groups. In addition, Wen and Zhang (forthcoming) find that the growth rates of investment in fixed assets among industries are not correlated to the marginal rates of return to capital from the industries. Instead, the investment level in fixed capital of each industry is significantly related to total capital stock of the industry and the sum of total profit and taxes. Hence, on the one hand, China has used preferential policies to attract foreign investment and enriched total investment. On the other hand, domestic resources for investment are being misallocated across different ownership groups and across industries. It is this severe misallocation of resources that makes China's prospects of rapid economic growth unclear.[8]

Review of the Changes in Transition and Development

Although China has achieved remarkable growth, the operation of the whole economy is still quite different from a well-functioning market economy and there is still a large distance or gap between China and developed countries in terms of per capita GDP.

Transition

All the transitions from a centrally planned economy to a market economy are based on the recognition that a market system is more efficient in utilizing scarce resources to meet consumers' demand for goods and services. The market as an information network is more efficient in coordinating rational self-interested behaviours and delivering information about resources and products through price signals. The results from the 21-year actual comparison between the central planning and market performance in China have added another credit to the market system.

A well-functioning market system is usually characterized by high productive efficiency, high distribution efficiency, high allocative efficiency, fast technology progress and good product performance through putting into effect the basic economic decisions about what to produce, how to produce it and how products and income are distributed among buyers and sellers. Empirical studies indicate that there is improvement in productive efficiency and technology progress in the state and collective sectors alongside the transition towards a market system in China. In addition, the market may function well in final goods distribution as there are abundant and diversified consumption goods distributed widely according to the market principles. Furthermore, upgrading of a product to a higher product quality with reasonable price increases is common in many product markets. Hence the market may be functioning in product performance as well. However, in a system of incomplete markets, the market may not exert its full function. Even worse, the market can misallocate resources in an incomplete market system. In China's case, the following are some of the causes that may have hindered sound market functioning.

First, the capital allocation mechanism and poor labour market not only impede firms from adopting optimal input combinations to achieve production efficiency according to market signals in the short run, but also severely obstruct firms in adjusting their size according to changes in the market situation and their own performance in the long run.

Second, in a market economy with profit-maximizing producers, the willingness to pay for intermediate goods should be equal to the marginal return to the intermediate input. However, when managers of SOEs do not maximize profits and they are facing a soft budget, the demand (the willingness to pay) for the intermediate goods from the state and non-state sectors is not comparable in terms of economic return generated by the intermediate goods. In the unified intermediate goods market, the demand from the state and non-state sectors is not distinguishable and the intermediate goods are allocated to buyers according to their willingness to pay. Hence the allocation of intermediate goods through the market can be inefficient when SOEs' objective is not profit maximization and their budgets are soft. The fact that, among domestic enterprises, less efficient SOEs are the main investment entities in adopting advanced technology indicates inefficiency in resource allocation.

Third, a lack of an established social welfare system becomes a barrier for inefficient SOEs to exit from the market although it might prevent a decrease in work incentives of low-income earners.

Fourth, explicit barriers of entry to resource extraction, telecommunications, insurance, banking, securities, audio visual elements, professional service sectors and some other sectors or state ownership of banks may hinder the emergence of potentially more efficient firms in certain industries.

Fifth, an immature market for land use rights and a lack of land market with the distribution form of the land use rights under HRS does not allow farm size to be optimally endogenized in the agricultural sector. Although because of high population density, small-scale production with a high utilization rate of fertilizers would be an optimal agricultural production mode for China, which is similar to Japan, production scale should be endogenized instead of being restricted by distributed size of land.[9]

Sixth, with non-profit-maximizing SOEs as main investors in the economy and a lack of legal protection of private property, the operation of the market itself cannot breed domestic entrepreneurship.

The development experience of developed countries suggests that a well-functioning market system is usually based on good infrastructure such as good legal, transport and communication systems. While transport and communication systems can be endogenously improved during the development process, a good legal system which legitimates and protects private property and freedom of contract is regarded as essential for a market system to exercise its full functions. In 1999, a clause was added to provision 6 of the Amendment of the Chinese Constitution which states that the People's Republic of China is to be ruled by laws and China should be seen as a socialist country with a sound legal system. In the same amendment, individuals, private economic organizations and other non-state-owned economic entities are regarded as important components of a socialist market economy. Meanwhile, the Individual Invested Enterprise Law of the People's Republic of China has taken effect since 1 January 2000. In addition, the first comprehensive Contract Law of the People's Republic of China was passed in March 1999.[10] Recently, the Chinese government revealed that private property rights are soon going to be made legitimate and protected through legislation. Yet the government has been investing in infrastructure for triggering investments from the non-state sectors since the end of 1997. These will be supportive moves towards further market development.

Development

When China started the economic reform in 1978, its per capita GDP was US$150 at 1995 prices, which located it at the lower end of the low-income economies group in the world. After 20 years of rapid economic growth, its per capita GDP reached US$680 in 1997, putting it in the upper end of the low-income economies. Many economists expect that China will enter the middle-income economies group by 2010, although it is still far away from the high-income economies. From per capita GDP of US$150 to US$680, China has been making progress in fostering industrialization and the rise of modern industries. In this process, China has experienced many structural changes and regional developments of its own character under favourable international conditions in addition to the above-mentioned institutional transitions towards a market economy.

According to Kuznets (1966), there is a trend of moving away from agriculture in the industrial structure in the modern economic growth stages of Western economies. During the past 20 years, China has experienced similar changes in industrial structure, as shown in Figure 9.2. In 1978, the share of primary industry, secondary industry and tertiary industry in GDP was 0·28, 0·48 and 0·24 per cent, respectively. By 1997, the share of agriculture had decreased to 0·19 per cent, while the share of industry and services increased to 0·49 and 0·32 per cent, respectively. However, compared with the growth experience of the 13 countries up to the 1950s or 1960s studied in Kuznets (ibid.), the increase in the share of secondary industry in Chinese GDP is not outstanding, while the increase in the share of tertiary industry is unusually large.[11] What causes the difference between China's structural change and the

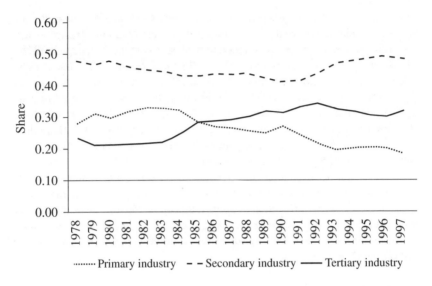

Source: *Statistical Yearbook of China* (1998).

Figure 9.2   Share of three sectors in GDP at current prices

earlier experience of developed countries? Is it that China is developing in a different global economic environment dominated by service industries and information technology, or is it because there are factors in China's economy that restrict growth of the secondary industry? In either case, or both, it seems that more studies are needed to find out the reasons.

Along with the industrial structural change, there is the same trend in the change of labour force distribution among the three sectors, as shown in Table 9.5. From the table, we can see that, in 1978, the primary industry absorbed 71 per cent of total employment while the secondary and tertiary industries had 17 per cent and 12 per cent of total employment, respectively. However, in 1998, employment in the primary industry dropped to 50 per cent of total employment while employment in the secondary and tertiary industries increased to 24 and 27 per cent of total employment, respectively. As with structural change, the increase in the share of the tertiary industry in total employment is more significant than the increase in the share of the secondary industry, yet there are arguments that the secondary and tertiary industries did not absorb enough surplus labour from the primary industry[12] because of the household registration system and other restrictive factors.[13]

Table 9.5   *Employment in three sectors (in 10 000 persons) and their share in total employment*

	1978	1980	1982	1984	1986	1988	1990	1992	1994	1996	1998
Total	40 152	42 361	45 295	48 197	51 282	54 334	56 740	65 554	67 199	68 850	69 957
	1	*1*	*1*	*1*	*1*	*1*	*1*	*1*	*1*	*1*	*1*
Primary industry	28 313	29 117	30 853	30 862	31 212	32 197	34 049	38 349	36 489	34 769	34 838
proportion	*0·71*	*0·69*	*0·68*	*0·64*	*0·61*	*0·59*	*0·60*	*0·58*	*0·54*	*0·50*	*0·50*
Secondary industry	6 970	7 736	8 377	9 622	11 251	12 188	12 158	14 226	15 254	16 180	16 440
proportion	*0·17*	*0·18*	*0·18*	*0·20*	*0·22*	*0·22*	*0·21*	*0·22*	*0·23*	*0·24*	*0·24*
Tertiary industry	4 869	5 506	6 065	7 713	8 819	9 949	10 533	12 979	15 456	17 901	18 679
proportion	*0·12*	*0·13*	*0·13*	*0·16*	*0·17*	*0·18*	*0·19*	*0·20*	*0·23*	*0·26*	*0·27*

Source: Data before 1985 are from *Statistical Yearbook of China* (1993); data of 1986, 1988 and 1990 are from *Statistical Yearbook of China* (1996); data of 1992 are from *Statistical Yearbook of China* (1997); data of 1994 and 1996 are from *Statistical Yearbook of China* (1998); data of 1988 are from *Statistical Yearbook of China* (1999).

From 1978 to 1998, the shift of surplus labour from agriculture into industry was mainly through self-employment, employment in private or individual businesses, employment in TVEs and temporary employment in SOEs, where TVEs were the main economic organizations which absorbed the largest amount of surplus labour from the agricultural sector. In 1998, of 492·8 million employed rural citizens, 0·88 million people worked as employers of private business, 19·4 million people were self-employed persons, 25·6 million people were employees in private business or individuals, 125·4 million were employees in TVEs and 321·5 million were the labour force in the agricultural sector. In 1996, about 80 million rural citizens worked in the industrial sector in the TVEs alone.[14]

TVEs have been regarded as an unexpected success in terms of their fast growth, their increasing contributions to GDP, especially gross domestic product of the secondary industry, and high speed in absorbing surplus labour from the agricultural sector. Early in 1976, when the State Council approved of the Department of Agriculture and Forestry's setting up an enterprise management bureau of the people's communes, TVEs existed as collectives at either the town or the village level. However, TVEs stagnated from 1978 to 1983. With the success of agricultural reform, the emergence of large amounts of surplus labour from the agricultural sector, the effect of the emergence of individuals and the effect of fiscal decentralization, TVEs started their fast growth from 1984 with the emergence of private TVEs (including individuals and private joint enterprises). By 1997, TVEs produced 27 per cent of GDP and contributed 41 per cent to gross domestic product in the secondary industry. Collectives were the main form of TVEs up to 1995.

In 1996, after the Law of Township and Village Owned Enterprises of the People's Republic of China (the TVE law hereafter) was passed in October, many TVEs started to get rid of their 'red hats' and became private. The TVE law legitimates TVEs (no matter the ownership) as legal enterprise entities and important components in the national economy. As the development of TVEs from 1984 to 1995 was not planned by the central government, the law aimed to further support the development of TVEs. More importantly, the TVE law clearly stipulates that the property rights of private TVEs belong to their investors and gives collective TVEs and private TVEs equal ground in terms of legal protection of their property rights, their property, their managers and autonomy in management. In 1997, private TVEs surpassed collective TVEs in terms of the number of units, total employment and total value added, although collective TVEs still contributed more to industrial value added.

Although TVEs were not centrally planned, there were many factors promoting their development. Among earlier studies, factors such as sociological factors, conflict of interests between the central and local governments, risk-sharing behaviour between nominal owners and local governments in an imperfect market environment (Li, 1996), degrees of economic freedom, decentralization and market perfection have all been used to explain the success of TVEs. With the success of agricultural reform, surplus labour was released from agricultural production. Under the household registration system, and with the state ownership of urban land, it is unlikely that all the labour force released from agriculture will shift to industry through urban employment. After fiscal decentralization, local governments had the incentive to set up TVEs for absorbing the surplus labour, capitalizing the collective owned rural land and increasing income of rural citizens as the local governments were able to raise more taxes from the development of TVEs.

In addition to its implications in employment and the increase in technical efficiency of secondary industry, the development of TVEs is likely to have the following effects in China's future economic performance. First, further development of private TVEs may promote development of urban private enterprises. Domestic private enterprises are usually small, owing to capital constraints. If private TVEs can be treated equally with collective TVEs in capital financing, enlargement of private TVEs will speed up capital accumulation of the private entities and be helpful to the growth of the total private sector. According to APSEM (2000), many private TVEs are doing business well after getting rid of 'red hats'. Second, further development of TVEs under the present distortion in resource allocation would be harmful to technological innovation and invention. Although TVEs are producing more gross industrial output than SOEs, SOEs are investing more in fixed assets. Yet the average education level of employees in TVEs is usually lower than that of SOEs. In present-day China, TVEs have difficulty in competing with SOEs and joint ventures in attracting human capital. The high wages from joint ventures would attract the best human resources. A good geographic location of the SOEs and ample financing in applied research in SOEs would be more attractive than TVEs to educated potential employees. Hence the separation between the best human resources, the applied research and the major producer would be unfavourable to technological innovation and invention. Third, as a main economic entity in China's industrialization process, the location of TVEs would have retarded the urbanization process. After 1949, the distinction between urban and rural areas mainly served for administration purposes. According to development and trade literature (see Yang and Rice, 1994; Yang, 1998, for example), when the industry of a country develops with individual specialization and increased division of labour, producers will choose to locate at some central places where people are trading all kinds of goods together in order to save transport costs, if they are free to do so. By locating close to each other, the benefit from infrastructure investment will be more significant in reducing transaction and transport costs. Cities and the urbanization process will then emerge in this development process. Although the administrative urban areas of China are growing with the economic development, the urbanization process is much slower than the development of the industry.

Reviewing the development of TVEs, we can see that those TVEs whose locations are close to urban areas where industrial and urbanization levels are higher are more likely to be successful. This is why TVEs in eastern China are more successful than TVEs in western China, where resources might be more abundant. However, the development of TVEs is nationwide and many of them are located in the remote rural areas and decisions on their locations are not economic ones, as most location decisions would be restricted by the land attachment (land rights) (limited to the location of the village or the town). This indicates that transaction efficiency may not be improved fast enough in the industrialization process. It thus indicates welfare loss, as potential higher welfare would not be reached with the same production and resource input owing to location constraints.

This section has shown that China's transition from a centrally planned economy to a market economy is far from complete, as markets are incomplete and there are institutional restrictions obstructing a sound functioning of the market. In addition, there are some poorly matched aspects in the development process. From the earlier fast industrialization process of Western developed economies, we have observed that product diversity, increased productivity, technology progress and urbanization are different facets of industrialization. But in China, urbanization does not keep pace with product development and diversity. The distance from a complete market economy and well-coordinated development implies both problems in China's economic growth and the great scope for further growth if the problems can be resolved. Under these circumstances, what does the Chinese government plan to do for China's future economic growth?

3   CENTRAL PLANNING FOR FURTHER ECONOMIC REFORM AND ECONOMIC GROWTH

After the contractionary policy adopted in July 1993, China's economy slowed down from 1995 to 1997. In 1997, there was an obvious over-supply in the product market, with significant excess production capacity in many industries. Prices of many consumption goods started to decrease. The economy started showing signs of a recession. Confronting all these problems, some economists attributed the recession to the long-term contractionary policy, yet others thought that the recession was based on the long-run accumulated problems in microeconomic structure. As the effect of the adjustment of microeconomic structure and further economic reform would be mainly on long-run economic growth and many economic advisors to the government thought that macroeconomic policies were necessary to stimulate effective demand and short-run economic growth, macroeconomic measures have been adopted. Microeconomic structure adjustment and further enterprise reforms have been proceeding in parallel.

Macroeconomic Measures and their Effectiveness

Since 1998, expansionary fiscal and monetary policies have been adopted to stimulate investment, consumption and exports. In 1998, 58 billion yuan treasury bonds within the government budget and an additional 108 billion yuan treasury bonds outside the government budget were issued and lent to the local governments for infrastructure investment, where part of the additional 108 billion yuan was actually utilized in 1999.[15] Banks increased investment loans correspondingly. These investment loans are mainly used in infrastructure constructions such as the agricultural irrigation system, the transport and telecommunications system, environment protection, renovation of the power network, grain warehouses and urban public facilities.[16] The issue of treasury bonds in 1999 was of similar size to that in 1998. As a result, investment in fixed assets by state-owned enterprises increased by 19·5 per cent in 1998, while total investment in fixed assets in the economy increased by 14·1 per cent.[17]

Since 1998, the expansionary monetary policies adopted include increase of money supply, consecutive cuts in interest rates, policies for expansion of bank loans, and an increase in income of teachers and public servants. M1 and

M2 increased, with a growth rate of 11·9 per cent and 15·3 per cent, respectively, in 1998. In 1999, the government did not increase the rate of issuing treasury bonds to accelerate infrastructure investment. Instead, the central government increased its budget deficit to 150·3 billion yuan to support infrastructure investment. As a result, money supply accelerated in 1999. Interest rates were cut three times in 1998. The nominal interest rate on one-year term deposits dropped from 5·76 per cent to 3·78 per cent after the three cuts. As consumer prices generally decreased in 1998, a cut of nominal interest rates had little effect. Hence the interest rate was lowered further in June 1999. Policies on the expansion of bank loans include the special loans for infrastructure investment, consumer loans for car and housing starting in 1998, further expansion of consumption loans under the guidelines issued by the People's Bank of China in 1999, and policies for increased loans to small businesses by commercial banks. However, under these expansionary monetary policies, commercial banks still ran into difficulty issuing loans, as not many firms were prepared to invest in the current economic environment, with severe excess production capacity. Without housing tax cuts and with all kinds of charges on buying new commercial residential units, the number of vacant new houses accumulated with the rapid development of the real estate industry from 1992 to 1995 did not decrease with the housing loan policy. Instead, more vacant housing appeared and even the development of the real estate sector slowed down. Prices of consumption goods kept falling. Only recently, the price of steel has risen as a result of industrial adjustment. Neither fiscal nor monetary policies had much effect in triggering private investment or consumption, although net exports increased by 25·5 billion yuan in 1998 with the pegged exchange rate.

As the lasting effect of China's expansionary fiscal and monetary policies is not significant, people have to think more about the microeconomic foundations.

Plans for Microeconomic Reform

Early in the third industry census in 1995, it was revealed that there was a large amount of excess production capacity in many industries. (See Table 9.6 for the utilization rate of production capacity for some final products.) The utilization rate of production capacity is lower than 50 per cent in some industries. This is the consequence of redundant investment since the 1980s due to the pursuit of short-run local benefits and the severe problems with the capital allocation mechanism. As most SOEs were making losses, the Ninth Five Year Plan for the National Social-Economic Development of the People's Republic of China and the Programme for the Long-Term Objectives by 2010 stipulated an SOE reform policy of 'grasping the big and letting go of the small' in 1995.

In the 'Report on the Work of the Government' presented at the second meeting of the Ninth National People's Congress (see *Gazette of the State Council of the People's Republic of China*, 1999, no. 2), accelerating the reform of SOEs is taken as one major task of the government, in addition to adopting a lasting fiscal policy to stimulate domestic effective demand, adjusting agricultural product structure and the structure of TVEs (including product structure and organization structure) and making efforts to increase exports.

As discussed in Wen *et al.* (1998), the performance of enterprises is not a simple management problem. It is determined by intrinsic incentive structure under different ownerships, coordination between nominal property rights and actual control rights within the firms and operation environment. Hence, whether the performance of SOEs can be improved is not only determined by reforms within the SOEs, but is also strongly related to the establishment of a complete market, including factor markets, improvement of the capital allocation mechanism and improvement of the social security system. However, among all the problems pointed out in the earlier sections, the existence of obvious excess capacity, obstacles presented by a poor social security system to SOE reforms and harmful effects of the governments' direct involvement in doing business have been recognized as either most urgent or solvable problems. Hence the government has plans to take measures partly to solve these problems.

To a very large extent, excess capacity is caused by redundant investment without market analysis. As a result, the government is now trying to use its control of bank loans and approval rights on industrial construction projects to prevent redundant investment in certain industries. Closing down of those small enterprises whose equipment is outdated, whose product quality is low, which are inefficient in utilizing resources and generate large amounts of air pollution is taken as one measure to solve the excess capacity problem. Because there exists significant excess capacity in many industries with increasing return to scale (the motor industry, for example: see Table 9.6), merging and restructuring of SOEs in these industries and the formation of enterprise groups are thought to be appropriate measures to improve production efficiency and competency of some medium and large-sized SOEs. After the formation of the enterprise groups, it is said that their future will be determined by their performance in future industrial competition.

In order to let the above-mentioned small enterprises go bankrupt, an improvement of the social security system is regarded as an urgent task, as accelerated unemployment would cause social instability. According to the 'Report on the Work of the Government', unemployment benefits to former SOE employees will come from three channels: one-third from SOEs, one-third from the social insurance system and one-third from the fiscal budget. After an employee is laid off from an SOE, he or she can gain a fraction of

Table 9.6　Utilization rate of production capacity of some durable houshold items, products of the motor industry and others

Product	Output (unit: one)	Production capacity (unit: one)	Utilization rate of production capacity
Video camera	46 251	354 250	0·13
Air conditioner	6 825 573	20 354 048	0·34
Copy machine	217 548	641 508	0·34
Video recorder	2 083 647	5 169 147	0·40
Washing machine	9 484 109	21 831 859	0·43
Car	1 452 691	3 285 365	0·44
Colour TV	20 577 363	44 676 468	0·46
Household refrigerator	9 185 441	18 208 325	0·50
Bicycle	44 722 490	81 993 181	0·55
Motor cycle	8 254 146	14 895 746	0·55
Camera	33 261 456	57 660 588	0·58
Vacuum cleaner	8 054 986	12 836 006	0·63
Household sewing machine	6 174 720	9 730 225	0·63
Tractor	2 126 250	3 235 116	0·66
Truck	37 284	53 820	0·69
Electric shower	1 397 931	1 989 069	0·70
Bus	2 395	2 901	0·83

Note: Both the output and production capacities are the amount at the end of 1995. Output is national total, while the production capacity is the total of independent accounting units at or above village level. There would be two opposite biases in the utilitization rate. The exclusion of the production capacity of those units under village level may raise the utilitization rate. And the fact that both statistics are at the end of 1995 may lower the capacity utilization rate, as some capacity would be newly installed.

Source: *The Data of the Third National Industrial Census of the People's Republic of China in 1995, Summary and Industry Volume.*

their basic wages from the enterprise within the first three years. If he or she has not found a new job within these three years, the former employer–employee relationship will be ended and the person should be paid unemployment benefit from social insurance institutions in the following two years. If the person cannot find a job within these two additional years, he or she should ask for a benefit based on the basic living expenses of urban citizens from the Department of Civil Administration. In addition to this three-channel security system, the central government will have a budget for professional retraining for laid-off employees to assist them in finding new jobs.

As one step for the government to distance itself from the business world and to establish a sound supervision system, all the departments of the State Council have severed relationships with formerly attached enterprises. The central government requires local government to reform in the same principle. In the 'Report on the Work of the Government', selection and supervision of the managers of SOEs are regarded as important issues in improving SOEs' performance.

In addition to the above measures related to SOE reform, the Chinese government links the reform on TVEs with the development of small cities and towns. Although in the latest revision of China's constitution there is a subtle change in stating the basic national task of China, from 'to concentrate on Chinese modernization of socialist style *according to the theory* of building up a socialist country with Chinese character' to 'to concentrate on Chinese modernization of socialist style *along the path* of building up a socialist country with Chinese character', state and public ownership of production factors are still regarded as the basis for a socialist economic system.

In 1999, China's Agenda 21 highlighted the significance of the establishment of sound legislation and legal enactment systems, optimal extraction of natural resources, protection of the natural and ecological environment, population control, improvement of health condition and balance in regional development for sustainable economic development.

In the frequent bilateral negotiations with the United States, European countries and other WTO members, China has been confronting increasing pressure to reduce import tariffs and permit competitive entry of foreign enterprises into many Chinese industries. Since 1999, many new policies and regulations have been quickly issued for further opening the economy. With its effect on access to the WTO, competition in the Chinese market will be rapidly strengthened. This globalization trend provides China with great opportunities and even greater challenges as developed countries are much advanced in technology and China still lacks a strong class of good domestic entrepreneurs.

4   DETERMINANTS OF CHINA'S SUSTAINABLE GROWTH

Traditional theory on industrialization describes the growth of industrialization characterized by private capital accumulation, especially from the agricultural sector, absorption of surplus labour from the agricultural sector by the industrial sector, private investment in the industrial sector, technological progress and the growth of entrepreneurship in the evolution of economic organizations. Britain, the United States and France are some of the economies that have experienced this kind of industrialization. Industrialization mainly through private capital accumulation is based on institutional conditions such as the legal system, the establishment of a market system, and especially the mobility of production factors. This is one kind of industrialization. The other kind of industrialization is industrialization under government planning: the government uses its administrative power to mobilize resources and set up state enterprises to start its industrialization process. The former Soviet Union built up an industrial power 20–30 years after the Russian revolution which was competent in some ways when compared with the industries of Western industrial countries. China and India started to set up their industrial system under central planning from the 1950s to the late 1970s. Evidently, this kind of industrialization was based on introduction and imitation of advanced technology and industrial organization. Before transition and reform in these three countries, the industrialization process did not bring a high living standard to their citizens.

Yet there is the other kind of industrialization that lies in between: the domestic private and government sectors developed simultaneously. Germany and Japan experienced this kind of industrialization process. When Germany and Japan started their industrialization process there were two significant conditions. First, the market was developed to a certain degree and production factors were mobile. Second, there was rapid accumulation of domestic private capital and effective entrepreneurial responses to the development of a merchandized economy. From the history of the above-mentioned countries, we see that establishment of a market system, factor mobility, private capital accumulation and effective entrepreneurial responses to the development of a merchandized economy are important conditions for a simultaneous increase in the industrialization level and in the living standards of the people in an economy. We have seen in section 2 that China's market is still incomplete. In addition, there are institutional factors that can obstruct sound market functioning in the economy. So are there factor mobility, fast private capital accumulation and effective entrepreneurial responses to the market economic development of Chinese style in the economy?

Factor Mobility

Before China's economic reform, production factors were mobilized through central planning and administration. They were not allocated into different production according to factor productivity. Although the success of the reform in the past two decades would have been impossible without the recognition that ideology should not be an obstacle to China's economic development, Chinese history since 1949 and the socialist theory on state and public ownership of production factors as the basis of socialism do hinder the sound functioning of the market based on the mobility of production factors. In fact, state control of production factors has been affecting the effectiveness of resources allocation, the location of industrial firms according to economic principles and equity of income distribution.

Capital mobility

As China is a country with a high population density, an effective allocation of capital is extremely important for sustainable economic growth and the growth of the nation's wealth, because of its scarcity. Owing to the fact that any government would have the objective and incentive to increase both fiscal revenue and returns to capital in the economy, it is impossible for state capital to be allocated according to the marginal rate of return to capital within the state sector with the state ownership of most banks. In fact, Wen and Zhang (forthcoming) find that investment in fixed capital across different industries within the state sector is significantly and positively related to total fixed capital stock of the industry and the pre-tax profits of the industry. The positive correlation between investment in fixed assets and pre-tax profits provides partial evidence that the government pursues both fiscal revenue and profits of SOEs. The positive correlation between investment and total fixed capital stock may be due to two reasons: first, a big industry within the state sector may have weighty lobbying and bargaining power in collecting capital funds for investment;[18] second, many investment projects cannot be finished within one year and they usually last for several years. Although the capital allocation in the private and foreign sector should pursue the marginal return to capital, our cross-industry study shows that there is no significant positive correlation between investment in fixed capital and marginal return to capital in the whole economy. To a large extent, inefficiency in capital allocation is due to limited mobility of capital resources.

Right at the beginning of the economic reform, China started its banking system reform. With the People's Bank of China (PBC) being separated from the Ministry of Finance in 1978 (becoming the country's central bank in 1983), several banks were established to manage the banking services in different areas in 1979. For example, the Agricultural Bank of China mobilized and directed financial resources from within the rural sector and rural industries. The Bank of China was separated from the PBC and dealt with foreign exchange businesses and settled international accounts for China. The People's Construction Bank of China (PCBC) managed budgetary grants and absorbed domestic deposits for enterprise investment in fixed assets. The China International Trust and Investment Corporation (CITIC) specialized in services for joint ventures. In the 1980s and 1990s, more state and local government-owned banks were established, either for specific purposes or for local development under local government advice. There are several characteristics of these state or provincial banks: first, they have the monopoly power in the specific area in which they are operating, although a rise in the number of banks has strengthened competition in general banking services; second, their lending behaviour comes under either the central or the local government policy guidance, depending on their ownership; third, officials at the different levels can have a say in deciding those to whom a loan should be made, owing to the ownership of these banks.

Although the establishment of the Shenzhen and Shanghai share markets in 1992 introduced another financing channel for enterprises, the division of banking services among different banks limited capital mobility across the industrial sectors. With the existence of a few private banks (such as Mingshen Bank) and foreign banks (for example, Bank of Australia and New Zealand),[19] the monopoly power held by the state and provincial banks with government intervention more or less limits capital mobility across industries, across different ownership types and across regions. More importantly, bank managers would pursue fringe benefits including economic rents in addition to the benefits of the bank's performance. Hence there is a large volume of bad loans in China at present,[20] in addition to the redundant investment without market analysis, as verified by ample excess capacity in many industries.

Although modern economic development can be proceeded with mobilizing international capital, to use a preferential policy to attract foreign capital on the one hand and to waste domestic capital resources on the other hand can lead to fast growth in GDP but slow growth in national wealth.[21] With China's accession to the WTO, more foreign banks and private banks will be allowed to enter China's financial sector. However, in the circumstance where there is no sound legal enforcement system and loss-making firms cannot go bankrupt according to the Corporate Act of the People's Republic of China (*Gazette*, 1994, no. 30), whether foreign banks can operate their business well in China is still a question to ponder upon. Foreigners will be very cautious in doing business in China. Meanwhile emergence of more domestic private banks will be limited by legalized domestic private capital accumulation. Hence whether China can break the monopoly power in the banking industry and improve the efficiency of capital allocation is a key determinant of China's sustainable growth both in GDP and in national wealth. Strengthening the legislative and legal enforcement systems can be helpful in breaking the monopoly power in the financial sector, improving efficiency in capital allocation and increasing the probability of sustained fast growth of GDP. If the legislative and legal enforcement systems can be reinforced, to stock-list state and provincial banks by selling some of the shares to China's residents simultaneously with an introduction of competition can be helpful in increasing the probability of sustained fast growth of national wealth. The government can choose to withdraw gradually from the commercial banking sector by reducing its ownership of banks and let domestic commercial banks operate like Western cooperatives to guarantee increases in fiscal revenue from taxation when both GDP and national wealth experience fast growth.

Labour mobility

Before the economic reform, China's labour force was largely immobile. With the household registration system, urban and rural labour forces are separated. In the case of urban adults, they were allocated to different SOEs through central administration channels. Jobs were usually permanent. In the 1970s, collective units attached to different administration districts in cities provided another channel for youth employment. The rural labour force was restricted to the affiliated production team. The first reform in utilizing the labour force occurred in urban areas with the introduction of contract employment in the state sector, with some of the new employees in SOEs working under these contracts. Later on, some information centres for human resources were set up to provide labour demand and supply information. With the permission and development of non-state enterprises, self-employment as individuals, employment in private business, employment in joint ventures and employment in 100 per cent foreign enterprises have been providing more channels for mobilizing human resources. In the 1990s, many kinds of databases of specialized human resources for people who have passed standardized examinations were set up as well. As a result, people with high education levels are largely mobile in the economy now. However, owing to the history of permanent jobs and social welfare provided in the SOEs, urban workers with a lower education level lack the incentive and spirit to seek new employment opportunities even if they are widely available. Instead, many surplus labour workers from rural areas have stronger incentives either to find an opportunity for self-employment or to work in the non-state sector in the urban area. But with the household registration system, labour mobility from rural to urban areas is strongly limited.

As discussed in section 2, the fast development of TVEs has been attributed to the large amount of surplus labour which is scantily mobile to the urban area and which also becomes the main channel for absorbing surplus labour from the agriculture sector. As one of the few ways of benefiting from collectively owned land beside agricultural production with limited employment opportunities in the urban area, TVEs seem to be a good choice to Chinese rural citizens. However, rural infrastructure development was unable to keep pace with the development of TVEs because the location of TVEs to their towns or villages implies high costs in infrastructure development. Hence the household registration system with the collective ownership of land postpones China's urbanization. This is also one reason for insufficient demand for household electrical appliances in rural areas, and therefore a reason for ample excess capacity in these industries.

In recent years, the Chinese government has emphasized infrastructure development in the rural areas and the development of small cities and towns. Furthermore, the household registration system in these small cities and towns will be put into practice. However, this urbanization process cannot be as economical as the urbanization from the agglomeration of industries, as the latter has significant economies of scale. More importantly, how many TVEs can survive in the near future, when a large number of foreign enterprises will set up in China and choose their location according to economic principles? This will be a real problem, quite apart from the dominant position in technology and management knowledge of these foreign enterprises. When China enters the WTO, there will be more employment opportunities in the old or newly established urban areas where infrastructure is better than that in the rural areas where most TVEs are now located. Then there will be demand for a large amount of rural labour migration to these areas, and restructuring and relocation of TVEs will be inevitable if TVEs want to survive.

Although China has a uniquely large population, the aging of the population under the present population control policy will be another problem for sustained fast economic growth. The 'one couple, one child' policy accelerates the aging of the population and the dependency rate of the economy. In 10 to 20 years, the burden on the social security system will increase significantly. Then, whether China can have high saving and investment rates as it has had during the past two decades will be another determinant of sustained fast growth, although international capital mobilization may alleviate the seriousness of the problem.

Private Capital Accumulation and Entrepreneurship

The development experience of developed countries shows that entrepreneurship in seeking profit-making opportunities is essential for the development of a market economy as it is this profit seeking that leads to an effective allocation of resources in the economy. In the 19th century, the entrepreneur was seen as an individual proprietor who supplied most or all of the factors of production, but especially managerial expertise. Hence the development of the entrepreneurs and the accumulation of legalized private capital are strongly related to each other. The entrepreneurial function is sometimes regarded as a fourth factor of production in addition to natural resources, labour and capital. For the entrepreneurs to be able to find and grasp profit-making opportunities in market competition, they have to have the following attributes. First, they are familiar with the law of the market and try to win in market competition through efficient business operation and management according to the law of the survival of the fittest. Second, they have a knowledge of modern science and technology and capability in business management and the ability to exploit it: making production and enterprise organization decisions according to their production and management knowledge. Third, they have good perception and prediction about the evolution of the market and have a high spirit of innovation, including innovation through R&D in technology, exploration of new markets, adoption of new materials in production and innovation in their enterprise organization and regulations. Fourth, they are part of the business culture: be proud of making profits, have a strong commitment to fulfilling contracts, take customers as masters, have the courage to take risks, believe in equal opportunity and value of freedom, and deal well with employer–employee relationships.

Owing to a shortage of proprietors who have both wealth and modern management expertise, there has been a fast development of large corporations with a separation of ownership from control since 1930. The separation of ownership from control in large joint-stock companies influences the incentives of economic agents within organizations, and managers may not pursue profit maximization which is the interest of the owners as the latter can claim residual income while managers of corporations are usually awarded according to their reported performance. King and Pitchford (1998) show that, if there are perfect accounting measures and all kinds of incentive mechanisms can be designed and adopted without costs, ownership itself should not have efficiency implications. However, in reality, there is no perfect accounting measure and design and implementation of some incentive mechanisms can be very costly,[22] and private ownership would be more efficient. Hence the existence of a group of proprietors would be the easiest way to achieve efficient resource allocation, while improvement of the accounting system towards perfection and design and adoption of incentive-compatible mechanisms to coordinate managers' and owners' interests are a second-best solution when there is not enough integration of private wealth and modern management knowledge.

According to earlier empirical studies on the household survey data of 1988 and 1995, income distribution was becoming more and more unequal along several dimensions in China's economy (see Khan *et al.*, 1999; Li, 1999, for example). The rural–urban income gap has been widened. There are also significant regional disparities of household income. Most importantly, according to a decomposition study based on reported incomes, four sources of income (wages, pensions, the rental value of owned housing, and housing subsidy) account for 93·7 per cent of the overall income inequality among urban households. On the one hand, urban poverty has been worsened by a large number of worker lay-offs from SOEs in recent years and by the yet to be improved social welfare system. On the other hand, income of managers and workers in the foreign-related sector (either pure foreign-owned enterprises or joint ventures), in monopolized industries of the state sector (the banking industry, for example) and in the individual and domestic private sectors has greatly increased and is higher than that in the other sectors. Hence there is accumulation of private capital. There is also a large literature on rent-seeking behaviour in China which indicates a large amount of private capital accumulation belonging to government officials at all kinds of levels (see Tinari and Lam, 1991; Liew, 1993; Harris and Lockwood, 1997; Yao, 1997, for example).[23] Unfortunately, this trend of private capital accumulation may not breed entrepreneurship (see Zhang, 1999).

In the 20 years of market-oriented economic reform with strengthened market competition, it is fair to say there have been many managers in China's enterprises (even in SOEs and TVEs) having good management knowledge. The success of the Changhong colour TV company in the Chinese TV market, competition with many joint ventures and huge excess capacity in the industry is one example that shows some managers in SOEs not only have a good knowledge about the law of the market, but also know how to exploit the first mover advantage in the market.[24] In the fast development of TVEs and individuals, there are also some entrepreneurs of the type 'the farmer turned entrepreneur'. However, these kinds of domestic managers are few in the domestic big and medium-sized enterprises. As an example, there were 115 colour TV production lines introduced into China in the 1980s and most domestic colour TV companies did not survive the ensuing market competition. Furthermore, SOE managers do not have to face hard budgets and even most managers of TVEs, owing to an imperfect market,[25] have to seek risk sharing with local government officials by inviting them to join the companies.

In 1999, when fiscal policy adopted from 1998 did not trigger domestic private investment and banks could not make many loans, the government did issue policies to encourage state-owned banks to lend money to domestic private enterprises. However, there were not much response from the domestic private sector. Except for the macroeconomic environment, the sluggish response from private businesses also sends out a signal that there is a lack of entrepreneurs with innovative ideas in the economy. After all, the relationship with government officials was formed into a business culture in China under the imperfect market situation. Most business managers are proud of making profits as a result of their relationship with government officials, instead of their innovation in production or management approaches, or exploitation of new products or markets. Even managers of foreign-owned enterprises sometimes have to learn China's business culture to operate within it. This might be one reason why joint ventures on average could do better than pure foreign-owned enterprises in the first half of the 1990s.

Hence, in present-day China, government officials who are generally wealthy usually do not have enough entrepreneurial experience of rigid market competition, while genuine entrepreneurs who do have entrepreneurship skills are few in the economy. This divorce of wealth and management knowledge hinders an emergence of a new class of proprietors. In these circumstances, Chinese domestic enterprises are likely to lose their first mover advantage if the domestic private sector does not grow very rapidly, before the economy is wide open to rigorous global market competition. In 1999, the government was inviting foreign experts to set up a new accounting system and assigning central government representatives to those big SOEs which badly need supervision. On the one hand, the representatives can go back and bring administrative intervention into these enterprises. On the other hand, as the development of the principle of agent theory indicates, improvement of the accounting system and coordinating owners' and managers' interests are only a second-best solution. Hence, how fast China's private sector can grow before the economy is widely opened up will determine the performance of domestic enterprises in global rigorous competition, subsequently affecting the growth of national wealth.

Optimal Utilization of Natural Resources

Malthus (1798) and Ricardo (1895) regarded the existence of so-called 'over-population' and the persistent pressure on maintaining a subsistence living standard from population growth in the context of scarce natural resources, mainly land, as significant problems in economic development. In the late 1950s and 1960s, when the Chinese population grew fast and a large part of the population suffered from famine, the theory of Malthus became well known in China. The Chinese government started population controls in the mid-1970s. Because of its uniquely large population, China's stable supply of agricultural products has always been a concern during the reform period. With the development of TVEs and the real estate sector, a reduction of arable land in the 1990s made the government adopt the protection of arable land as the most important task in land management reform. It has not been widely realized that industrial agglomeration and rapid urbanization that are based on the economic choice of enterprise locations would reduce the probability of the loss of arable land compared with a fast rural industrial development.

Unlike the present Chinese situation, industrialization of developed countries relieved the pressure of population on fixed land with technology progress, as Schumpeter summarized (1943, p.116): 'Technological progress effectively turned the tables on any such tendency, and it is one of the safest predictions that in the calculable future we shall live in an *embarras de richesse* of both foodstuffs and raw materials, giving all the rein to expansion of total output that we shall know what to do with. This applies to mineral resources as well.' Nevertheless, Schumpeter's generalization of the statement to mineral resources seemed to be optimistic. Even though there are pioneering studies such as Hotelling (1931), Scott (1955) and Herfindahl and Kneese (1967) on natural resources, these studies passed largely unnoticed when they appeared. Only in the 1970s, especially after the oil crises in 1973/4 and 1981, was a substantial effort made to reconstruct an economic theory in the light of resource exhaustibility. (See the Royal Economic Society, 1974; Kemp and Long, 1980, 1984; Ray, 1984; Cecen, 1991; Levin, 1993; Hartwick, 1995, for detailed surveys and the development of the theory.)

In the classical view, the literature that was developed on survival problems has two main concerns: (a) whether a positive level of consumption or output could be sustained if production requires the input of a raw material derived from an exhaustible resource stock, if the available stock is finite and non-augmentable, and (b) with or without technical progress, what are the conditions for sustaining a positive living standard? Without technical progress, the answers to the survival problems usually depend on the substitution elasticity between the raw materials derived from the resource and capital input, or the elasticities of output with respect to inputs. With technical progress, the possibility of a positive and growing level of per capita consumption is then up to the rate of technical progress. Closer to Schumpeter's theory, the experience of developed countries shows that a positive living standard could not only be maintained, but the living standards in most economies have also improved with population growth owing to the substitution of labour for resources, the substitution of capital goods for resources and the invention or improvement of the technology of substitutable raw materials. Therefore further theoretical and practical concerns address the optimal exploitation of exhaustible resources for a long-term economic growth.

According to the above economic theory and development experiences of developed countries, should China worry about the constraints of natural resources on its sustainable economic growth? In its present situation, the answer is yes, as there is a huge waste of natural resources through redundant investments which developed countries did not experience. In addition, the separation of the main investment entities, the best human resources, from the main production units would hinder either fast development of applied research or the applicability of scientific research. As a matter of fact, the Chinese government has a much louder voice on the significance of reasonable utilization of natural resources than on the significance of the improvement in its capital allocation mechanism for sustainable economic growth. But, as discussed in the earlier sections, with an efficient capital allocation mechanism based on a competitive capital market, redundant investments would not happen to such an extent in China. In 1999, the Chinese government encouraged foreigners to tap its mineral resources. In addition, the introduction of advanced technology will speed up after China gains its WTO membership. Hence the pressure on the constraints of natural resources will lessen in the future.

According to historical observations and recent economic development theory (Boserup, 1981; Murphy *et al.*, 1989; Chandler, 1990; Yang and Ng,

1993; World Bank, 1995; Wen, 1997; Wen and King, 1998; Sachs and Warner, 1999), there are two kinds of economic development: population push and transaction pull. A high population density and low per capita endowment of natural resources of a country would make the benefit from adoption of advanced technology and development in infrastructure more significant than in an economy with a low population density and high per capita resource endowment. In addition, a large population implies great scope for coordinating division of labour and thus evolution in division of labour and chances of innovation based on development of specialized knowledge. Improvement in infrastructures including the legal, transport and telecommunication systems can reduce unit transaction costs and promote fast productivity progress based on evolution in division of labour and accumulation of knowledge. But to what extent improvement in the transport system can improve unit transaction efficiency will depend on the location of economic agents involved in transactions. Furthermore, there is an essential difference between a simple adoption of advanced technology and innovation and invention based on specialization and evolution in division of labour: the former is limited by availability of advanced technology outside the economy, while the latter would provide unlimited sources of technological progress based on accumulation of total knowledge with individual specialization and evolution in division of labour.[26] Owing to the globalization trend and public goods character of human knowledge, the distinction between development based on simple adoption of advanced technology and the development based on innovation and invention implies that the former would make the economy always a follower in the global economy, while the latter could have a chance of taking over technology leadership in the global economy in the future.

5   CONCLUSIONS

Despite the fact that there are many urgent problems in the economy, China's entrance to the WTO is very likely to bring into China rigorous market competition and a faster GDP growth due to great scope for further economic development. These outcomes depend on how fast the legal system and social security system can be improved. Although some economists (for example, Maddison, 1998) pointed out that the genuine annual growth rate of China's GDP could be exaggerated by 2 to 3 per cent, China's economy in terms of GDP will grow faster than its present speed as long as its legal enforcement and social security systems can be quickly improved. However, how fast China's national wealth can grow and whether China will always be a follower in the global economy will depend on whether there will be substantial changes in China's capital allocation mechanism and whether there will be accelerated development of the domestic private enterprises before China opens its economy wide to the rest of the world.

NOTES

1. The Chinese government launched a contractionary policy (a so-called rectification and adjustment programme) in July 1993 after the overheating in investment in 1992 and 1993. We see the effect of the policy on the economy in 1995. By 1997, it was claimed that the soft landing of the economy had been accomplished.
2. See Naughton (1994), Lin (1995), Jefferson and Singh (1999), for example.
3. The dual track system introduced in 1984 regulates that the output under plan should be sold at the planned price and the output beyond plan can be sold at floating prices within 20 per cent differences from the planned price.
4. See Jefferson *et al.* (1999), Duncan and Huang (1998) and Wu (1996) for a detailed survey.
5. See Jefferson *et al.* (1999), Zheng *et al.* (1998) and Murakmi *et al.* (1994).
6. See Jefferson *et al.* (1999), Wen *et al.* (1998) and Murakmi *et al.* (1994).
7. From bilateral negotiation documents between China and the United States, China and Australia, China and European Countries for China to join WTO, we can see that China will open more industries to foreign investment and cut tariffs of agricultural and industrial products to a large extent.
8. Many economists cast doubt on China's prospects of sustained economic growth after examining investment behaviour in China. See Rawski (1999) for example.
9. According to Wen (1993), there were experiments in some counties of China which tried to increase farm operation scale through government intervention. Plots were taken away from farmers before expiration of contracts and reassigned to a small number of pre-selected farm households. Governments at county or township level provided them with large subsidies in order to keep them in business. However, it should be noted that this inefficiency from increased land scale would be different from consequences of increase in production scale endogenized through market process if there were a well established land, capital and labour market. Hayek stressed that consequences generated from market system are not things that policies can purport to achieve as the needs of everybody change over time. Technically, restrictions on factor distributions make feasible production smaller and usually make best available choice suboptimal.
10. There were the Economic Contract Law, the Law on Economic Contract Involving Foreign Business and the Technology Contract Law of the People's Republic of China. However, none of them can be compared with a unified contract law. With the Contract Law of the People's Republic of China being effective from 1 October 1999 on, the former three contract laws in specific areas have been abandoned.
11. According to the growth experience of the 13 countries studied in Kuznets (1966), in the industrialization process, when the share of the primary industry in GDP declines, there will be significant increase in the share of the secondary industry, while the share of the tertiary industry will vary slightly, in other words, the secondary industry will experience the fastest growth while the tertiary industry grows with a speed similar to the GDP growth rate. However, in the post-industrialization period, the tertiary industry should grow with the highest speed and become the largest sector in the economy.
12. See Liu, *et al.* (1999) for example.
13. The other restrictive factors include the welfare benefits, such as low-priced housing, medical subsidies and cheaper tuition to urban citizens. Although farmers have the right to claim residual income from using the arable land under the HRS, they will not only lose the benefit from using the arable land, but also have no right to enjoy the welfare benefits of urban citizens if, as rural citizens, they migrate to urban areas without urban household registration.
14. See *Township and Village Owned Enterprises' Yearbook of China*, 1997.

15.	Of the 108 billion yuan treasury bonds outside the budget, 100 billion were issued by the Department of Finance as special bonds to commercial banks. Commercial banks increased 100 billion yuan investment loans correspondingly.
16.	See the State Council of the People's Republic of China (1999).
17.	Figures given in the *Statistical Yearbook of China*, 1999 are rather different. According to the *Statistical Yearbook*, the growth rate of total investment in fixed assets was 13·9 per cent in 1998, while the growth rate of total investment in fixed assets by the state-owned units was 17·4 per cent. The growth rate of total investment in fixed assets by collectively owned units, individuals and other types of ownership were 8·9, 9·2 and 11·6 per cent, respectively.
18.	As shown in the empirical work done by Lin and Chen (forthcoming) since firm size is an important determinant of CEOs' total emolument in China's stock-listing companies, managers of SOEs would have a strong incentive to lobby and bargain for more financial resources instead of spending their efforts on reducing production costs.
19.	Only in April 2000, did seven foreign banks obtain permits for Renminbi (Chinese currency) business.
20.	For a detailed description of the way the bad loans were formed, how serious the bad loan problem is in the economy and an evaluation of the approach adopted by China to solve it, see Bonin and Huang (2000).
21.	I am not trying to put foreign investment and domestic private investment on an equal footing here. Foreign investment can bring advanced management knowledge, although advanced technology can be purchased in both kinds of investment. However, domestic capital should be utilized efficiently when there is a need to mobilize international capital.
22.	By way of example, we see in China that some SOEs are making apparent losses due to imperfect accounting measures. Furthermore, owing to ideological obstacles, it is almost impossible for the government to design and adopt an incentive mechanism to stimulate managers of SOEs to behave in the interest of owners. As a result, managers of SOEs are more interested in rent-seeking and fringe benefits.
23.	Many publications on rent-seeking behaviour in China do point out that it is the ownership and institution setting during the transition which provides a lot of rent-seeking opportunities. To fight bribery, the legal channel is not the only approach. To stock-list state banks and let the government withdraw from business operation will reduce rent-seeking opportunities to a great extent.
24.	For the detailed story, see Zhu (1997).
25.	See Li (1996).
26.	It is this difference that makes Krugman call the four small Asian dragons 'paper tigers'.

REFERENCES

The Asia Pacific School of Economics and Management (APSEM), the Australian National University (2000), 'China Private Enterprise Study', mimeo, a Technical Report, APSEM, ANU.

Bai, C., D. Li, and Y. Wang, (1997), 'Enterprise productivity and efficiency: when is up really down?', *Journal of Comparative Economics*, 24(3), 265–80.

Bonin, J. and Y. Huang (2000), 'Dealing with the Bad Loans of the Chinese Banks', working paper, Economics Department, Wesleyan University and Research School of Asian and Pacific Studies, Australian National University.

Boserup, E. (1981), *Population and Technological Change, A Study of Long-Term Trends*, Chicago: University of Chicago Press.

Cecen, A.A. (1991), 'Optimal growth with exhaustible resources and foreign technology in a small open economy', *Journal of Economic Development*, 16(2), 169–80.

Chandler, A.D. Jr. (1990), *Scale and Scope*, Cambridge, Mass.: Harvard University Press.

CIESIN (2000), 'Priority Programme for China's Agenda 21', http://sedac.ciesin.org/china/policy/acca21.

Dong, F. and Z. Tang (1992), *Reform of China's State Owned Enterprises: Institutions and Efficiency*, Beijing: China Planning Press (in Chinese).

Duncan, R. and Y. Huang (1998), *Reform of State-owned Enterprises in China: Autonomy, Incentive and Competition*, Canberra: NCDS Asian Pacific Press, ANU.

The Editing Committee of the 'Township and village owned enterprises' Yearbook of China' (1997, 1998), *Township and Village Owned Enterprises' Yearbook of China*, Beijing: the Chinese Agricultural Publishing House.

Harris, N. and D. Lockwood (1997), 'The war-making state and privatization', *Journal of Development Studies*, 33(5), 597–634.

Hartwick, J.M. (1995), 'Constant consumption paths in open economies with exhaustible resources', *Review of International Economics*, 3(3), 275–83.

Herfindahl, O.C. and A.V. Kneese (1967), 'Depletion and Economic Theory', in M.M. Gaffney (ed.), *Extractive Resources and Taxation*, Madison, Wis.: University of Wisconsin Press, pp. 63–90.

Hotelling, H. (1931), 'The economics of exhaustible resources', *Journal of Political Economy*, 38, 137–75.

Jefferson, G.H. and I. Singh (1999), *Enterprise Reform in China: Ownership, Transition and Performance*, Oxford: Oxford University Press.

Jefferson, G.H., I. Singh, J. Xing and S. Zhang (1999), 'China's Industrial Performance: A Review of Recent Findings', in G.H. Jefferson and I. Singh (eds), *Enterprise Reform in China: Ownership, Transition and Performance*, Oxford: Oxford University Press, 1999, pp. 127–52.

Jin, H. and Y. Qian (1998), 'Public vs. Private Ownership of Firms: Evidence from Rural China', *Quarterly Journal of Economics*, 113(3), 773–808.

Kemp, M. and N.V. Long (eds) (1980), *Exhaustible Resources, Optimality and Trade*, Amsterdam: North-Holland.

Kemp, M. and N.V. Long (eds) (1984), *Essays in the Economics of Exhaustible Resources*, Amsterdam: North-Holland.

Khan, A.R., G. Griffin and C. Riskin (1999), 'Income Distribution in Urban China During the Period of Economic Reform and Globalization', *Americam Economic Review*, 89(2), 296–300.

King, S. and R. Pitchford (1998), 'A Normative Theory of Private versus Public Asset Ownership', work in progress, Department of Economics, University of Melbourne and Faculty of Economics, ANU.

Krugman, P. (1994), 'The maths of Asia's miracle', *Foreign Affairs*, 73(6), 63–78.

Kuznets, S. (1966), *Modern Economic Growth – Rate, Structure, and Spread*, New Haven: Yale University Press.

Levin, R.A. (1993), 'Optimal Depletion of an Exhaustible Resource under Changing Market Structure', PhD dissertation, University of New Mexico.

Li, D. (1996), 'A theory of ambiguous property rights in transition economies: the case of the Chinese non-state sector', *Journal of Comparative Economics*, 23(1), 1–19.

Li, S. (1999), 'Changing Income Distribution in China', in R. Garnaut and L. Song (eds), *China: Twenty Years of Economic Reform*, Canberra: Asia Pacific Press, pp. 169–184.

Liew, L.H. (1993), 'Rent-seeking and the two-track price system in China', *Policy Choice,* 359–75.

Lin, J.Y. (1992), 'Rural reform and agricultural growth in China', *The American Economic Review*, 82(1), 34–51.

Lin, J.Y. (1995), 'Endowments, technology, and factor markets: a natural experiment of induced institutional innovation from China's rural reform', *American Journal of Agricultural Economics*, 77(2), 231–42.

Lin, S. and Z. Chen (forthcoming), 'State-owned Enterprise Reform, Ownership Structure and Managerial Incentive', in P. Lloyd and X. Zhang (eds), *China in Global Economy*, London: Edward Elgar.

Liu, G.G., L.L. Wang and J.W. Li (1999), *China in Year 2000: Analysis on the Economic Situation and Economic Forecast* (Economic Blue Book), Beijing: The Publishing House of Chinese Social Science.

Maddison, A. (1998), *Chinese Economic Performance in the Long Run*, Paris/Washington, DC: OECD.

Malthus, T.R. (1798) (1966), *First Essay on Population*, London: Macmillan.

Murakami, N., D. Liu and K. Otsuka (1994), 'Technical and allocative efficiency among socialist enterprises: the case of the garment industry in China', *Journal of Comparative Economics*, 19(3), 410–33.

Murphy, K., A. Shleifer and R. Vishny (1989), 'Industrialization and the big push', *Journal of Political Economy*, 97, 1003–26.

National Statistics Bureau of the PRC (1997), *Market Statistical Yearbook of China*, Beijing: China Statistical Publishing House.

National Statistics Bureau of the PRC (various years), *China Statistical Yearbook of Investment in Fixed Assets*, Beijing: China Statistical Publishing House.

National Statistics Bureau of the PRC (various years), *Statistical Yearbook of China*, Beijing: China Statistical Publishing House.

Naughton, B. (1994), *Growing Out of Plan: Chinese Economic Reform, 1978–1993*, New York: Cambridge University Press.

Rawski, T.G. (1999), 'The Political Economy of China's Declining Growth', paper presented at 11th Annual International Conference of the Chinese Economic Studies Association of Australia, Melbourne, University of Melbourne.

Ray, D. (1984), 'Survival, growth and technical progress in a small resource-importing economy', *International Economic Review*, 25(2), 275–95.

Ricardo, D. (1895) (1969), *The Principles of Political Economy and Taxation*, 3rd edn, London: Dent.

The Royal Economic Society (1974), *Review of Economic Studies, Symposium on the Economics of Exhaustible Resources*, Oxford: Blackwell.

Sachs, J. and A. Warner (1999), 'The big push, natural resource booms and growth', *Journal of Development Economics*, 59(1), 43–76.

Sachs, J. and W.T. Woo (1997), 'Understanding China's Economic Performance', NBER Working Paper, 5935, February.

Schumpeter, J.A. (1943), *Capitalism, Socialism and Democracy,* London: Allen & Unwin.

Scott, A. (1955), *Natural Resources: The Economics of Conservation*, Toronto: University of Toronto Press.

The State Council of the People's Republic of China (1981–99), *Gazette of the State Council of the People's Republic of China*, various issues, the General Office of the State Council of the People's Republic of China, Beijing.

The Third National Industrial Census Office (1997), *The Data of the Third National*

Industrial Census of the People's Republic of China in 1995, Summary and Industry Volume, Beijing: Chinese Statistical Publishing House.

Tinari, F.D. and D.K.K. Lam (1991), 'China's Resistance to Economic Reforms', *Contemporary Policy Issues*, 9(3), 82–92.

Wen, G.J. (1993), 'Total factor productivity change in China's farming sector: 1952–1989', *Economic Development and Cultural Change*, 42(1), 1–41.

Wen, M. (1997), 'Infrastructure and evolution in division of labour', *Review of Development Economics*, 1(2), 191–207.

Wen, M. and S. King (1998), 'Push or Pull? The Relationship beween Development, Trade and Resource Endowment', working paper no. 653, Department of Economics, University of Melbourne.

Wen, M. and X. Zhang (forthcoming), 'Capital Allocation in China', in P. Lloyd and X. Zhang (eds), *Modelling the Chinese Economy*, London: Edward Elgar.

Wen, M., D. Li and P. Lloyd (1998), 'Ownership and Technical Efficiency: A Cross-section Study on the Third Industrial Census of China', Asian Economics Center working paper no. 5, Department of Economics, University of Melbourne.

The World Bank (1995), *World Development Report 1995: Workers in an Integrating World*, Oxford: Oxford University Press.

Wu, Y. (1995), 'Productivity growth, technological progress, and technical efficiency change in China: a three-sector analysis', *Journal of Comparative Economics*, 21, 207–29.

Wu, Y. (1996), *Productivity Performance in Chinese Enterprises: An Empirical Study*, New York: St. Martin's Press.

Xu, D. and G. Wen (eds) (1996), *Reform of China's State-owned Enterprises*, Beijing: China Economy Press (in Chinese).

Yang, X. (1998), *The Principle of Economics*, Beijing: The Publishing House of Chinese Social Science.

Yang, X. and Y.K. Ng (1993), *Specialization and Economic Organization – A New Classical Microeconomic Framework*, Amsterdam: North-Holland.

Yang, X. and R. Rice (1994), 'An Equilibrium Model Endogenizing the Emergence of a Dual Structure between the Urban and Rural Sectors', *Journal of Urban Economics*, 25, 346–68.

Yao, S.T. (1997), 'Corruption and Anti-corruption Movement: The Modelling and Analysis of the Situation in China', *Australian Economic Papers*, 36, 156–65.

Zhang, W. (1999), *The Theory of the Firm and China's Enterprise Reforms*, Beijing: Peking University Press (in Chinese).

Zheng, J., X. Liu and A. Bigsten (1998), 'Ownership Structure and Determinants of Technical Efficiency: An Application of Data Envelopment Analysis to Chinese Enterprises (1986–1990)', *Journal of Comparative Economics*, 26, 465–84.

Zhu, W. (1997), *China's Economy with Excess Capacity*, Hong Kong: Wide Angle Press Ltd.

10. The crisis of success and feedback quality in managing economic crisis

Xiaokai Yang

1 INTRODUCTION

There are two different ways to explain the Asian financial crisis. One is to attribute this crisis to moral hazard caused by the state monopoly of the banking sector and cronyism. The other emphasizes financial insurance provided by the International Monetary Fund (IMF) assistance funds (a review of the two approaches can be found in Radelet and Sachs, 1998; Stiglitz, 1998). The first method cannot explain why China, which has serious moral hazard caused by state-owned firms and the state monopoly of the financial sector, was not seriously affected by the Asian financial crisis and why the financial crisis in South Korea was partly caused by the liberalization reforms. The second method, by playing down the role of moral hazard in causing the financial crisis, cannot explain why Taiwan, which successfully reduced moral hazard by liberalizing the financial sector, prior to the liberalization of international capital flows, was not seriously affected by the Asian financial crisis either (Shea and Yang, 1994).

This chapter addresses the questions using several general equilibrium models with endogenous network size of division of labour. In section 2, we review two general equilibrium models that formalize the notion of the crisis of success. In the models with endogenous network size of division of labour, the trade-off between positive network effects of division of labour on aggregate productivity and reliability of the network implies that, as the risk for each transaction declines, the equilibrium network of division of labour will expand. The enlarged network of interdependent trade partners will raise aggregate productivity, on the one hand, and reduce coordination reliability of the network of industrial linkages, on the other. Hence increasing aggregate risk of coordination failure of the expanding network of division of labour is a consequence of successful economic development. The increasing aggregate risk of coordination failure of the trade network may occur in the absence of failure of fundamental institutions. In other words, the increasing aggregate risk of a financial crisis might be called a crisis of success. In section 3, we review two Lio models with endogenous networks of division of labour and insurance. The models specify the trade-off between positive effects of insurance in reducing risk of coordination failure and moral hazard caused by the insurance to investigate the efficient balance of the trade-offs among economies of division of labour, coordination reliability and moral hazard. The models illustrate that each of the two sides of the policy debate on the Asian financial crisis should be complemented by its opponent. In section 4, we use a cobweb model with endogenous network size of division of labour to formalize the trade-off between incentive provision generated by sensitive feedback and stability of the feedback mechanism.

2 TRADE-OFFS BETWEEN RELIABILITY AND THE POSITIVE NETWORK EFFECTS OF DIVISION OF LABOUR

In this section, we use a number of Smithian models of endogenous network size of division of labour to study the trade-offs among positive network effects of division of labour on aggregate productivity and coordination reliability of the network. We first consider the Yang and Wills model (1990) which introduces a transaction risk into each transaction in a model of endogenous specialization. We then consider a model with two alternative ways to reduce aggregate transaction risk. One of these reduces transaction risk by deepening an incumbent trade relationship and the other by broadening potential trade relationships.

The Yang–Wills model specifies trade-offs among positive network effects of division of labour on aggregate productivity, transport costs and aggregate transaction risk. The story behind the algebra runs as follows. There are economies of specialization for many *ex ante* identical consumer-producers. This implies that, if each consumer-producer specializes in producing a single good and then exchanges it for all other goods from other specialists, aggregate productivity for the economy is high, but each individual has to trade with many different specialists. If each individual self-provides all goods, aggregate productivity is low, but no transactions and related costs occur. In addition to the trade-off between economies of division of labour and transport costs, each transaction involves a risk of delivery failure. A Cobb–Douglas utility function implies that utility is zero if the amount of any goods consumed is zero. Hence, if an individual purchases $n-1$ goods and the risk of delivery failure of each good is $1-\theta$, then the total risk for her or him to receive 0 utility is $(1-\theta)^{n-1}$. As transport efficiency is improved, the scope for trading off economies of division of labour against transport costs and transaction risk is enlarged, so that the equilibrium network of division of labour and related extent of the market expand, productivity increases and the efficient aggregate risk of coordination increases. If the risk of coordination failure for each transaction is reduced owing to, say, more secured property rights, the extent of the market, the network size of division of labour, and productivity will rise too. However, if the direct positive effect of the higher reliability of each transaction on the aggregate reliability of the network of division of labour is outweighed by its indirect negative effects through increasing the number of transactions, the aggregate reliability decreases.

We present a simplified version of the Yang–Wills model. Consider an economy with M *ex ante* identical consumer-producers. The decision problem for a person selling good i is:

Max: $V_i \equiv Eu_i = u_i P + 0(1 - P)$ (expected utility)

s.t. $u_i = x_i (kx_r^d)^{n-1} x_j^{m-n}$ (utility function)

   $P = \theta^{n-1}$ (reliability of $n - 1$ transactions)   (10.1)

   $x_i + x_i^s = l_i - \alpha, \, x_j = l_j - \alpha$ (production function)

   $l_i + (m - n)l_j = 1$ (endowment constraint of time)

   $p_i x_i^s = (n - 1)p_r x_r^d$ (budget constraint)

where $x_i, x_j, x_i^s, x_i^d, l_i, l_j, n, P$ are decision variables, θ and k are parameters, p_i is the price of good i. $V = Eu_i$ is expected utility, which is a weighted average of u_i and 0, where the weights are P and $1 - P$, respectively. We have used the symmetry of the model; that is, tastes and production and transaction conditions are the same for all goods. Hence the amounts of goods purchased, x_r^d, are the same for all r, the amounts of self-provided goods, x_j, and the amounts of labour allocated to the production of non-traded goods, l_j, are the same for all j. Coordination reliability of division of labour P is the probability that all goods purchased are received; $1 - \theta$ is the probability that the individual fails to receive a good from a purchase contract. We assume that the failure of a seller to deliver the good to the buyer is an event that is independent of the failure of any of the other goods. Therefore θ is the probability that the buyer receives the good and $P = \theta^{n-1}$ is the probability that she or he receives all $n - 1$ goods purchased. $1 - P$ is the probability that she or he fails to receive at least one of all goods that she or he buys. Since for the Cobb–Douglas utility function an individual's utility is zero if the quantity of any good consumed is zero, a consumer-producer will receive 0 utility at probability $1 - P$ and receives u_i at probability P.

α in the production functions is a fixed learning cost in each activity, l_i and l_j are respectively the amount of labour allocated to produce the traded good i and the non-traded goods j. We may call l_i an individual's level of specialization.

Assume that prices are sorted out through a Nash bargaining mechanism which generates the same utility between *ex ante* identical individuals who have the same disagreement point. As shown by Yang and Wills (1990), this establishes the utility equalization conditions which, together with the market clearing conditions, will generate the same equilibrium as in a Walrasian regime. The equilibrium has equal prices of all traded goods and an equal number of sellers for each traded good, $N = M/n$, because of symmetry. With these results, the equilibrium values of decision variables can be solved as follows.

For any $i = 1, 2 \ldots, n$

$$x_i = x_r^d = x_j = [1 - \alpha(m - n + 1)]/m \,\forall r \in R, j \in J$$
$$x_i^s = (n - 1)[1 - \alpha(m - n + 1)]/m$$
$$l_i = \alpha + (n/m)[1 - \alpha\,(m - n + 1)] \tag{10.2}$$
$$P = \theta^{n-1}$$
$$V \equiv Eu_i = \{1 - \alpha(m - n + 1)/m\}^m(k\theta)^{n-1}$$
$$n = m + 1 - (1/\alpha) - [m/(\ln k + 1n\theta)] \tag{10.3}$$

The comparative statics of the general equilibrium are:

$$dn/d\theta > 0, \quad dn/dk > 0, \tag{10.4a}$$
$$dP/d\theta = (\partial P/\partial\theta) + (\partial P/\partial n)(dn/d\theta) < 0, \text{ if and only if}$$
$$(\partial P/\partial\theta) < |(\partial P/\partial n)(dn/d\theta)| \tag{10.4b}$$
$$dP/dk = (dP/dn)(dn/dk) < 0 \tag{10.4c}$$
$$dV/d\theta = \partial V/\partial\theta > 0, \quad dV/dk = \partial V/\partial k > 0. \tag{10.4d}$$
$$dl_i/d\theta = (dl_i/dn)(dn/d\theta) > 0, \quad dl_i/dk = (dl_i/dn)(dn/dk) > 0, \tag{10.4e}$$
$$dx_i^s/d\theta = (dx_i^s/dn)(dn/d\theta) > 0, dx_i^s/dk = (dx_i^s/dn)(dn/dk) > 0 \tag{10.4f}$$
$$dN/d\theta = (dN/dn)(dn/d\theta) < 0, \quad dN/dk = (dN/dn)(dn/dk) > 0 \tag{10.4g}$$

(10.4a) implies that the equilibrium number of traded goods, n, which represents the equilibrium level of division of labour, increases as the reliability of each transaction increases, or as the anticipated risk of coordination failure of each transaction caused by endogenous transaction costs falls.

(10.4b) implies that, as the reliability of each transaction rises, total reliability P would fall if the negative effect of the increase in θ, $(\partial P/\partial n)(dn/d\theta)$, outweighs its positive effect, $\partial P/\partial\theta$. Otherwise, total reliability rises. Here, $(\partial P/\partial n) < 0$ and $(dn/d\theta) > 0$. Since $1 - P$ can be considered as aggregate risk of coordination failure caused by anticipated endogenous transaction costs, (10.4b) can be interpreted in another way. It means that total endogenous transaction costs in terms of the aggregate risk increase as the endogenous transaction cost, $1 - \theta$, for each transaction falls if the positive effect of the fall on the total endogenous transaction costs through its impact on the number of transactions outweighs its direct negative effect on total endogenous transaction costs. Otherwise, total endogenous transaction costs decrease with the endogenous transaction cost for each transaction. Because of the connection between total endogenous transaction costs and the degree of softness of the budget constraint, this result implies that the budget constraint may become increasingly soft as the endogenous transaction cost for each transaction falls.

(10.4c) implies that, as the exogenous transaction cost coefficient, $1 - k$, is reduced, or as transaction efficiency k rises, total anticipated endogenous transaction costs $1 - P$, or the aggregate risk of coordination failure, increases (or aggregate reliability P falls). This is because, as exogenous transaction efficiency is improved, the benefit of increasing division of labour rises in comparison to increasing endogenous and exogenous transaction costs, so that total endogenous transaction costs may increase to the degree that the increased endogenous transaction costs are outweighed by the increased economies of division of labour that are exploited.

(10.4d) means that, as the endogenous transaction cost for each transaction falls (or as the coordination reliability for each transaction rises), or as exogenous transaction efficiency is improved, expected real income V goes up. We have used the envelope theorem to get this result.

(10.4e) and (10.4f) imply that, as the reliability of each transaction r rises, or as exogenous transaction efficiency k is improved, each individual's level of specialization and per capita trade volume all go up. Because of economies of specialization, the result implies that labour productivity of each traded good goes up and the degree of self-sufficiency falls.

(10.4g) implies that, as the reliability of each transaction θ goes up (or as the anticipated endogenous transaction cost for each transaction falls), or as exogenous transaction efficiency is improved, the number of sellers of each traded good, which represents the degree of competition, goes down. This results in a fall of aggregate reliability and a rise in total anticipated endogenous transaction costs.

This prediction invalidates the belief that more secured property rights and reduced transaction risk for each transaction will always reduce the aggregate risk of coordination failure that results in economic crises like the Great Depression in the 1930s and the Asian financial crisis in 1997. A high aggregate risk of coordination failure can be interpreted as a risk of mass unemployment as all individuals will be forced to choose autarky when coordination of the division of labour breaks down. Hence it is possible that more secured property rights promote economic development, on the one hand, and increase the aggregate risk of economic crisis, on the other. A devastating consequence of the Great Depression was the major reason it gave for communism to spread in many countries after World War II. But in the long run, the striking difference in development performance between the capitalist system and the Soviet-style system shows that the cost of economic development caused by the greater aggregate risk of coordination failure associated with a large network of division of labour may be worth paying. From the experience of the recent Asian financial crisis, we may obtain a better understanding of the trade-off between the positive effect of the evolution of the division of labour on economic development and its effect on the risk of coordination failure.

A more general version of the model with endogenous θ can be found in Yang and Wills (1990) or in Yang and Ng (1993, ch. 10). The endogenization of θ is a feature of the economic literature on the trade-off between economies of division of labour and coordination reliability that distinguishes this literature from the engineering literature on reliability. A survey on the literature of endogenous specialization can be found in Yang and Ng (1998).

In particular, if the risk of coordination failure for each transaction can be reduced by inputting resources, that risk then becomes an endogenous decision variable. The risk of coordination failure of division of labour can be reduced by allocating resources to the specification and enforcement of contractual terms related to the transactions at the cost of rising exogenous transaction costs in specifying and enforcing property rights. We may consider the welfare losses caused by the risk of coordination failure as anticipated endogenous transaction costs caused by the opportunistic behavior. Thus we have a trade-off between the exogenous transaction costs of specifying and enforcing property rights and endogenous transaction costs. We can then see that the efficient trade-off between endogenous and exogenous transaction costs in the market place may involve imperfect specification and enforcement of property rights. The trade-off between exogenous and endogenous transaction costs is referred to by Milgrom and Roberts (1992, pp.277, 377) as the trade-off between influencing cost and distortions caused by rigid rules reducing employees' activities to influence the decisions of a manager.

Sachs and Yang (2000, ch. 10) consider two ways to reduce risk of coordination failure or to reduce the endogenous transaction costs in each transaction. The first is to allocate more resources to reducing the risk of coordination failure of each incumbent transaction. The second is to allocate more resources to cultivating more potential relationships which are in parallel connection with an incumbent relationship. This will increase the number of parallel connections for each incumbent transaction and reduce the risk of coordination failure of the transaction. In other words, extensive connections with many potential partners yields competitive pressure on the incumbent partner, so that the individual can turn to one of the potential partners when the incumbent one fails to deliver what the person needs. Mathematically, the total risk of coordination failure of each transaction is $(1 - \theta)^N$ when there are N potential trade partners and each of their deliveries is realized with probability θ. Then total reliability of each transaction $P = 1 - (1 - \theta)^N$ can be raised either by reducing the risk of coordination failure with the incumbent partner, $1 - \theta$, or by increasing the number of potential partners, N. Note that θ is between 0 and 1 and P increases as θ or N increases.

For a non-trivial transaction cost in keeping a potential relationship, there is a trade-off between costs in deepening incumbent relationships and costs in broadening potential trade connections. Hence each buyer's efficient number of potential sellers of a good with whom she or he keeps in touch may be smaller than the number of all sellers of the good in the market. Sachs and Yang (ibid.) use a model of endogenous specialization to formalize this trade-off in addition to the trade-off between economies of division of labour and all kinds of transaction costs. The story behind the algebra runs as follows.

The inframarginal comparative statics of general equilibrium in the Sachs and Yang model (2000) generate the following interesting results. As the parameter that represents efficiency in specifying and enforcing property rights is increased, the equilibrium level of division of labour and per capita real income go up. But two types of changes in transaction reliability may take place in response to improvement in specification and enforcement efficiency. Individuals can either divert resources from specification and enforcement to raising the level of division of labour in production, or allocate the resources that are saved by the more effective specification and enforcement of rights to raising the degree of precision of the specification and enforcement of property rights in each transaction. These two responses are to some extent substitutes in raising per capita real income.

If the first generates a greater net benefit than the second, an improvement in specification and enforcement efficiency will generate a lower reliability of each transaction and thereby a higher aggregate risk of coordination failure when it promotes division of labour and economic development. If the second method is better, then an improvement in specification and enforcement efficiency will raise the level of division of labour and the reliability of each transaction, meanwhile generating a higher or a lower aggregate risk of coordinate failure. Its effect on aggregate risk of coordination failure is parameter value-dependent since the positive effect of an increase in the number of transactions on the aggregate risk may or may not outweigh the negative effect of an increase in the reliability of each transaction.

For a large value of the cost coefficient for deepening the incumbent relation relative to the cost coefficient for widening potential relations, 'classical contracts' with many potential trading partners (similar to perfect competition) may occur at equilibrium. For a small value of the deepening cost coefficient, 'relational contracts' without potentially alternative trading partners may occur at equilibrium. Again, this model shows that, as the efficiency coefficient of deepening incumbent trade relationships or that of broadening potential trade relationships increases, aggregate productivity and aggregate risk of coordination failure of a larger network of division of labour will increase side by side.

3   THE TRADE-OFF BETWEEN COORDINATION RELIABILITY AND MORAL HAZARD CAUSED BY INSURANCE

Another institution that can be used to reduce the risk of coordination failure of a large network of division of labour is insurance. In this section, we shall use Lio's model of endogenous specialization to show why insurance can promote division of labour and economic development. Then the trade-off between risk sharing and incentive provision is introduced to investigate the function of incomplete insurance in reducing endogenous transaction costs caused by moral hazard and in promoting economic development. Since incentive provision is associated with well-specified and enforced property rights, we have a trade-off between the positive effect of insurance on reliability of network of division of labour and the negative effect of insurance on the precision of enforcement of property rights. This trade-off implies that development implications of property rights are much more complicated than many economists have realized.

The Lio model (1996, 1998) shows that complete insurance can alleviate the adverse effect of transaction risk on expected utility, thereby increasing the equilibrium level of division of labour and related aggregate productivity and the efficient aggregate risk of coordination failure. In other words, insurance may increase rather than decrease aggregate risk of a financial crisis.

Consider the model in section 2. In each transaction, transaction efficiency k takes on a great value at probability θ and a small value at probability $1 - \theta$. The transaction risk may be caused by traffic accidents or by opportunistic behaviour that takes place with a probability. Moreover, we assume that all consumer-producers are risk-averse to the same degree, or they have *ex ante* identical strictly concave utility functions. In the model, there is a trade-off between economies of division of labour and coordination reliability, in addition to a trade-off between economies of division of labour and exogenous transaction costs.

If an insurance company collects a premium from each individual and compensates her or him in the event of low transaction efficiency, each individual will have the weighted average of the two levels of transaction efficiency for certain by pooling risk. Such an institution of insurance will certainly promote division of labour and productivity progress if all individuals are risk-averse. It will promote many other structural changes associated with the evolution in division of labour. More interestingly, the improved transaction conditions enlarge the scope for trading off economies of division of labour against transaction risk, so that the equilibrium and efficient aggregate risk of coordination failure increase. Also a decrease in the risk of coordination failure for each transaction may increase the efficient aggregate risk of coordination failure for the same reason. This story is formalized in the following Lio model (1998). The decision problem for each consumer-producer selling good i is specified as follows.

Max: $E u_i = E \{x_i \Pi_{r \in R}(k_r x_r^d) \Pi_{\in J} x_j\}^{1/\rho}$ (expected utility)

s.t. $x_i + x_i^s = l_i - \alpha, \ x_j = l_j - \alpha$ (production functions)

$l_i + (m - n)l_j = 1$ (endowment constraint) (10.5)

$p_i x_i^s = (n - 1)p_r x_r^d$ (budget constraint)

where x_i is the amount of good i self-provided, x_r^d is the amount of good r purchased, k_r is the transaction efficiency coefficient for good r, R is the set of $n - 1$ goods purchased, J is the set of $m - n$ non-traded goods, n is the number of traded goods, x_j is the self-provided amount of non-traded good j, x_i^s is the amount of good i sold, l_i and l_j are respective levels of specialization in producing goods i and j, and p_i and p_r are respective prices of good i and r. It is assumed that each individual is endowed with one unit of non-leisure time; α is the fixed learning cost in each production activity. We will see later that parameter $\rho > 1$ relates to the degree of risk aversion. The larger the value of ρ, the more risk-averse is the individual, since a larger value of ρ implies a more concave utility function. The endowment constraint and the budget constraint in (10.5) are obtained using the symmetry.

The transaction efficiency coefficient is

$$k_r = \begin{cases} k_H \text{ with } \theta \\ k_L \text{ with } 1 - \theta \end{cases} \qquad (10.6)$$

where $\theta \in (0, 1)$ is the probability that transaction efficiency is high, $k_H > k_L$, $r \in R$. That is, there is transaction risk. It is not difficult to see that a special case of the Lio model for $\rho = 1$, $k_L = 0$ is the model in section 2. Inserting all constraints into the utility function, the constrained maximization problem in (10.5) can be converted to a non-constrained maximization problem.

$$\text{Max: } Eu_i = WP, \ P \equiv E(\Pi_{r \in R} k_r)^{1/\rho} \qquad (10.7a)$$

where x_i^s, l_i and n are decision variables, P can be interpreted as the aggregate reliability, or $1 - P$ can be interpreted as the aggregate transaction risk, and

$$W \equiv \{(l_i - \alpha - x_i^s) \ [x_i^s/(n - 1)]^{n-1} \ [(1 - l_i)/(m - n) - \alpha]^{m-n}\}^{1/\rho}. \qquad (10.7b)$$

Also, it can be shown, using symmetry, that $p_i/p_r = 1$ in equilibrium.

The number of k_r is $n - 1$. Suppose that s of them take on value k_H and $n - 1 - s$ of them take on value k_L, while s can take on value from 1 to $n - 1$.

Here, k_H takes place with probability θ and k_L takes place with probability $1 - \theta$. Therefore the $n - 1$ of k_r follows a binomial distribution. The probability for $n - s$ of k_r to take on value k_H and for $s - 1$ of k_r to take on value k_L is

$$P_s = C_{n-1}^{s-1} \theta^{n-s} (1 - \theta)^{s-1} \tag{10.8}$$

where C_{n-1}^{s-1} is $s - 1$ combinations of $n - 1$ elements. Following a binomial formula, it can be shown that

$$
\begin{aligned}
P &= E \left(\Pi_{r \in R} k_r \right)^{1/\rho} = \Sigma_{s=1}^{n-1} P_s (k_H^{n-s} k_L^{s-1})^{1/\rho} \\
&= C_{n-1}^0 \theta^{n-1} k_H^{(n-1)/\rho} + C_{n-1}^1 \theta^{n-2} (1 - \theta) k_H^{(n-2)/\rho} k_L^{1/\rho} + \\
&\quad \ldots + [C_{n-1}^{n-1} (1 - \theta)^{n-1} k_L^{(n-1)/\rho}] \\
&= [\theta k_H^{1/\rho} + (1 - \theta) k_L^{1/\rho}]^{n-1}
\end{aligned}
\tag{10.9}
$$

where P_s is given by (10.8) and the final equality in (10.9) is given by the binomial formula. Having inserted (10.9) into (10.7), we can express Eu_i as a function of l_i, x_i^s and n. Letting the derivatives of Eu_i with respect to the three variables equal 0 yields the solutions for the corner equilibrium values of all endogenous variables when insurance is absent.

$$
\begin{aligned}
l_i &= [n + \alpha(n^2 - mn + m - n)]/m \\
l_j &= \{1 + \alpha(n - 1)\}/m \\
x_i &= x_r^d = x_j = [1 - \alpha(1 + m - n)]/m, \; x_i^s = (n - 1)x_i/n \\
n &= (1 - {}^1\!/_\alpha) + m\{1 - 1/\ln[\theta k_H^{1/\rho} + (1 - \theta)k_L^{1/\rho}]\} \\
Eu &= \{[1 - \alpha(1 + m - n)]/m\}^{m/\rho}[\theta k_H^{1/\rho} + (1 - \theta)k_L^{1/\rho}]^{n-1} \\
P &= [\theta k_H^{1/\rho} + (1 - \theta)k_L^{1/\rho}]^{n-1}.
\end{aligned}
\tag{10.10}
$$

Differentiation of the corner equilibrium values of the endogenous variables with respect to parameters k_s ($s = H, L$), θ, ρ yields the comparative statics of the corner equilibrium with no insurance.

$$dn/dk_s > 0, \quad dn/d\theta > 0, \quad dn/d\rho < 0 \tag{10.11a}$$

$$dl_i/dk_s > 0, \quad dl_i/d\theta > 0, \quad dl_i/d\rho < 0 \tag{10.11b}$$

$$
\begin{aligned}
&d[M(n - 1)x_r^d]/dk_s > 0, \quad d[M(n - 1)x^d]/d\theta > 0 \\
&d[M(n - 1)x_r^d]/d\rho > 0,
\end{aligned}
\tag{10.11c}
$$

$$dEu/dk_s > 0, \quad dEu/d\theta > 0 \tag{10.11d}$$

$$
\begin{aligned}
&dP/dk_s = (\partial P/\partial k_s) + (\partial P/\partial n)(\partial n/\partial k_s) < 0, \text{ and} \\
&dP/d\theta = (\partial P/\partial \theta) + (\partial P/\partial n)(\partial n/\partial \theta) < 0
\end{aligned}
\tag{10.11e}
$$

where $(n - 1)x_r^d = x_r^s$ is each individual's aggregate purchase volume and $M(n$

$-1)x_r{}^d = Mx_r{}^s$ is the aggregate demand for all goods in the market, which is the extent of the market. We have used the envelope theorem to obtain (10.11d). To obtain (10.11e), we have used the solution of n, given in (10.10), and the fact that $\alpha m<1$ if the solution of l_j, given in (10.10), is between 0 and 1.

The comparative statics imply that, as transaction efficiency k_H and k_L rises, or as the probability of a high transaction efficiency, θ, increases (or as the risk of a low transaction efficiency decreases), or as the degree of risk aversion ρ falls, the following phenomena concur. The level of division of labour, n, increases. This implies increases in the number of markets for different goods, in diversity of structure, in market integration and in production concentration. Aggregate coordination reliability of the network of division of labour, P, decreases, or aggregate risk of coordination failure of the network of division of labour increases. This is quite counter-intuitive: an increase in coordination reliability of each transaction or a decrease in transaction risk of each transaction will increase aggregate transaction risk! The logic behind this result is that, as transaction conditions for each transaction, k_s, are improved, or as the risk of coordination failure of each transaction $1 - \theta$ decreases, the scope for trading off economies of division of labour against transaction risk is enlarged, so that individuals can expand the network of division of labour to exploit more economies of division of labour, so that they can afford more risk of coordination failure of the network of division of labour.

Each individual's level of specialization increases. This implies increases in productivity, in the extent of the market, in the extent of endogenous comparative advantage, in aggregate demand and in per capita real income. An interesting interpretation of an increase in k is a decrease in tax rate. Also an increase in θ can be interpreted as a more stable tax rate. Mokyr (1993, pp.46–58) provides historical evidence that a stable and non-predatory tax system is essential for economic development. Sachs and Warner (1995, 1997) provide empirical evidence that economic development performance negatively relates to the transaction risk caused by institutional deficiency. They use an institution quality index to measure this.

Now we assume that there is an insurance company from which individuals can buy an insurance contract. No matter what the level of transaction efficiency, an individual buying insurance must pay a premium π. If transaction efficiency is low, or is k_L, the insurance company pays the individual c. Hence the individual's expected utility is

$$Eu_i = W[\theta(k_H - \pi)^{1/\rho} + (1 - \theta)(k_L - \pi + c)^{1/\rho}]^{n-1} \qquad (10.12)$$

where the non-random variable W is given in (10.10b). If the insurance is complete and the market for insurance is competitive, the insurance company's expected profit must be 0. The company receives premium π at probability 1 from the individual and pays the individual c at probability $(1 - \theta)$. Therefore the complete insurance and 0 profit condition requires

$$\pi = (1 - \theta)c. \qquad (10.13)$$

Inserting this expression into (10.12) and letting the derivative of Eu_i with respect to c equal 0 yields each individual's optimum insurance policy $c = k_H - k_L$. Plugging the optimum policy c into (10.13) yields the optimum premium:

$$\pi^* = (1 - \theta)(k_H - k_L). \qquad (10.14)$$

Inserting the optimum premium and policy back into (10.12) gives the expected utility in the presence of insurance:

$$Eu_i = W[\theta k_H + (1 - \theta)k_L]^{n-1/\rho}. \qquad (10.15)$$

This result says that, no matter what the level of transaction efficiency, an insured person always gets the utility level at the weighted average of the high and low transaction efficiencies $\theta k_H + (1 - \theta)k_L$. That is, the insured individual avoids all risks. Such insurance is called *complete insurance*. We now consider the function $f(k) = k^{1/\rho}$, which is the part of the utility function that involves uncertainty. The function is concave in the random variable k if $\rho > 1$. A comparison between Eu in (10.10) and Eu in (10.15) indicates that an individual gets $f(Ek) = [\theta k_H + (1 - \theta)k_L]^{1/\rho}$ if she or he is insured, and she or he gets $Ef(k) = \theta k_H^{1/\rho} + (1 - \theta)k_L^{1/\rho}$ if she or he is not. Since, for a strictly concave function $f(k)$, the value of the function at the weighted average of two contingent transaction efficiencies is greater than the weighted average of the values of the function at the two contingent transaction efficiencies, (10.15) is certainly greater than the expected utility in the absence of insurance.

The first order conditions for maximizing (10.15) are exactly the same as those for (10.10), except for the first order condition for the equilibrium n. These conditions yield the local equilibrium with insurance.

$$
\begin{aligned}
l_i' &= [n' + \alpha(n'^2 - mn' + m - n')]/m \\
l_j' &= [1 + \alpha(n' - 1)]/m \\
x_i' &= x_r^{d'} = x_j' = [1 - \alpha(1 + m - n')]/m, \quad x_i^{s'} = (n' - 1)x_i'/n' \qquad (10.16) \\
n' &= (1 - 1/\alpha) + m\{1 - 1/\ln[\theta k_H + (1 - \theta)k_L]\} \\
Eu' &= \{[1 - \alpha(1 + m - n')]/m\}^{m/\rho}[\theta k_H + (1 - \theta)k_L]^{(n'-1)/\rho} \\
P' &= [\theta k_H + (1 - \theta)k_L]^{n-1/\rho}
\end{aligned}
$$

Primes on the variables denote corner equilibrium values with insurance. The differentiation of the corner equilibrium values of the endogenous variables with respect to parameters k, θ, ρ indicates that the comparative statics in (10.11) hold for the case with insurance. A comparison between the corner equilibrium in (10.13) and that in (10.19) given below indicates

$$n' > n, \quad l_i' > l_i, \quad P' > P, \quad Eu' > Eu, \quad Mx_i^{s'} > Mx_i^s \qquad (10.17a)$$

$$\mathrm{d}n'/\mathrm{d}k_s > 0, \quad \mathrm{d}n'/\mathrm{d}\theta > 0, \quad \mathrm{d}Eu'/\mathrm{d}k_s > 0, \quad \mathrm{d}Eu'/\mathrm{d}\theta < 0$$
$$\mathrm{d}P'/\mathrm{d}k_s < 0, \quad \mathrm{d}P'/\mathrm{d}\theta < 0. \qquad\qquad\qquad\qquad (10.17b)$$

This implies that the expected utility with insurance is greater than that with no insurance. As shown by Lio, all individuals will choose insurance in a general equilibrium. The corner equilibrium with no insurance is not a general equilibrium. (10.17) implies also that the level of division of labour for society, individuals' levels of specialization, productivity, aggregate coordination reliability of the network of division of labour and the extent of the market are all greater in the corner equilibrium with insurance than in the corner equilibrium with no insurance.

The complete insurance in this model is equivalent to the complete insurance in an economy with a soft budget constraint associated with government subsidies. But, in this model, it is assumed that the risk of low transaction efficiency is exogenously given, independent of the effort devoted to reducing such risk. Hence complete insurance does not generate moral hazard. But we know that complete insurance in a Soviet-style economy indeed generates tremendous moral hazard problems. Lio (1996) endogenizes the risk of a low transaction efficiency and investigates the relationships between the level of division of labour, incomplete insurance and complete insurance that generate moral hazard and endogenous transaction costs.

There are two opposite views of the Asian financial crisis in 1997. According to one of them, the financial crisis was caused by moral hazard associated with cronyism and complete insurance of loans provided by the government. The other view (Radelet and Sachs, 1998; Stiglitz, 1998) holds that, as the network of trade expands, aggregate risk of coordination failure inevitably increases even if moral hazard is not that serious. Hence policy missteps and hasty reactions by the governments and by international organizations may miss the efficient balance of the trade-off between insurance and incentive provision. For instance, the overemphasis of the financial reform programmes which reduce moral hazard when insurance should receive more attention added to the virulence of the banking panics.

We can apply Lio's models to assess this view. According to (10.11e) and (10.17b), it is obvious that, even if moral hazard is absent, the aggregate risk of coordination failure $1 - P$ increases as transaction conditions are improved or as the risk of coordination failure for each transaction decreases. This is because, as the risk of coordination failure for each transaction reduces, the scope for trading off economies of division of labour against aggregate risk is enlarged, so that individuals can afford a higher risk. Hence choosing a higher aggregate risk of coordination failure is associated with economic development generated by evolution of division of labour, and it is efficient. This explains why a more successful developed economy has a higher risk of having an episode like the Asian financial crisis than a less developed economy. This is why Radelet and Sachs call the 1997 Asian financial crisis a 'crisis of success'. The higher risk is efficiently chosen, just like choosing the higher risk of being killed by driving a fast car on the freeway.

This implies that moral hazard is not the whole of the story. This is why more moral hazard generated by complete insurance in China and in the Soviet Union does not necessarily imply more risk of a financial crisis occurring. The Lio model (1996; see Yang, 2000, ch. 17) with moral hazard indicates that the efficient way to handle the Asian financial crisis is to balance efficiently the trade-off between risk sharing and incentive provision in reducing the risk, rather than paying too much attention to one of them.

If the time lag between financial decisions and economic fundamentals is considered, we may have another trade-off between the strong incentive created by sensitive feedback and the stability of the financial market. Financial reforms may increase the sensitivity of the feedback mechanism. But too sensitive feedback may make overshot more likely to occur. Sometimes, too sensitive feedback may generate overreactions that create a financial crisis. We consider such a model in the next section.

4   THE TRADE-OFF BETWEEN INCENTIVE PROVISION AND STABILITY

The Asian financial crisis was correlated with high international capital mobility. Aghion *et al.* (1998) develop a cobweb model to explain why great capital mobility in a developed international financial market may decrease market stability. Their story runs as follows. If there is a time lag between economic performance and financial signals, there will be a trade-off between incentive provision, which can be increased by sensitivity of feedback between signals and players' actions, and stability of the feedback process, which will be decreased by increasing the sensitivity. A feedback system that is not sensitive to signals (as in a socialist system) will fail to provide enough incentive for economic development. But a too sensitive feedback process will generate non-convergent fluctuations, an explosion, or a chaotic process. In the model of Aghion *et al.*, the degree of feedback sensitivity is represented by a feedback sensitivity coefficient in a difference equation that relates signals to players' actions via a time lag between the two variables. High capital mobility in a developed international financial market is associated with a large value of the coefficient. This high mobility implies that any trivial positive signal can attract capital from all countries in the world, and thereby create a huge inflow of capital within a very short period of time. Any trivial negative signal can have a huge opposite effect, which can generate a panic flight of capital (explosion or chaos in the non-linear difference equation).

This trade-off between incentive provision and stability implies that it is not efficient to have an extremely high power incentive. Russia liberalized its capital account prior to privatization reforms. This significantly increased the sensitivity of the feedback mechanism. Privatization reforms further increased the sensitivity, which is good for providing incentives, but not good for stability. Of course, corruption and money laundering were the source of negative signals. South Korea liberalized its capital account prior to substantial reduction of moral hazard caused by cronyism. Without the moral hazard caused by opportunism, sensitive feedback itself may not make trouble, just like what happens to the highly developed financial market in Taiwan and in Western Europe. But moral hazard itself is not enough to explain South Korea's financial crises, since moral hazard in China, which was not greatly affected by the Asian financial crisis, is even greater than in South Korea. Some economists explain the financial crises in Russian and Asia using the conventional models of moral hazard. But the models cannot explain why the crises occurred when liberalization and privatization were implemented. Lio's models (1996, 1998) and the model of Aghion *et al.* show that the trade-offs between reliability, transaction costs and economies of division of labour and between incentive provision, sharing risk and stability can explain the crises better. In the rest of this section, we use a cobweb model to illustrate the story behind the model of Aghion *et al.*

Consider the Smithian model with endogenous specialization in Sachs and Yang (2000, example 4.2). An individual's decision problem based on the CES (constant elasticity substitution) utility function is:

Max: $u = [(x^c)\rho + (y^c)\rho]^{1/\rho}$ (utility function)

s.t. $x^c \equiv x + kx^d$ $y^c \equiv y + ky^d$ (definition of quantities to consume)

     $x + x^s = l_x{}^a$ $y + y^s = l_y{}^a$ (production function)

     $l_x + l_y = 1$ (endowment constraint)

     $p_x x^s + p_y y^s = p_x x^d + p_y y^d$ (budget constraint)

where x and y are respective amounts of the two goods self-provided, x^s and y^s are respective quantities of the two goods sold, x^d and y^d are respective quantities purchased, l_x and l_y are respectively quantities of labour allocated to the production of the two goods; p_i is the price of good i, which is a given parameter in a Walrasian regime. The optimum decisions in the various configurations are summarized in Table 10.1, where $p \equiv p_y/p_x$ and $\rho \in (0, 1)$.

Table 10.1   Corner solutions in four configurations

Configuration	Quantities self-provided	Supply functions	Demand functions	Indirect utility function $u(p)$
A	$x = y = 0.5^a$	0	0	$2(1 - pa)/\rho$
(x/y)	$x = [1 + (k/p)^{\rho/(1-\rho)}]^{-1}$	$x^s = [1 + (p/k)^{\rho/(1-\rho)}]^{-1}$	$y^d = x^s/p$	$[1 + (k/p)^{\rho/(1-\rho)}]^{(1-\rho)/\rho}$
(y/x)	$y = [1 + (kp)^{\rho/(1-\rho)}]^{-1}$	$y^s = [1 + (kp)^{-\rho/(1-\rho)}]^{-1}$	$x^d = py^s$	$[1 + (kp)^{\rho/(1-\rho)}]^{(1-\rho)/\rho}$

Configuration A is autarky where each individual self-provides x and y. Configuration (x/y) denotes that an individual produces and sells good x and buys good y; (y/x) denotes that an individual produces and sells good y and buys good x. The corner equilibrium relative price in structure D consists of configurations (x/y) and (y/x) is $p = 1$, given by the utility equalization between the two configurations.

We now introduce the discrete time dimension into the model. There is a one-period time lag between changes of the relative number of individuals choosing professional occupations (x/y) and (y/x) in response to the difference in utility between the two occupations. Hence

$$M_x(t) - M_x(t - 1) = \beta[u_x(t - 1) - u_y(t - 1)] \qquad (10.18)$$

where t denotes the time period and β is the sensitivity coefficient of changes in the number of specialist producers of x in response to the difference in utility between two occupation configurations. $M_i(t)$ is the number of specialist producers of good i in period t. The indirect utility function u_i for a specialist producer of good i is given in Table 10.1. Since $M_x(t) + M_y(t) = M$ where population size M is a given parameter, changes in $M_x(t)$ are proportional to changes in $M_y(t)$ in the opposite direction. For simplicity, we assume that $M = 1$. Further, there is a one-period time lag between changes of relative price of good y to good x in response to changes in excess demand for good y. Hence

$$p(t + 1) - p(t) = \alpha[M_x(t) y^d(t) - M_y(t)y^s(t)] \qquad (10.19)$$

where $M_y(t) = 1 - M_x(t)$ and $y^d(t)$ and $y^s(t)$ are given in Table 10.1; α is the sensitivity coefficient of changes of relative price in response to excess demand for good y. Equations (10.18) and (10.19) constitute a second order non-linear system of difference equations in p and M_x. Assume that the initial state of the system is given by $M_x(0) = M_0$, $p(0) = p_0$, and $p(1) = p_1$. Then the dynamics and comparative dynamics of this system can be given by simulations on the computer. Figure 10.1(a) gives the results of the simulations for $\alpha = 0.6$, $\beta = 0.2$, $\rho = 0.6$, $k = 0.6$, $M_0 = 0$, $p_0 = 0.2$, and $p_1 = 0.21$. In panel (b),

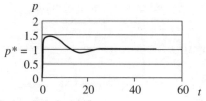

(a) $\alpha = 0.6$, $\beta = 0.2$, $\rho = 0.6$, $k = 0.6$

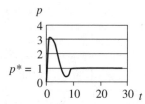

(b) $\alpha = 1.61$, $\beta = 0.2$, $\rho = 0.6$, $k = 0.6$

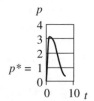

(c) $\alpha = 1.62$, $\beta = 0.2$, $\rho = 0.6$, $k = 0.6$

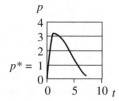

(d) $\alpha = 0.6$, $\beta = 0.3$, $\rho = 0.6$, $k = 0.6$

(e) $\alpha = 0.6$, $\beta = 0.2$, $\rho = 0.6$, $k = 0.601$

*Figure 10.1   Trade-off between sensitive incentive and stability of feedback
            mechanism*

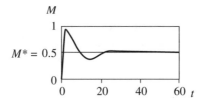

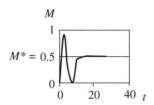

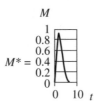

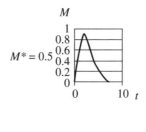

α is increased to 1·61 and other parameters are unchanged. In panel (c), α is increased to 1·62 and other parameters are unchanged. In panel (d), all parameter values are the same as in panel (a) except that β increases from 0·2 to 0·3. In panel (e), all parameter values are the same as in panel (a) except that k increases from 0·6 to 0·601.

A comparison of the time paths of relative price p and the numbers of x specialists M in panels (a) and (b) shows that, as the feedback sensitivity parameter α increases from 0.6 to 1.61, the convergence of the feedback process to the static equilibrium (steady state, $p = 1$ and $M_x = 0·5$) becomes faster. Panel (c) shows that, as the sensitive coefficient α reaches the threshold level, 1·62, the number of specialist producers of x becomes negative after several rounds of feedback. A comparison between panels (b) and (d) shows a similar result of an increase of value of sensitivity parameter of β from 0·2 to 0·3 with unchanged α = 0·6. The negative number of specialists in an occupation is not feasible. Hence this implies a breakdown of the division of labour and all individuals have to choose autarky, even if the static equilibrium is the division of labour (utility in the structure with the division of labour is higher than in autarky). This panic rush of individuals from the occupation configuration producing x to that producing y as M_x tends to 0 looks like the panic rush of investors from one country to the other in a highly integrated world market with a very high level of international division of labour. A comparison between panels (b) and (e) shows that an increase in the trading efficiency coefficient k has the same effect of an increase in feedback sensitivity parameters. Also, as k reaches a threshold, the system will overshoot and never reach the steady state.

The results are very intuitive. If the system starts from a non-equilibrium state, then one occupation generates more utility than the other, so that individuals will shift from the latter to the former. This will adjust aggregate demand and supply of a traded good and thereby excess demand for this good. The relative price will change in response to the change in excess demand. The indirect utility functions in different occupations will change in response to this change in relative price. This will again cause changes in the relative number of specialists in the two occupations if the steady state is yet to be achieved. In this feedback process, the more sensitive the feedback, the faster the convergence of fluctuations towards the steady state. But if the feedback is too sensitive, the system may overshoot, so that the steady state can never be reached. A larger trading efficiency coefficient has an effect similar to that of a larger feedback sensitivity coefficient. It can speed up the convergence of the feedback before a threshold is reached. A very high trading efficiency may generate overshoot that paralyses the feedback mechanism.

This model can be used to explain fluctuations of excess demand for professionals, such as lawyers and accountants, with a time lag between education and professional work. Also it can explain the financial crisis caused by liberalization reforms that increase sensitivity coefficients or trading efficiency by raising the mobility of capital, goods and labour.

Liberalization and privatization reforms will increase feedback sensitivity coefficients or the trading efficiency coefficient. This will make the convergence of the economic system towards equilibrium faster, but will also increase the risk of overshoot that reduces the realized level of division of labour and related trade. It can be shown that, for the same feedback sensitivity coefficient and trading efficiency, the larger the initial difference between value of price and its static equilibrium level, the more likely the feedback system may break down by overshoot. This explains why Taiwan was not greatly affected by the Asian financial crisis.

Taiwan implemented liberalization and privatization reforms of its financial sector before liberalizing its capital account. This ensured a low moral hazard caused by state monopoly of the financial sector. This implies that the initial difference between prevailing market prices and its static equilibrium level was not great when feedback sensitivity was raised by liberalization reforms. China had very high moral hazard, but since it had a very small feedback sensitivity coefficient due to the government's tight control of the capital account, it was not greatly affected by the Asian financial crisis either. In contrast, South Korea liberalized its capital account before the great moral hazard in its state-monopolized financial system was significantly reduced. Hence the initial difference between the market price and its static equilibrium level, which relates to moral hazard, and the feedback sensitivity and trading efficiency coefficients, which relate to the openness of the financial market, are two major determinants of the trade-off between incentive provision and stability. Thus the different cases of Taiwan, China and South Korea can all be explained by the cobweb model. The story suggests that the sequence of liberalization and privatization reforms makes a difference. In the literature of engineering, the degree to which the feedback system achieves the efficient balance of the trade-off between feedback sensitivity and stability is referred to as feedback quality. The major task in macroeconomic policy making is to raise feedback quality.

5 CONCLUDING REMARKS

This chapter investigates the trade-offs among positive network effects of division of labour on aggregate productivity, coordination reliability of the network, positive effects of insurance on the reliability, moral hazard caused by insurance, stronger incentive provided by sensitive feedback, and stability of the feedback mechanism. It is shown that decreases in transaction risk in each trade connection may efficiently increase aggregate risk of economic crisis. Liberalization reforms may improve incentive provision at the cost of stability of the feedback mechanism in the market. The efficient policy regime should not eliminate aggregate risk; rather it should find the efficient balance point of the trade-offs and improve the quality of the market feedback mechanism. Our analysis suggests that the sequence of reforms is important for achieving the efficient balance of the trade-offs. Liberalization of the domestic financial market should be implemented before liberalization of international capital flows.

NOTE

I am grateful to Steven Radelet, Jeff Sachs and Monchi Lio for helpful discussion. The remaining errors are solely mine.

REFERENCES

Aghion, P., P. Bacchetta and A. Banerjee (1998), 'Capital Markets and the Instability of Open Economies', working paper, presented at Harvard University and MIT Growth and Development Seminar.

Lio, M. (1996), 'Three Essays on Increasing Returns and Specialization: A Contribution to New Classical Microeconomic Approach', PhD dissertation, Department of Economics, the National Taiwan University.

Lio, M. (1998), 'Uncertainty, insurance, and division of labour', *Review of Development Economics*, 2, 76–86.

Milgrom, P. and J. Roberts (1992), *Economics, Organization and Management*, Englewood Cliffs: Prentice-Hall.

Mokyr, Joel (1993), 'The New Economic History and the Industrial Revolution', in J. Mokyr (ed.), *The British Industrial Revolution: An economic perspective*, Boulder/Oxford: Westview Press.

Radelet, Steven and Jeff Sachs (1998), 'The Onset of the East Asian Financial Crisis', paper presented to the National Bureau of Economic Research Currency Crisis Conference, Cambridge.

Sachs, J. and A. Warner (1995), 'Economic Reform and the Process of Global Integration', *Brookings Papers on Economic Activity*, 1.

Sachs, J. and A. Warner (1997), 'Fundamental sources of long-run growth', *American Economic Review, Papers and Proceedings*, 87, 184–8.

Sachs, J. and X. Yang (2000), *Development Economics: Inframarginal versus Marginal Analyses*, Cambridge, Mass.: Blackwell.

Shea, Jia-Dong and Yang, Ya-Hwei (1994), 'Taiwan's Financial System and the Allocation of Investment Funds', in Joel Aberbach, David Dollar and Kenneth Sokoloff (eds), *The Role of State in Taiwan's Development*, Armonk: M.E. Sharpe, pp. 193–230.

Stiglitz, Joseph (1998), 'Sound Finance and Sustainable Development in Asia', Keynote Address to the Asia Development Forum, The World Bank Group, Internet.

Yang, X. (2000), *Economics: New Classical Versus Neoclassical Framework*, Cambridge, Mass.: Blackwell.

Yang, X. and S. Ng (1998), 'Specialization and Division of Labor: a Survey', in K. Arrow, Y.-K. Ng and Xiaokai Yang (eds), *Increasing Returns and Economic Analysis,* London: Macmillan.

Yang, X. and Y.-K. Ng (1993), *Specialization and Economic Organization, a New Classical Microeconomic Framework*, Amsterdam: North-Holland.

Yang, X. and I. Wills (1990), 'A Model Formalizing the Theory of Property Rights', *Journal of Comparative Economics*, 14, 177–98.

11.   The Asia recovery: the road and obstacles ahead

Tran Van Hoa

In the first half of 2000, there were signs that the Asia recovery had started. This can be seen from a number of general aspects, as judged from various reports and statistics published by the national and international organizations involved in the crisis analysis and management advice. First, further impact and contagion of the crisis in the Asian region had been reportedly arrested. Second, emergency loans earmarked by such institutions as the International Monetary Fund as financial assistance for some crisis economies had been repaid or even not been used owing to improvements in the countries' budgetary situations. Third, growth and other economic activities, especially exports, in most of the crisis economies in Asia had resumed, albeit at a hesitant pace and much lower rate than that attained by these economies in the three decades or so before July 1997.

From other relevant perspectives (such as the social and political situations or even a closer look at economic and financial activities at the sectoral level), however, it would be rather premature to predict that the Asian crisis countries have completely left the turmoil behind and even escaped its long and dark shadow in the months or years to come. There are many reasons for this assessment.

First, at the regional level, the Bank for International Settlements (BIS) which was set up to promote cooperation among the major central banks around the world reported in July 2000 that, in the first three months of 2000, international bank lending to Asia fell by 2 per cent, as companies repaid foreign debt and demand for new bank loans remained weak. In fact, lending to Asia fell by US$6·0 billion in this quarter, to US$297 billion, with US$1·6 billion coming from bank loan repayments. Since foreign bank loans have been a main source of funds to support development, growth and technology transfer in Asia, a shortage of these funds in the region would not bode well for its prospects in expanding trade, improving living standards, enhancing national and individual welfare, and participating in international economic integration and globalization.

Second, at the national level, the huge costs (estimated to be about

US$1 billion for the part played by Australia alone) of restoring and maintaining peace and reconstructing the country of East Timor after the ethnic, religious and racial bloodbaths in late 1999 were seen as a new and additional burden on the countries in the region at a time (the post-crisis period) when they were least able to afford it. East Timor was not the only problem affecting a full economic recovery by the crisis countries in Asia in 2000.

At the time of writing, the Asian crisis economies were still individually beset by problems that had the potential to seriously hinder their recoveries. Indonesia was still a country deeply embroiled in religious and ethnic riots, vicious and widespread independence movement unrest, general mistrust of the government, power struggles among major political parties and lingering corruption. As an example, in mid-2000, the Indonesian government's Supreme Audit Agency reported that the country was facing US$16 billion in potential losses owing to the misuse of emergency loans and financial abuses and that this involved Bank Indonesia officials and several prominent business groups.

Malaysia was still a country paralysed by internal political turmoil, alleged cronyism and emerging ethnic armed violence, in addition to a severe skilled labour shortage for its information technology-based economic development plan. In Korea, the restructuring of the banking and financial system and the *chaebols* or big corporations, the main targets of the country's reform programme during the crisis, has not been regarded by international economists as very successful.

The Philippines was still troubled by slow growth and the emergence of zealous freedom fighters who have resorted to violence and kidnapping of foreign tourists to support their causes. Even Vietnam, which, after many years of negotiations, signed a historic trade agreement with the United States early in July 2000, still felt negatively affected by the Asia meltdown and uncomfortable with free market reforms. It was quite apprehensive about the possible adverse consequences of this trade agreement and the perceived high costs and uncertain benefits (economic and social) of its accession to the World Trade Organization in the near future.

Late in 1999, Thailand was regarded, in the reports prepared by staff of the international organizations, as a country with fairly successful economic and financial reforms and one in which the impact of the Asian crisis was not serious in an average context. However, this reported perception (and that of similar reports and assessments for other crisis countries in Asia) was seen by economic and financial experts in Thailand and overseas as superficially investigated, inappropriately analysed and dangerously misleading. In a country with 80 or more per cent of its population living and working in the traditional ages-old way in the rural area, the impact of a major modern economic or financial crisis was necessarily centred on the urban population. As a result, the weighted average impact on both the urban and the rural populations of that country must be negligible. The cruel facts in the case of Thailand are that business people and their relatives still continue to commit suicide, even publicly, as a result of hardships and problems brought about by the Asia crisis, and strong growth in some sectors of the economy (such as exports) without equally strong transmissions of the benefits to other major sectors is not sufficient to rescue the economy from the shadow of depression or stagnation to a full recovery.

The role played by Japan, the second-largest economy in the world after the United States, in the Asia crisis and in the economic recovery in major crisis countries should not be underestimated. It has been recognized that, while Japan's often generous foreign aid is important as a stop-gap measure to help Asian development, the Asia recovery crucially depends on what will happen in the Japanese economy, especially in regard to its fiscal and monetary policy. In mid-2000, however, Bank of Japan governor Masaru Hayami stipulated that Japan's emergency fiscal and monetary policy measures, that include a zero per cent interest rate policy, may have to be tightened as soon as possible to the normal positive level. The effect of such a shift in policy may result in depressing private demand and therefore stifling growth not only in Japan but also in the neighbouring countries in Asia and beyond. Even in Japan, the country's Economic Planning Agency director-general, Taichi Sakaiya, and a number of cabinet ministers had urged caution in this policy shift since it was too early to be optimistic about the government's efforts to make private demand take over from government spending as the engine of growth for the economy.

The above observations and discussions seem to indicate that, despite the good signs of an upswing in various economic and financial activities, as reported by national and international organizations, a full recovery for major economies in crisis or in transition in Asia may not be able to eventuate for some time in the future.

Index